DATE DUE

Reciprocity and the
North Atlantic Triangle
1932–1938

Reciprocity and the North Atlantic Triangle

1932–1938

By RICHARD N. KOTTMAN

Iowa State University

Cornell University Press

ITHACA, NEW YORK

To My Parents

Elmer and Dorothea Bokemeier Kottman

Acknowledgments

This account is rooted in the belief that if historians are to render
balanced judgments about the American foreign policy record in
the 1930's they must consider the broad range of problems that
concerned Washington and not just render post mortems on such
related topics as the wisdom of the neutrality legislation or the
responsibility for the disaster at Pearl Harbor. Many of the problems of the decade remain unexplored because they do not fit the
more spectacular or lurid pattern dealing with American involvement in the Second World War. One neglected dimension
which this book describes is the effect of the reciprocal trade
program on the relationship among the North Atlantic nations,
the United Kingdom, Canada, and the United States. Though a
nearly forgotten subject now, in the thirties the program of expanded trade was Secretary of State Cordell Hull's answer to
international pleas for world peace. Because Hull believed, in
particular, that trade agreements with Canada and the United
Kingdom were imperative if his prescription were to be given a
fair test, the American government expended a great amount of
time and work to bring them about. An understanding of Washington's relations with the United Kingdom or Canada during
this period is impossible unless these relations are viewed in the
perspective of the American experiment in reciprocity.

Spending the summer of 1964 in the Washington area as a Visiting Lecturer at the University of Maryland afforded me the initial opportunity to develop the project. I owe a debt, therefore, to Professor Donald W. Giffin of the Department of History of the University of Maryland, who was especially helpful during those summer months.

In Washington and Ottawa, the personnel of the National Archives, the Manuscripts Division of the Library of Congress, and the Public Archives of Canada were most helpful, cooperative, and courteous. In the early stages of my research the counsel of the late E. Taylor Parks, then Chief of the Research Guidance and Review Division of the Historical Office of the Department of State, was invaluable. Mrs. Patricia Dowling of the Diplomatic, Legal, and Fiscal Branch, National Archives, patiently made available to me countless boxes of State Department documents.

The staffs of several libraries were extremely competent and cooperative: Franklin D. Roosevelt Library, Houghton Library of Harvard University, Douglas Library of Queen's University (Kingston, Ontario), North Texas State University Library, University of Iowa Library, Iowa State University Library, and the Harriet Irving Library (formerly the Bonar Law-Bennett Library) of the University of New Brunswick. Dr. Gertrude E. Gunn, Librarian of the Harriet Irving Library, merits particular mention for expediting my research. Mr. J. R. H. Wilbur, of the Department of History, University of New Brunswick, who had worked extensively in the Richard B. Bennett Papers, graciously shared with me his knowledge of the collection, of Bennett, and of Canadian politics. Elizabeth B. Drewry, Director of the Franklin D. Roosevelt Library, promptly responded to my requests for the filming of selected items in the Roosevelt collection.

I am indebted to two former colleagues at North Texas State University. Professor William Kamman read the chapter on the

World Monetary and Economic Conference and offered useful comments. Professor William T. Hagan, now Chairman of the Department of History at State University College, Fredonia, New York, not only subjected portions of the manuscript in their early form to his critical eye, but also set an example of scholarship and professional integrity which I have attempted to emulate.

Grants from the North Texas State University Faculty Research Committee, chaired by the Dean of the Graduate School, Robert Toulouse, freed me from teaching duties, making possible later trips to Canada, Washington, and Boston.

I want to thank the Honorable Francis B. Sayre and the Honorable William Phillips, both of whom permitted me to quote from their private collections, and Mrs. Albert Levitt, who approved my use of the J. Pierrepont Moffat Papers. Moreover, Mr. Phillips read the chapter on the Canadian-American trade agreement of 1935 and kindly answered several questions.

Chapter 3 is a slightly expanded version of an article which appeared in the September, 1965, issue of *The Journal of American History*. The editor, Professor Martin Ridge, granted permission for me to use the article in the altered form.

Others, too numerous to acknowledge, have also devoted time in my behalf. To them I can in this impersonal way only express my sincere gratitude.

Finally, no debt is so great as that I owe my wife, Anne Martin Kottman; her loving understanding made my task infinitely more pleasant.

RICHARD N. KOTTMAN

Ames, Iowa
June 1967

Contents

*Reciprocity and the
North Atlantic Triangle
1932–1938*

Introduction

For the past two decades diplomatic historians have been investigating facets of American diplomacy in the thirties pointing toward the gradual involvement of the United States in the Second World War. The themes of their books are familiar to specialist and general reader alike—the evolution of frictions with Japan from the Manchurian crisis to the attack on Pearl Harbor; the responses of the Roosevelt Administration to the Italo-Ethiopian and Spanish Civil wars; the attempts by Congress to insulate America against entanglement in another European slaughter; the struggle between nationalists and interventionists to define American vital interests and how best these interests could be promoted in light of catastrophic events in Europe; and the partnership established with Great Britain after 1939, highlighted by the repeal of the arms embargo, the destroyer-bases deal, lend-lease, and German-American naval skirmishes in the North Atlantic.

The same historians, however, have generally neglected those aspects of American diplomacy that seemingly had little bearing on American entry into the war. Apart from treating the attempts at Far Eastern cooperation, the development of joint defense of North America, and St. Lawrence Seaway negotiations—and the first two of these were germane to the drift of Washington toward belligerency—they have written little of the relations of the United States with the United Kingdom and Canada before 1941. The present study aims to rescue from undeserved neglect one important dimension of these relations and, by focusing on it, to provide glimpses of the larger question of North Atlantic Triangle diplomacy.

Washington's relations with London and Ottawa suffered from the breakdown of trade following the economic collapse of 1929. American officials at least thought that restoration of trade among them was central to any détente. Study of the negotiation of the three reciprocal trade agreements that did so much to heal the wounds contributes to greater understanding not only of Anglo-American and Canadian-American relations—and corractives are needed—but also of the entire period, for much of its diplomacy is mirrored in the American attempt to resolve the world's political problems through the revival of international commercial activity. In addition to pointing out the relationship between the trade negotiations and the well-known contemporary developments, this book views the leaders of the three countries in a slightly different context: its emphasis is on the immensity of the economic and political problems these men faced, the pressures to which they were subjected when making their decisions, and their uncertainties and apprehensions as they sought to restore order to a world disrupted by depression and the political frustrations it released. Confronted by unprecedented international disturbances and upheavals, these leaders groped for answers. On more than one occasion, as they improvised policies to cope with the problems, their patience wore thin. Certainly the leaders in Washington were guided neither by principles slightly treasonous nor by rules laid down by an omniscient President or Secretary of State. In short, the goal of this study is understanding, not value judgment; to show why the governments acted as they did, not to determine whether they acted wisely or stupidly. That these men made mistakes in the pursuit of their responsibilities is obvious; to understand their motivations is instructive.

Undeniably the Great Depression contributed markedly to—if it did not itself create—the environment in which nationalistic regimes in Germany and Japan gained power. Attributing the economic plight of their people to past sins committed by other parties, these governments set out to square accounts through vigorous political and economic programs. Territorial questions were made to order for Nazi propaganda, but almost as easily the Reich could contend that it had to be freed of the shackles placed on its economic expansion by the "have" nations of the Atlantic. This meant German acquisition of land in Europe. A minor but an occasionally convenient goal was the restoration of colonies lost at Paris or of a reasonable substitute. Obviously, the Nazis argued, Germany ought not to be disarmed while its neighbors were free to enlarge their military establishments. Repudiating the controls laid down in 1919, Berlin turned to rearmament, which stimulated the economy, eliminated the unemployment problem, and fortified the nation against foreign encroachments. Most important of all, a strengthened military could underwrite the expansion that was supposedly indispensable to the economic health of Germany.

Their passionate pleas contained elements of truth, leading some influential individuals to agree that the settlement of Versailles had imposed on Germany harsh conditions and inequities that must be remedied. Prominent Conservatives in Great Britain—officials like Neville Chamberlain, Lord Halifax, Samuel Hoare, Sir John Simon, and Stanley Baldwin, and private citizens like Geoffrey Dawson of the London *Times,* the Astors, and Thomas Jones, Baldwin's confidant—sought closer Anglo-German ties. Disdainful of the French and suspicious of the

Soviets, these Tories defended, condoned, and rationalized Hitler's actions as natural responses to legitimate grievances stemming from 1919 and to realistic fears of a militarized and militant Communist Russia.

Meanwhile, Japanese nationalists saw their economy suffer from tariffs and other restrictions to the successful marketing of their exports. Promising that a thrust into China would bring prosperity and stability, they gradually assumed a commanding position in their government. The establishment of Japanese hegemony in China had been denied before by Western nations, but the depression, rendering Japan's antagonists momentarily inert, put a different complexion on its prospects. By skillful exploitation of frustrations and of Japanese love of country, the nationalists overcame the opposition of those politicians whom they considered to be weak and unpatriotic, who had groveled to the West by accepting restrictions on trade and by agreeing to limitations on naval arms, and who still urged caution. Now was the time to bring Japanese order to East Asia. Inaction would mean vassalage.

The consequences of the economic debacle were not so severe in Great Britain. No Rightist coup took place, and J. Ramsay MacDonald, the Laborite Prime Minister, qualifies as neither a Lenin nor a Stalin. Yet, the depression produced fundamental economic changes and created political problems for foreign governments. The pleas of Joseph Chamberlain and the Tariff Reform League for protection of domestic interests and the demands for Empire Free Trade, having been turned down early in the century, now gathered influential support. Accordingly, the United Kingdom built tariff walls around the Isles, cooperated in efforts to promote economic unity within the Commonwealth, and sought to stimulate exports by negotiating bilateral trade agreements. Apprehensive of both the Japanese expansion and the German challenge in Europe, but particularly of the latter,

Whitehall, if somewhat halfheartedly, chose a policy of rearmament as the only feasible means of protecting its far-flung interests.

Beginning in 1933, Secretary of State Cordell Hull sponsored the reciprocal trade program as America's contribution to the restoration of international harmony and stability. He believed that the most pressing need in the world was the return of prosperity. In prosperous times revolutionary movements, whether of the Left or Right, had little attraction and could not for long command mass followings. The road to prosperity and thus to political tranquility lay in increasing the flow of trade among nations. For this to happen, governments had to lower drastically the restrictions they had recently raised in nationalistic rages. Because of the unconditional most-favored-nation principle incorporated in them, trade agreements between the United States and foreign countries could provide the impetus. In his assault on trade barriers, Hull solicited the cooperation of Great Britain. An Anglo-American trade agreement not only would be to the financial advantage of both nations, but if these trading giants joined forces in the removal of the economic causes of political tension and war, they could lay the foundation for a more orderly, prosperous, and peaceful world.

During much of the decade, however, there was only a modicum of cooperation between London and Washington. Tariffs, discriminations, and the bad feeling aroused during the World Monetary and Economic Conference, characteristic of the early years, gave way in England to reluctance to jettison British trade policies and follow the "enlightened" leadership of the United States. As a result, trade agreement negotiations made little headway. This sluggishness was particularly offensive to the Secretary of State, who hoped that a pact would clean the slate of annoyances in Anglo-American relations. Nor could the two countries agree on Far Eastern policy. Japanese penetration into

China met no united response: Secretary of State Henry L. Stimson's attempts in 1932 to obtain British support against the Manchurian policies of Japan were thwarted by an admixture in the United Kingdom of economic uncertainty and political conservatism. It is doubtful, however, whether the United States would have done much even had Sir John Simon, then British Foreign Secretary, been more cooperative. Perhaps Stanley Baldwin, the most powerful force in the Cabinet at this time, was correct when he said, "You'll get nothing out of Washington but words, big words, but only words." [1] After 1934, Whitehall's campaign for collaboration in the Far East fared little better. Wanting to avoid a situation in which it might find itself the leader of an anti-Japanese coalition, the United States resisted these initiatives. [2] In 1937, Prime Minister Neville Chamberlain rejected an overture for a meeting with Franklin D. Roosevelt, and the following year his disarming reply to the President's flirtation with the idea of a world peace conference killed that plan. [3]

The following pages thus reveal the great gap that existed between British and American policies. Whenever London made an initiative to close that gap, Washington was unreceptive;

[1] Thomas Jones, *A Diary with Letters, 1931–1950* (London, 1954), 30.

[2] Armin Rappaport, *Henry L. Stimson and Japan, 1931–33* (Chicago, 1963), 18–20; Dorothy Borg, *The United States and the Far Eastern Crisis of 1933–1938* (Cambridge, 1964), *passim*.

[3] For discussions of Roosevelt's proposed conference, see William L. Langer and S. Everett Gleason, *The Challenge to Isolation, 1937–1940* (New York, 1952), 19–32; Donald F. Drummond, *The Passing of American Neutrality, 1937–1941* (Ann Arbor, 1955), 62–65; United States Department of State, *Foreign Relations of the United States: Diplomatic Papers, 1937*, I (Washington, D.C., 1954), 665–670, and *Foreign Relations of the United States: Diplomatic Papers, 1938*, I (Washington, D.C., 1955–1956), 115–132 (hereafter cited as *Foreign Relations*, followed by year and volume and page numbers of document).

when Washington made its move, London had embraced other alternatives. Anglo-American cooperation on the major issues was nonexistent. The trade agreement negotiations offer an excellent subject for a case study of that unfortunate—and perhaps tragic—phenomenon.

Anglo-American disunity cannot be traced to lack of dialogue. Principal spokesmen of the two countries talked much about the necessity of collaboration. Whenever they discussed specifics, however, they found fundamental differences in international outlook. The United States proposed economic rehabilitation through revived trade as the key to resolving the more explosive problems of the world. In the friendlier atmosphere created by the increased flow of goods among nations, governments could reduce expenditures on armaments; prosperous and disarmed, they would dismiss thoughts of war. The first priority was a broad attack on the economic causes of political tensions. Once these causes were removed, Germany and Japan would again take their places in the international community as respectable and respected nations. Political cooperation, particularly commitments to check aggressive moves in Europe or Asia, was anathema to the American people, if not to the Roosevelt Administration as well.

While not denying economics as a factor in the world's disorder, the United Kingdom thought of its origins as political and relied on political solutions. Germany and Japan, intent on altering in their own favor the balance of power in Europe and Asia, could be restrained either by reasonable settlements or by expanded armaments, but not by the possible political consequences of trade agreements. Anthony Eden, British Foreign Secretary, and Neville Chamberlain, Chancellor of the Exchequer, told Norman H. Davis in April of 1937 that because any retreat from the present rearmament program would be construed as inability on the part of Great Britain to sustain it, they wanted no disarmament discussions for the moment.[4] Moreover, since economic activity had been greatly reduced by depression and there was greater need to protect domestic interests, the British chose not to negotiate a trade agreement precipitately. London—or at least Chamberlain—preferred to cope with the challenges confronting it in Europe and the Far East by close political association with the United States, but encountered Washington's aversion to actual or potential commitments. Deprived of guarantees and doubtful of American staying power, the British clung to their policies of rearmament, political appeasement, and nationalistic trade pacts.

To some American officials, the picture reflected was that of American friendship taken for granted by Whitehall regardless of the latter's policies. No more succinct statement of this attitude was made than by J. Pierrepont Moffat, a career officer in the Department of State who in 1936 was serving as Consul General in Australia. He noted in October of that year, "At present she [Great Britain] thinks she can count on our help politically, and yet hit us below the belt commercially all over the world." Moffat predicted that there would have to be "some sort of showdown" between the two nations.[5]

----

[4] Memorandum of conversation between Anthony Eden and Norman H. Davis, April 9, 1937; Davis to Roosevelt, April 13, 1937; and memorandum of conversation between Neville Chamberlain and Davis, April 26, 1937, Norman H. Davis Papers, Library of Congress, Box 55.

[5] Moffat's first letter on the subject, written to Davis on June 19, 1936, asserted that "in matters of trade London is bitterly hostile. . . . I have reluctantly reached the conclusion that Britain is using her financial pressure to make preferential bargains, and that despite lip service to the Secretary's ideals, she is really fighting his theory of equality of commercial treatment to the last ditch. Thus British commercial interests have been unrelenting in their propaganda that Australia should restrict American imports and divert them to Great Britain." On July 29, Davis replied to Moffat by writing, "I think you have sized up correctly the British tactics, and particularly the fact that their political policy does not always

The "showdown"—if it can be called that—came in 1938. With the passage of each month, time was getting short for Washington and London to compose their differences and present a more united front to the world. Both sides had to decide whether the fruits were worth the risks and sacrifices. On November 17, Sir Ronald Lindsay, British Ambassador to the United States, and Cordell Hull expressed the decision by signing a trade agreement. The new era in Anglo-American collaboration, which became so evident after the outbreak of war in September, 1939, had its origin in this reciprocity pact, though the causal relationship might easily be exaggerated. The happy ending of the protracted negotiations removed from the purview of Anglo-American relations their most divisive issue, undoubtedly facilitating later political maneuvers by the two governments. At the time, however, the political significance was not so evident. The identification of the trade pact with future political rewards was an American pastime; Hull repeatedly stressed that international peace depended on its successful negotiation. While the Secretary of State justified the proposed arrangement in economic terms, he also called again and again for London to see its far-reaching political implications. But the British refused to join Hull in singing its political praises. They measured the accord by economic criteria, accepting or rejecting proposals on that basis. Rapprochement with Germany was their pressing ambition, and as they sought in their own way to avert what could only be a calamitous war, they assigned the trade pact a lower priority.

---

jibe with their trade policy. I was particularly struck by this when in London this last time." Davis was not certain "that the divorcement of trade and financial policies from political policies is deliberate, because there is undoubtedly friction between the Foreign Office . . . and the Treasury and the Board of Trade." The quotes in the text were extracted from Moffat to Davis, Oct. 7, 1936, Davis Papers, Box 41.

In 1939, when the Conservatives realized that their efforts had ended in failure, they found friendlier relations with Washington, now imperative, to be more feasible because of the reciprocity agreement. Chamberlain had seen this—he occasionally nodded to the political motivations underlying a trade pact—but the effect of the accord on the Anglo-American partnership was mostly a fortuitous one rather than the outcome of a conscious maneuver by the leadership in Whitehall.

Another dimension in the evolution of Anglo-American economic solidarity is the closer relationship formed during this same period between the United States and Canada. As a result, the Ottawa-London-Washington bonds were strengthened. Canada made noteworthy contributions to the development of an Anglo-American entente. Not only was the Dominion an interpreter for the United States in British official circles, but it also played a more tangible role in making possible an Anglo-American trade agreement. In retrospect, the year 1935 marks the turning point in relations between Ottawa and Washington. The Canadian election in October brought the Liberals to power, and for the first time in the twentieth century a Democratic president and a Liberal prime minister simultaneously headed their respective governments. The outlook was for improved communication between the two capitals. Their low-tariff tradition made the Democrats more popular in Canada than the historically protectionist party of Lincoln. United States officials preferred the low-tariff, American-leaning Liberals to the Conservatives. Nearly a year before the Dominion election, Warren Robbins, then American Minister in Canada, wrote to Franklin D. Roosevelt that the Liberals were "inclined far more than the other party to play the game with us." [6] In November, Ottawa concluded a trade accord with Washington. Although the nego-

[6] Robbins to Roosevelt, Dec. 18, 1934, Franklin D. Roosevelt Papers, Franklin D. Roosevelt Library, Hyde Park (on microfilm).

tiations had been begun by the Conservatives, success had eluded them, and the Liberal regime of Mackenzie King received credit for terminating a trade war and weakening the imperial preference system. In 1938, Canada released Whitehall from certain legal obligations preventing the conclusion of the United States–United Kingdom pact. A second Canadian-American agreement was signed forthwith, and, symbolically at least, a more powerful and closely linked North Atlantic Triangle had taken form.

Any analysis of Canada's role in the diplomacy of the thirties is incomplete, however, without reference to another factor. The Canadian electorate in 1935 had placed in office a prime minister who, like a majority of Americans, balked at having his government involved in a foreign war in which the interests of Canada were not clearly defined and at making political commitments that could easily lead to entry into a war alien to those interests. He thus took his government down foreign policy paths quite similar to those being traveled by the United States. The Prime Minister's isolationism, along with the anti-British variation of O. D. Skelton, the Under Secretary of State for External Affairs, tells much about the friendlier north-south contacts and the contribution of the Dominion to the trade negotiations of 1937–1938.[7]

As political association followed the Anglo-American economic rapprochement, Canadian-American reciprocity also had its ramifications. In 1938, President Roosevelt assured Canadians that the United States would not be a disinterested spectator were Canada to be threatened by invasion, and in 1940 the two

[7] See James Eayrs's essay, "'A Low Dishonest Decade': Aspects of Canadian External Policy, 1931–1939," in Hugh Keenleyside *et al.*, *The Growth of Canadian Policies in External Affairs* (Durham, 1960), 59–80; also Eayrs's *In Defense of Canada: Appeasement and Rearmament* (Toronto, 1965).

governments committed themselves to joint defense of North America. The trade accords of 1935 and 1938 helped temporarily to remove irritants that had hampered relations between the countries especially since the First World War and its aftermath. Many Canadians had felt that Americans were ignorant of or indifferent to their interests, expecting the Dominion to follow supinely Washington's pursuit of its foreign policy goals. Certainly the trade agreements, which recognized the interrelationship of the two economies, blunted the first charge, and the establishment of the Joint Defense Board resulted in bilateral military consultations and decisions which squared well with the second.

Although their primary intention was to increase the flow of trade within the three-nation bloc, the accords of 1938 contributed to a new political climate in the three capitals and thus were integrally related to the development of the North Atlantic unity that confronted the challenges of Germany and Japan between 1939 and 1941.

Chapter 1

Erecting Tariff Walls
around the British Empire

This study begins with the response to the Great Depression by the three governments. As one means to combat the economic downturn, Congress in 1930 passed, and President Hoover signed into law, the Smoot-Hawley tariff. Opposed by both economists and diplomats, it raised duties to their highest levels in American history. In the campaign of 1928 the Republicans had promised to alleviate farm distress, that embarrassing domestic problem of the twenties, by raising tariffs, but they had failed to implement their platform pledges during the special congressional session of 1929. The Great Crash of October, portending at least temporary economic dislocations, provided the needed impetus for the Grand Old Party to carry through with its traditional anti-depression weapon.

As early as November, 1928, William Phillips, the United States Minister to Canada, had warned the State Department, and subsequently Hoover and leading members of Congress, of the probable reaction in the Dominion to any raising of American tariffs affecting Canadian farm products. Following passage of the Smoot-Hawley Act the predicted wave of resentment swept this nation whose prosperity was so dependent upon trade with its southern neighbor. The embarrassed Liberals, despite tariff retaliation in the Dunning Budget of 1930, watched the Conservatives, capitalizing on this sentiment, win an electoral victory in July of that same year. Richard B. Bennett, the New Brunswick–reared lawyer who had promised to blast his way into world markets, became Prime Minister. The protectionist Conservatives, a party traditionally wary of close relations with the United States and fond of the imperial link, retaliated even further against the entry of American goods into the Dominion. They increased tariffs, empowered the Minister of National Revenue arbitrarily to valorize imports, passed an excise tax, and, finally, promoted greater imperial trade at the expense of American exporters.[1]

In the United Kingdom a combination of effects of the depression and the Smoot-Hawley Act prompted a reversal of the tariff

---

[1] The most useful sources for background material are the following: J. F. Parkinson, "Memorandum on the Bases of Canadian Commercial Policy, 1926–38" (mimeo.; Canadian Institute of International Affairs, 1939), 6–55, 85–144, 156–174; A. E. Safarian, *The Canadian Economy in the Great Depression* (Toronto, 1959), 13–82, 97–116, 137–145; Hugh L. Keenleyside and Gerald S. Brown, *Canada and the United States* (rev. ed.; New York, 1952), 276–302. There is a fuller treatment of the economic problems between 1928 and 1933 in Richard N. Kottman, "Canadian-American Relations, 1927–1941" (Ph.D. diss., Vanderbilt University, 1958), 151–234. William Phillips' first warning, following a conversation with Mackenzie King shortly after the presidential election, was transmitted in Phillips to Secretary of State Frank B. Kellogg, Nov. 19, 1928, Department of State Records, National Archives, Washington, D.C., File No. 711.42157 Sa 29/543 (Department of State documents are hereafter cited by title, number where applicable, date, and file number). Phillips has related an interesting account of his trip to Washington, just before Hoover's inauguration, where he met with the President and key congressmen (*Ventures in Diplomacy* [Boston, 1952], 146–147).

policy that had been in effect generally since 1846. The abandonment of free trade began in 1931 with two emergency measures: the Abnormal Importations Act which granted the President of the Board of Trade discretionary authority to impose duties on a wide variety of commodities; and the Horticultural Products Act which empowered the Minister of Agriculture to levy tariffs on fruit and vegetables. Under both laws imperial imports entered Great Britain duty-free, compounding the problem for American exporters. The great victory for the protectionists came in February, 1932, with the Import Duties Act, a permanent law making nearly all imports into the United Kingdom dutiable at 10 per cent ad valorem. The original bill, which embraced Dominion items as well, drew criticism from Bennett. He wired his friend Lord Beaverbrook, the Canadian-born British publisher, that "we are greatly perturbed. Undoubtedly effect of suggested action will be to create an atmosphere that will render successful conference [imperial gathering at Ottawa] difficult if not impossible." His endeavors, coupled with pressure from the Empire Free Trade enthusiasts within the Cabinet, brought results. In Parliament Neville Chamberlain, the Chancellor of the Exchequer, announced that "neither the general nor the additional duties shall become operative before the Ottawa Conference has been concluded." The Canadian Prime Minister immediately sent Beaverbrook, an Empire Free Trader himself, his "heartiest congratulations with sincere gratitude for your untiring and successful efforts. We are greatly heartened by Chamberlain's speech." In its final form, the measure granted tariff immunity to Dominion imports until November 15, 1932.

The Import Duties Act also created the Import Duties Advisory Committee, a body which could recommend tariff increases above the 10 per cent level. Its first recommendation, accepted by the Treasury Department in 1932, resulted in duties of 20 per cent to 33⅓ per cent. By the end of 1938 nearly 180 other orders had raised specific schedules.[2]

The major blow to foreign exporters was inflicted at the Imperial Economic Conference in Ottawa. There the nations of the Empire extended and strengthened the preference system. Imperial preferences had been in effect since the late nineteenth century with Canada and its famous Prime Minister, Sir Wilfrid Laurier, pioneering the effort. Although Joseph Chamberlain had wanted the Empire to carry this principle even further and adopt commercial union, his campaign fell far short of his imperialistic ambition. In 1919, the United Kingdom had granted preferences on a few items but, due to their limited application, had hardly bothered American businessmen. Fortunately for American farmers, Parliament had refused to tax the importation of food. Because of the agreements negotiated in the Canadian capital, the picture changed appreciably. For the next five years

[2] A few tariffs had been imposed in the United Kingdom between 1846 and 1931, notably the McKenna duties of 1915, which were still existent when Parliament passed the measures mentioned in the text, and the Safeguarding of Industries Act of 1921. For a discussion of the development of British commercial policy, see Carl Kreider, *The Anglo-American Trade Agreement: A Study of British and American Commercial Policies, 1934–1939* (Princeton, 1943), 10–15, 19–25, 83–86. In a chapter entitled "Great Britain Adopts Protection," Joseph M. Jones relates these measures to the Smoot-Hawley tariff (*Tariff Retaliation: Repercussions of the Hawley-Smoot Bill* [Philadelphia, 1934], 211–246). Bennett's telegrams to Beaverbrook, February 2 and 5 respectively, are quoted in Lord Beaverbrook, *Friends: Sixty Years of Intimate Personal Relations with Richard Bedford Bennett* (London, 1959), 67–68. Keith Feiling writes, "Only Canadian remonstrance had brought about the decision of no duties on the Dominions till after Ottawa" (Feiling, *The Life of Neville Chamberlain* [London, 1946], 205). For Chamberlain's speech of February 4 in Parliament, see Great Britain, *Parliamentary Debates,* House of Commons, 5 series, Vol. 261, p. 291 (hereafter cited as follows: volume number, *H. C. Deb.* 5 s., page number).

American exporters helplessly saw trade diverted to imperial channels.

The Ottawa Conference of 1932 and its results were largely the work of Richard B. Bennett. A supporter of Joseph Chamberlain's ideas of closer economic union as early as 1911, Bennett was by 1930 a strong advocate of an imperial preference system.[3] His actions in London at the Imperial Conference of 1930 were consistent with his maturing philosophy of trade within the Empire, although other forces as well might have influenced his behavior. He knew that the free-trade Labor Government of Ramsay MacDonald would never embrace such a plan. Possibly encouraged by the more "Tory" wing of the British Conservative party who wanted to embarrass the incumbents and hasten the day when a national election would turn them out of office, he had pressed the Laborites to favor the Dominions with the passage of a tariff levying 10 per cent duties against all foreign imports. James H. Thomas, Secretary of State for Dominion Affairs, responded in the House of Commons with the biting remark that "there never was such humbug" as Bennett's proposals.[4] The Canadian Prime Minister's principal accomplishment

[3] For Bennett's early views, see Beaverbrook, *Friends,* 23–33.

On July 25, 1932, J. W. Dafoe wrote to Thomas B. Roberton, an assistant editor of the *Free Press,* that "in 1930 [referring to the conference in London] Bennett put over his demands in the expectation that he would put the Labor gov't in a hole and help the Tories. I thought then that Amery was jogging his elbow." While this statement of a political opponent obviously cannot be considered "proof," subsequent developments at Ottawa suggest that something quite similar lay behind the activities of Bennett and Amery in 1932 (John W. Dafoe Papers, Public Archives of Canada, Ottawa [microfilm, reel no. M–76]). See also the discussion of this question in Alfred Eugene Morrison, "R. B. Bennett and the Imperial Preferential Trade Agreements, 1932" (M.A. thesis, University of New Brunswick, 1966), 71–81, 89–94.

[4] Thomas made the comment on November 27, 1930 (Great Britain, 245 *H. C. Deb.* 5 s., 1550).

in London was passage of a resolution that imperial trade matters be examined at a special conference sometime within the next year.

In February, 1931, Canada suggested that the conference meet the following August, but George William Forbes, the Prime Minister of New Zealand, wired Bennett that he doubted whether his government could attend such a gathering in 1931. "In August," he explained, "Parliament will be in session and General Elections are probable towards the end of the year." That the political complication was a convenient excuse for a New Zealand Cabinet that frowned on the idea for another reason is evident in Forbes's further comment that the recent proceedings in London had convinced it "that there is no possibility of any effective consideration at Ottawa of a general system of Imperial Preference embracing the United Kingdom, and this being the case . . . [his colleagues] feel deliberations of forthcoming Economic Conference will not have sufficient application to the Dominion of New Zealand to warrant any alteration of date to suit their convenience." [5] Economic uncertainties in Australia, prompting a similar message from Canberra, and, particularly, the continued refusal of the British Labor Government to accede to the Bennett program combined to force postponement.[6]

[5] George William Forbes, Prime Minister of New Zealand, to Bennett, March 7, 1931, Richard B. Bennett Papers, Vol. F–100. This collection is housed in the Harriet Irving Library (formerly the Bonar Law-Bennett Library), University of New Brunswick, Fredericton, New Brunswick. I am grateful to the Harriet Irving Library for permission to consult and quote from the Papers of R. B. Bennett.

[6] See Bennett statement June 8, 1931, in Canada, *House of Commons Debates* (hereafter cited as Can. *H. of C. Debates*), III, 2374–2375. A few days before, the American Minister in Ottawa had written, "It is more or less openly admitted that last autumn Mr. Bennett suggested the adjournment of the Imperial Conference to Ottawa in the firm belief that by the summer of 1931 the Conservative Party would have been returned

The British electorate removed a key obstacle in October, 1931, when it placed in power a national government headed by Ramsay MacDonald but dominated by Conservatives. So happy was Bennett that he congratulated Stanley Baldwin upon his "magnificent victory which makes Empire economic association a certainty." [7] Within twenty-four hours he had invited the members of the Empire to meet in Ottawa as early as possible. After further delays and a trip by the Canadian Prime Minister to Great Britain, representatives from nine Empire countries convened in July, 1932, to seek more stable markets within this family of nations.

By July, 1932, conditions had changed markedly from what they had been in 1930. The depression had worsened, making agreements within the Empire more urgent but also more difficult to reach. Under pressure from domestic interests that wanted either greater protection or else no reductions in the tariff schedules, delegates were forced to adopt much tougher bargaining tactics. Every indication is that Bennett had hardened in the interval. With a new government that had embarked on a policy of protection, and with the expiration date for Dominion free entry fixed for November, Great Britain could bar-

---

to power in Great Britain. Since this event has not as yet taken place the futility of dealing with the Labour government is becoming increasingly emphasized" (Hanford MacNider to Secretary of State, no. 377, May 29, 1931, 842.9111/53). The situation in Australia in 1931 and early 1932 is mentioned in Raymond A. Esthus, *From Enmity to Alliance: U.S.-Australian Relations, 1931–1941* (Seattle, 1964), 12. The importance of the Labor Government's opposition to Bennett's proposals is discussed in Ray Atherton, Counselor of United States Embassy in London, to Secretary of State, no. 167, June 18, 1932, 841.01 Imperial Economic Conference–Ottawa/97. For a general account of the Canadian Prime Minister's role at the London conference of 1930, see W. K. Hancock, *Problems of Economic Policy, 1918–1939*, Vol. II of *Survey of British Commonwealth Affairs* (New York, 1940), 212–213.

[7] Bennett to Baldwin, Oct. 28, 1931, Bennett Papers, Vol. F–189.

gain more effectively with the Dominions.[8] Leopold S. Amery, a staunch Conservative protectionist, warned his friend Bennett that Liberals within the Government had successfully opposed tariffs on wheat and meat and that he could expect tough bargaining. He singled out J. H. Thomas as the principal adversary, for "his whole attitude is that of a Trade Union Leader thinking only of driving a bargain and of strengthening his position for such a bargain by depreciating everything the other side have ever done." [9]

The Ottawa Conference had great significance for both the United States and the British Empire, but it has thus far escaped the careful scrutiny of historians. While not all the evidence is available, enough has come to light to give a reasonably accurate description of what actually transpired in the Canadian capital during those frenetic days of July and August. The British delegation was a strong body including Stanley Baldwin, Neville Chamberlain, Walter Runciman, Lord Hailsham, J. H. Thomas, and several other Cabinet ministers. At Chamberlain's insistence, Baldwin headed the delegation.[10] Empire Free Trade, long championed by Beaverbrook, had few adherents in 1932. Instead, imperial preferences were thought to be more realistic because they rewarded interests within the Empire while they left still protected the manufacturers in the more industrialized Dominions. The issue was which method was better to effect closer economic union. Baldwin and his colleagues wanted pri-

---

[8] The Ottawa Conference and its preliminaries are discussed in Hancock, *Problems of Economic Policy, 1918–1939*, 198–230. See also Ernest Watkins, *R. B. Bennett: A Biography* (Toronto, 1963), 156–157, and Kreider, *The Anglo-American Trade Agreement*, 84.

[9] Amery to Bennett, March 4, 1932, Bennett Papers, Vol. F–91.

[10] Feiling, *Chamberlain*, 211. To his American friend, Abraham Flexner, Thomas Jones wrote in February, 1932, "S. B. [Stanley Baldwin, who that same day had paid Thomas a visit] himself may go to the Ottawa Conference as there is a doubt about J. H. T.'s [James H. Thomas] suitability " (T. Jones, *A Diary with Letters*, 27).

marily to lower the tariffs on imperial goods. As compensation for easier access in Dominion markets for their commodities, the British could guarantee continued free entry into the United Kingdom of the important exports of natural products from the Dominions.

The British delegation was confronted by formidable foes in Ottawa who adhered to a different program for a stronger imperial preference system. Both Richard Bennett of Canada and Stanley Bruce, the head of the Australian delegation, favored increasing preferences by retaining existing imperial levels and raising duties against foreign countries. For a more industrially developed economy, like Canada's, this method would afford Canadian industries greater protection from American imports, without opening the door to increased competition from the United Kingdom. Canadian industrialists, who wanted no foreign or imperial inroads into their domestic markets, had representatives in Ottawa keeping a watchful eye on the negotiations, applying pressure on Bennett to hold firm against major concessions, and maintaining links with the more conservative members of the Cabinet so that they would not be caught unawares by any developments. One important correspondent wrote how difficult it was for "anyone unfamiliar with the political milieu of Ottawa to realize what tremendous and varied pressure can be employed by industrial interests convinced that a diminution of their tariff preserves means, if not ruin, grave embarrassment. . . . [All] the massed resources of the high protectionist elements in Canada who feel their position threatened have been employed in Ottawa." In short, the British delegation found economic nationalism to be firmly entrenched in the two leading Dominions. The depth of this commitment became increasingly apparent with the passage of time.[11]

[11] See the perceptive article by George V. Ferguson in the Winnipeg *Free Press,* Aug. 27, 1932. The *Times* (London) of July 26, 1932, reported that the Canadian Manufacturers Association had a group of

Due in part to his close relationship with ultraconservative Tories in Great Britain, who seem to have convinced him that an uncompromising stand at Ottawa would suffice, Bennett and the British government were inadequately prepared for the conference. Whitehall had informed Bennett in February of the concessions it would seek, requesting similar information from the Dominion. In May, Thomas, dissatisfied that nothing concrete had been said about increasing United Kingdom exports to Canada, wired Bennett that "continuance of concessions within the framework of the Import Duties Act after the 15th of November could not be justified to public opinion and affected interests here unless balanced by reciprocal concessions." His colleagues were "somewhat concerned that, though time is running short, there has so far been no real indication of the attitude of the Dominion Governments as regards concessions which latter might be prepared to give in return for continuance of concessions under Imports Act."

Bennett never replied to these overtures, the preliminary work before the actual negotiations remained incomplete, and the United Kingdom delegates headed for the Canadian capital ignorant of "what they could receive . . . or what they would be expected to give." Shortly before his departure for Ottawa, Stanley Baldwin himself said that "no one knows what Bennett will do." [12]

---

officials in Ottawa acting as watchdogs of the conference proceedings. The quote in the text is from *ibid.*, Aug. 9, 1932.

[12] After the conference had ended, Dafoe synthesized the various attitudes and sentiments about it that he had gleaned from numerous sources. He wrote that "Bennett's cocky dictatorial attitude at opening thought to be . . . due in part to advice given him by Rothermere [Lord Rothermere, English newspaperman]. R. told him that the British ministers had no fixed programme and if he would take a strong line at the outset he could easily dominate the conference" (Dafoe Papers, reel no. M–76). Telegram, Thomas to Bennett, May 9, 1932, Bennett Papers,

The conference opened officially on July 21. In his initial speech, Bennett first reviewed the favorable developments since the London meeting for imperial economic unity, asserting that "our common need is now more urgent" and that "the time for action has arrived." He then endorsed trade expansion within the Empire and its beneficial effects on world trade in general. "Greater Empire markets," he declared, "mean as well greater world markets. . . . Closer Empire economic association does not mean in any sense world dissociation." To the United Kingdom, he offered an extended free list, retention of existing preferential rates, and increased preferences on certain items, through higher tariffs against third parties. At the same time, with the Canadian farmers—particularly wheat growers—clearly in mind, he requested continued free entry into Great Britain for Dominion natural products and extension of preferences to those natural and processed items not covered by the United Kingdom tariff. The Import Duties Act had exempted from taxation wheat and a few other commodities. Toward the end of his statement he exhorted that "the agreement should be an enduring one. This is not the time for ephemeral treaties."

Baldwin's opening address recorded support for achieving greater preferences by lowering intra-Empire tariff rates as opposed to the alternative of raising duties against foreign countries, for "we cannot isolate ourselves from the world." He argued that "no nation or group of nations, however wealthy and populous, can maintain prosperity in a world where depression and impoverishment reign" and called upon his fellow delegates to "aim at the lowering rather than the raising of barriers . . . and let us remember that any action we take here is bound to have its reactions elsewhere." Three weeks earlier, however, he

---

Vol. F–93; T. Jones, *A Diary with Letters*, 45–46; Winnipeg *Free Press*, Aug. 31, 1932.

had declared privately that at the conference he would "try and keep to the big things on which Canada can help us; iron and steel, coal, cotton, and wool. If we could divert some of her trade with America in these four groups it would help." [13]

Some months after its adjournment, Bennett took into his confidence a journalist who had covered the conference, and revealed to him the "inside story" of what actually had happened at Ottawa. According to the Prime Minister, he had undermined the position of the British delegation before it ever arrived in the capital. Together with Stanley Bruce and Leopold Amery—although Amery understandably remained silent in his memoirs—Bennett had been party to a combination directed to the defeat of any tariff reductions. Amery came to Ottawa as a lobbyist for both the Empire Sugar Federation and the Central Chamber of Agriculture. [14] During his stay he corresponded with the Prime Minister, urged him to remain firm, and gave him moral support. Bennett and Bruce "played ball from the beginning of the Conference," and by the end of July these two supporters of tariff exclusion had won all of the Dominions but New Zealand to their cause. By his own admission, Bennett was the spokesman in the clashes with the British, since Australia's hopes for a conversion loan from London later in the year inhibited Bruce. The Prime Minister was firmly convinced, therefore, that by being vigilant and unyielding he could get extremely favorable terms for Canadian goods imported into the United

[13] The texts of Bennett's and Baldwin's opening speeches are in Imperial Economic Conference, 1932, *Report of the Conference* (Ottawa, 1932), 67–74. See also *Times* (London), July 22, 1932. Relevant portions of the statements appear in *The United States in World Affairs: An Account of American Foreign Relations, 1932* (New York, 1933), 91–92. For Baldwin's earlier comment, see T. Jones, *A Diary with Letters,* 46.

[14] L. S. Amery, *The Unforgiving Years, 1929–1940,* Vol. III of *My Political Life* (London, 1955), 81.

Kingdom without paying an exorbitant price. The determining factor in his attempt to augment the Dominion's position in the British market without sacrificing Canadian industry would be his physical and mental ability to withstand the varied assaults of Chamberlain and Baldwin.[15]

During the first days of the conference, Bennett remained evasive as to what concessions Canada would grant on United Kingdom imports. He confined his offensive to pressuring the British delegation to embargo imports into Great Britain from the Soviet Union. The British, of course, "had financial commitments which would be jeopardised by such drastic action as a total prohibition of Russian imports." Although the Prime Minister "attached great importance to action against Russia," the Whitehall forces held firm.[16] This anti-Russian posture, which he assumed at his first meeting with Baldwin on the night of July 25, Bennett maintained throughout the week. On one occasion, he chose to harangue against the Soviet trade during an appearance before the Committee on Promotion of Trade within the Empire, the most important of the five committees established in the early proceedings. In the middle of this "oratorical flight," Runciman interjected "a caustic remark." As confirmed by Robert Manion, the party leader later in the decade, the "interruption was too much" for Bennett, and he "broke down for a moment to some extent in tears," the first of two such spectacles at the conference.[17] By the end of the month Canada,

[15] Grant Dexter to J. W. Dafoe, Oct. 16, 1932, Dafoe Papers, reel no. M–76.

[16] Feiling, *Chamberlain*, 213.

[17] Roberton to Dafoe, July 27, 1932, Dafoe Papers, reel no. M–76. The second breakdown came on the final Friday when, presented with evidence that the representative of British iron and steel interests had not consented to the Canadian withdrawal of the previous offer, he "broke down and cried. Herridge and Guthrie came in and carried him away" (Dafoe notes, Dafoe Papers, reel no. M–76).

accepting the British argument that London could not embargo Soviet imports, had reconciled itself to action against dumping only.

Meanwhile, on July 26, Bennett, together with Cabinet members C. H. Cahan and H. H. Stevens, discussed for the first time with the British representatives which products were to be covered by an agreement. As reported in the *Times* (London), the meeting "began the process of laying the cards on the table between the two countries, whose intentions hitherto have been most obscure." Two days later, the British published a statement calling upon the Dominion to adopt a competitive tariff system and to reduce duties on United Kingdom imports.[18]

As a first step, the Canadians wanted Whitehall, explicitly and unequivocally, to extend the principle of preferences to natural products. "It is idle to suggest that this Conference can reach an agreement of substantial consequence to us unless that principle is freely and unequivocally accepted," wrote one of Bennett's advisers. The British have "always known our position on this matter," he continued, "they, therefore, came to this Conference, we must assume, realizing that the principle must be accepted before business could be done. That principle still remains unaccepted. Manifestly, therefore, the first forward step to be taken is to dispose of it." Bennett was receiving advice also from William Herridge, the Canadian Minister to the United States and a brother-in-law, due to his recent marriage to the Prime Minister's sister. Herridge argued that a British proposal, containing "principles wholly antagonistic to the policy of the Conservative Party, but unfortunately highly acceptable to certain sections of Canada," was imminent. "For this reason," Herridge wrote, "I am firmly of the opinion that a definite proposal

[18] *Times* (London), July 28, 1932; *ibid.*, July 29, 1932.

should be made to the United Kingdom without any delay. However imperfect our proposal may be, we will fare better if we attack on it than if we are put in the position of defending ourselves against any proposal which they may make." [19] As the State Department would learn for itself in November, 1934, during the trade agreement discussions between Canada and the United States, Herridge had great faith in Bennett's ability to improve his political image in Canada by seizing the initiative from his antagonists and putting them on the defensive.

Impressed with this reasoning, the Prime Minister directed interested department officials to draft such proposals, which they did by "working night and day over the first long weekend." On August 4, Bennett relayed them to the British delegation. Subsequently this offer was referred to in at least one Canadian newspaper as the "Mickey Mouse" list because of its many "bizarre and silly articles." [20]

Contrary perhaps to the Prime Minister's expectations, the British found the Canadian position to be unsatisfactory.[21] Disappointed particularly with the absence of concessions on iron and steel products and textiles, they held that the Canadian offer was "quite inadequate to effect the Imperial purposes of the Conference expressed by the Prime Minister of Canada" in his

[19] Unsigned Memos, "Most Private and Confidential," no. 3, pp. 1, 3 (Bennett Papers, Vol. F–93); Herridge to Bennett, undated, *ibid.*

[20] Morrison, "Bennett and Imperial Preferential Trade Agreements, 1932," 138. In the words of Chamberlain, "Bennett came . . . to bring his offer. He adopted a very aggressive tone" (Feiling, *Chamberlain,* 213). For the reference to the "Mickey Mouse" list, see Winnipeg *Free Press,* Aug. 31, 1932.

[21] Dafoe notes, Dafoe Papers, reel no. M–76. Dafoe wrote, "Bennett's cocky dictatorial attitude at opening thought to be . . . due in part to advice given him by Rothermere. R told him that the British ministers had no fixed programme and if he would take a strong line at the outset he could easily dominate the conference."

opening address. Additional concessions had to be forthcoming if Canada expected Whitehall to grant the favors the Dominion sought.[22]

For the next few days the British maintained the pressure on Bennett to improve his proposals. Although the Canadian Prime Minister claimed later that he recognized the tactic as "flattery," Geoffrey Dawson, the editor of the *Times* (London) who was in Ottawa reporting developments directly to his readers, painted Bennett as one who had the task of repulsing the attacks of the high protectionists in his own party. "He is undoubtedly faced with the gravest crisis in his political career," wrote Dawson, "and his predicament, which is fully understood by the British Ministers, commands their sympathy." If he were to make "a brave stand for a policy of real Imperial cooperation," even at the expense of "the disintegration of his Cabinet and the construction of a National Government," this "would win for Mr. Bennett an assured place in the Valhalle of Imperial statesmen." [23]

By August 11, following information from Robert Manion that the "very best officials in the Customs Department" thought that the duties on steel and textiles were excessive, Bennett become convinced that some concessions had to be made or the conference might come to an end without an Anglo-Canadian pact.[24] He yielded on iron and steel, and was moving toward some reductions on textiles.

Alerted to developments, his ultraconservative colleagues, led by Cahan, rebelled, and the pressure groups representing Canadian manufacturers rose to the challenge. Returning to the issue of Soviet trade with Great Britain, they found in Bennett an

[22] "The Canadian Tariff Proposals—Note by the United Kingdom Delegation—Secret," Bennett Papers, Vol. F–93; *Times* (London), Aug. 10, 1932.

[23] Dexter to Dafoe, Oct. 16, 1932, Dafoe Papers, reel no. M–76; *Times* (London), Aug. 9, 1932.

[24] Manion to Bennett, Aug. 10, 1932, Bennett Papers, Vol. F–103.

amenable anti-Bolshevik who dutifully raised this topic again in the discussions with the British. Claiming that the earlier settlement would no longer suffice, he sought more effective measures against Soviet dumping in the United Kingdom market. The indignant British, thinking that the matter had been settled already, fought back, and acrimonious debates continued down to the very end of the negotiations, almost disrupting the conference at the eleventh hour.[25] There is evidence that Amery influenced this maneuver. On August 16, Manion informed Bennett that he had just seen Amery and that "something he has learned this morning convinces him that if we press hard enough, particularly with the assistance of some pressure from the other Dominions, we can get a three-cent duty on all meats except chilled beef, and he told me that I might pass this on to you." Amery thought also that the Canadians could get "20 per cent on lumber, plus restrictions on Russia. He is convinced that both of these can easily be carried in the English House of Commons. . . . He even thinks that the embargo on Russia could now be put through the House of Commons and would be given a wild demonstration." [26]

On August 18, with the two nations on the verge of agreement, Bennett withdrew certain concessions that he had earlier granted. The British had refused to accept the Canadian anti-Soviet policy, but there was something more fundamental in the Prime Minister's about-face. According to an authoritative account, the Canadian trade experts had agreed to the British request for reduction of the tariff on steel plates above a certain

[25] See the Ferguson article in the Winnipeg *Free Press,* Aug. 27, 1932, and telegrams of August 17 and 18 from Dexter in Ottawa to Dafoe, Dafoe Papers, reel no. M–76. In his notes on the conference, Dafoe wrote that "Cahan was in continuous open conversation with the textile people. He undoubtedly stood against change and textile people believe he saved the day for them" (*ibid.*).

[26] Manion to Bennett, Aug. 16, 1932, Bennett Papers, Vol. F–103.

size, thinking that the plates could not be manufactured in the Dominion. After this item had thus passed from the scene, a Canadian steel manufacturer informed Bennett that fabrication of such plates in Canada was feasible. The Prime Minister then shocked the United Kingdom delegation by removing it from the list of concessions, an action "Baldwin and Chamberlain never quite forgave." [27] Upon his return to London, Baldwin revealed to a friend, perhaps with some hyperbole, that "Bennett had a brain storm every day which wiped out what he had agreed to the day before." [28]

The negotiations became hectic and frenzied, since the conference, already once postponed, was scheduled to expire on August 20. On the next to last day the politicians, rather than the trade experts, worked until the early morning to reach agreement. Chamberlain reflected at the time that he hoped never "to go through such an experience again. I don't think I ever worked so hard in my life, for the heaviest of the strain fell on me." Lord Hailsham, who also bore much of the burden, "nearly collapsed on Friday night [August 19]." Stanley Baldwin wrote that "this has been a devil of a job." He confirmed that "the bulk of the negotiations have [sic] been done by Neville 'ably assisted' . . . by Hailsham." The Chancellor of the Exchequer admitted that "it was a d—d close-run thing"; the accord was reached "after a prolonged and desperate battle with Bennett." He had problems with the other Dominion representatives, but the principal antagonist remained the Canadian Prime Minister. Chamberlain recognized that the Australians and New Zealanders, while they caused anxieties, "had to think of their difficulties with their own people," and "were quite straightforward about it." On the other hand, "Bennett was a different proposition . . . he alternately

[27] Watkins, *Bennett,* 160–161. Morrison elaborates this point in "Bennett and Imperial Preferential Trade Agreements, 1932," 150–153.

[28] T. Jones, *A Diary with Letters,* 50.

blustered, bullied, sobbed, prevaricated, delayed, and obstructed to the very last moment." [29] He assigned "most of our difficulties . . . [to] the personality of Bennett. Full of high Imperial sentiments, he has done little to put them into practice. Instead of guiding the conference in his capacity as chairman, he has acted merely as the leader of the Canadian delegation." In this position, Bennett "has strained our patience to the limit." [30] Within a few days of the British delegation's return home, Stanley Baldwin told a friend that he "ought to have heard Neville at the Cabinet on Saturday telling the tale. When they heard what trouble we had with Bennett they swallowed all our discussions without a murmur." [31]

In the final analysis, however, the Canadian obtained essentially what he wanted—including most of the original requests—by convincing the British that if they refused to yield, he would let the conference collapse. After Bennett's behavior, the members of the United Kingdom delegation might have preferred collapse, but Prime Minister Ramsay MacDonald in London wired them to accept the altered version rather than return empty-handed.[32] As Bennett related to the reporter mentioned earlier, it was he, and not the British, who had postponed the end of the conference from August 18 to 20, who had delayed the special train carrying the British delegation to Quebec and had held up their ship, and, finally, who had threatened

---

[29] Iain MacLeod, *Neville Chamberlain* (New York, 1962), 160–161; T. Jones, *A Diary with Letters,* 49.

[30] Feiling, *Chamberlain,* 215.

[31] T. Jones, *A Diary with Letters,* 51.

[32] Watkins, *Bennett,* 161. In March, 1962, H. H. Stevens wrote Morrison that after Bennett withdrew the concessions on the plates, "the British Delegation contacted Ramsay MacDonald in London, suggesting they leave the Conference in protest, but MacDonald urged them to stay and sign the agreement no matter how unsatisfactory it might be" (quoted in Morrison, "Bennett and Imperial Preferential Trade Agreements, 1932," 150).

to sign agreements with the other Dominions only, thus killing an Anglo-Canadian pact, if they did not comply. Having no alternative if he wanted to salvage an agreement, "Baldwin came to Bennett." Great Britain accepted Canadian terms, and the accord was signed early Saturday morning. The protectionists had achieved the ultimate victory.[33] As John W. Dafoe, the Liberal editor of the Winnipeg *Free Press* and a political opponent of Bennett, wrote later, "In the end the British were bluffed into giving more than they wanted to give and taking a good deal less." [34]

By the terms of the final instrument, Canada increased and guaranteed for five years the margins of preference of 215 items imported from the United Kingdom, either through reductions of the preferential tariff (132) or through raising the rates on foreign imports (83). Iron and steel imports were made slightly easier, but one British objective, liberalization of the duties on textiles, was thwarted. Great Britain left Dominion imports on the free list, while agreeing to impose tariffs on importations of the same products from foreign countries. Bennett undoubtedly was proud of two other concessions directly affecting important constituencies. Whitehall granted a preference for the first time to wheat and promised to raise the margin on apples above the 10 per cent level. Moreover, the United Kingdom agreed in the accord not to lower preferences without the consent of Canada. The British achieved two partial victories in provisions dealing with the trade with Soviet Russia and future rates in the Cana-

[33] Dexter to Dafoe, Oct. 16, 1932, Dafoe Papers, reel no. M–76.
[34] Dafoe to Mary Craig McGeachey, Nov. 7, 1932, Dafoe Papers, reel no. M–76. In a similar vein, he wrote to C. L. Burton on October 22 that "at the last Bennett out-bluffed the British delegation. He made them believe that he was prepared to have the conference blow up if they did not fall in line with his views, and almost at the last moment they yielded, not having the courage to let the conference fail, and putting the responsibility of its failure upon Mr. Bennett" (*ibid.*).

dian tariff. Commercial ties with the Communists were retained, and Canada agreed to levy duties against British commodities sufficient only to equalize production costs in the two countries. A Tariff Board was established to revise rates consistent with the competitive principle, to review current rates, to inquire into any tariff increases, and to listen to appeals from British exporters. Unfortunately for these exporting interests, the conversion of the Canadians to a competitive tariff proved to be specious. Six other agreements were negotiated between Great Britain and the other Dominions which followed the general pattern of the Anglo-Canadian pact.[35]

With the closing of the conference, certain newspapers in the United Kingdom put a favorable complexion on the proceedings. In the words of the *Daily Telegraph* (London), "The finale of this great Conference was as happy as its inauguration." Developments at the last plenary session, highlighted by the signing of the various pacts, "leave no doubt as to the cordiality existing between the various delegations." Similarly, the *Morning Post* (London) termed Ottawa "an example to the whole world of what can be achieved by mutual confidence and conciliation." [36] Of course, nothing could be further from the truth.

In the process of reaching their accord, the Canadian and United Kingdom delegations had exchanged harsh words, creating an atmosphere of animosity, and bitterness had accompanied the actual signing. In his closing remarks, drawing an analogy between the weather in Ottawa at the time and the conference proceedings, Baldwin, in a moment of understatement, referred to "storms," "thunder and lightning," and how "we have very

[35] Imperial Economic Conference, 1932, *Report*. A summary of the agreement was printed in the New York *Times,* Aug. 22, 1932; the entire accord was published in October. See also *U.S. in World Affairs, 1932,* 94–96.

[36] *Daily Telegraph* (London), Aug. 22, 1932; *Morning Post* (London), Aug. 22, 1932.

nearly been washed out." He had no patent on understatement, however. Bennett declared in his final address, "There have been moments when I have been impatient, and, perhaps, intolerant." [37] What must have gone through the minds of the British delegation when they heard that admission! Both Neville Chamberlain and Walter Runciman, the President of the Board of Trade, supposedly had said publicly that the conference had been a mistake and that any good connected with the results had been nullified by the acrimony engendered in reaching them. Whether or not the statements had actually been made, the sentiments were those of all the British delegates.[38] Privately, on one occasion, Chamberlain had termed Bennett's position "modified humbug," and in a letter to a sister he had referred to the "outrageous provocation" to which he had been subjected. One source claimed that the "British visitors went home" regarding the Canadian Prime Minister either as a "mental case" or "a 'great big stiff.' Only he didn't say stiff." [39] In September, Baldwin, with no air of contradiction, quoted a Canadian Liberal's characterization of Bennett: "He has the manners of a Chicago policeman and the temperament of a Hollywood film star." [40]

That Bennett reciprocated these attitudes is attested by his appraisal of the delegation and its tactics. Bennett felt that Baldwin, while a "splendid public man," was basically "weak . . . deficient in the strength to resist a well-equipped determined opponent." He described J. H. Thomas in much the same language as had Amery, as an "ignorant, trade union demagogue type." The Canadian Prime Minister found Neville Chamberlain "a very great disappointment." Not only did Bennett con-

---

[37] Imperial Economic Conference, 1932, *Report*, 150–151, 156.

[38] New York *Times*, Aug. 20, 1932.

[39] MacLeod, *Chamberlain*, 161; Roberton to Dafoe, July 27, 1932, Dafoe Papers, reel no. M–76; Dafoe to Roberton, Sept. [undated], *ibid.*

[40] T. Jones, *A Diary with Letters*, 52.

sider the present Chancellor of the Exchequer intellectually inferior to Joseph Chamberlain, his famous father, but he also felt that the future sponsor of appeasement had "stabbed" him "in the back" by authoring the editorial attack in the Montreal *Gazette.* On August 10 this Conservative newspaper had argued that "the impasse which has been reached is attributable very largely to . . . [Bennett's] disposition to keep the preparation of Canada's case and the actual negotiations wholly in his own hands." This idiosyncrasy made him prone "to the commission of mistakes, and it is an open secret that mistakes have been made." [41] Bennett could not easily forgive or forget the "threats and abuse" directed his way by the British delegation, particularly the "despicable campaign to discredit" him in his own country.[42]

Throughout these proceedings, the United States government maintained an official posture of neutrality, but not of disinterest. Before the conference began, the State Department in conjunction with the Commerce Department mapped strategy. Pierre Boal, who within a few days departed for Ottawa to become the American Chargé at the Legation, called a meeting with Henry Chalmers of the Commerce Department's Division of Foreign Tariffs. The State Department spokesman stressed two points: the delicacy of the situation for American interests, and the necessity of close cooperation between the two departments. Boal emphasized that, as the United Sates was "the big outsider who would be principally affected" by the forthcoming agreements, it must "avoid the evidence of too great an interest" in the conference. The delegates at Ottawa, in his opinion, "would be watching" the American reaction to the proceedings, and if Washington became overly sensitive about any specific action, this would likely "crystallize their attitudes in favor of it."

[41] Montreal *Gazette,* Aug. 10, 1932.
[42] Dexter to Dafoe, Oct. 16, 1932, Dafoe Papers, reel no. M–76.

Both Chalmers and a subordinate official noted that irresponsible press coverage and the conspicuous activities in Ottawa of representatives of American businesses posed the real danger. The Commerce Department subsequently instructed its district managers to discourage these firms or associations from sending observers to the Canadian capital. To avoid "duplication of effort" at Ottawa, representatives of the two departments agreed that daily meetings between their people in the Canadian capital be held to review past and to outline future coverage.[43]

This circumspection explains the absence in State Department files of confidential and revealing reports by the foreign service officers. Even governmental pressure, however, could not keep affected American interests out of Ottawa. Stanley Baldwin subsequently reported that "American influence is of course very strong in Canada and we believe that it was doing its utmost to thwart us."[44]

When the terms of the various agreements were published, experts in the State Department calculated, and predicted quite accurately, the probable economic consequences to American business in Canada and the United Kingdom.[45] No formal communication to Ottawa or London was forthcoming at any time as the imperial delegates applied the capstone to their retaliation against the Smoot-Hawley Tariff Act. Opinions from Washington would have accomplished nothing. Certainly the United States recognized that the nations of the Empire, being autono-

[43] Henry Chalmers, Division of Foreign Tariffs, Department of Commerce, to Lynn Meekins, Commercial Attaché, Ottawa, July 13, 1932 (Department of Commerce, Bureau of Foreign and Domestic Commerce, Record Group 51 [National Archives], File No. 441); memorandum to all District Offices, from John Matthews, Jr., Assistant Director, Bureau of Foreign and Domestic Commerce, July 16, 1932, *ibid.*

[44] T. Jones, *A Diary with Letters,* 50.

[45] Pierre de L. Boal to Secretary of State, no. 1080, Oct. 20, 1932, 841.01 Imperial Economic Conference–Ottawa/204.

mous entities, could do as they saw fit without obtaining clearance from Uncle Sam. Moreover, Boal was probably correct: pressure from the State Department at this moment, given the nationalism prevalent in both countries, very likely would have strengthened the resolve of those who wanted to close the Empire even more to American exports.

In November, 1932, the British Parliament gave its approval to the Ottawa agreements and raised the duties on foreign imports as promised in them, thus putting the stamp of finality on this solution to imperial economic problems.[46] As a result, not only were formidable barriers to closer trade relations with the United States created, but also an atmosphere of suspicion, ill will, and defiance. Unquestionably the American Congress had precipitated the tariff responses in both Canada and the United Kingdom. Shortly before the Ottawa Conference, the American chargé in the Canadian capital reported a "quiet but definite undercurrent of antagonism and bitterness towards the United States trade policy" whenever comments were made of the impending gathering.[47] On August 16, Boal wrote Moffat from Ottawa that "most of the people I have talked to have not failed to refer to our tariff and to accuse it of starting the world movement toward restriction of trade." [48]

Once the mistakes were known, it was no easy task to rectify them, as Hull learned in 1933. In all three countries interests which had received this tariff protection fought diligently to retain it. In Great Britain the innovation captured converts other than just representatives of those businesses which benefited from the decrease in competition from the United States. To

[46] Kreider, *The Anglo-American Trade Agreement,* 22, 85.

[47] B. Reath Riggs to Secretary of State, no. 789, May 4, 1932, 841.01 Imperial Economic Conference–Ottawa/49.

[48] Boal to Moffat, Aug. 16, 1932, J. Pierrepont Moffat Papers, II, Houghton Library, Harvard University; this collection is quoted by permission of the Harvard College Library.

many the tariff was a necessary defensive precaution that their government had to adopt in order to survive in a highly nationalistic world. Walter Runciman, a former free trader, had "lost all hope of curbing the growing economic nationalism" which had left London no alternative but to abandon tradition.[49] As the thirties progressed, and as the United States, having done penance for its economic sins, sought to improve trade between the two peoples, the British government was not particularly interested in a return to the policies followed before 1931. After 1934, the year the Roosevelt Administration won an epochal victory for economic internationalism with the Trade Agreements Act, Washington moved in the direction of liberalized trade, while Whitehall moved in the opposite direction, content with its new policy and intent on negotiating trade agreements more bilateral in nature than those endorsed by Secretary of State Hull.

The situation differed in Canada, because even the Bennett government quickly appreciated the close commercial ties between the two nations and pressed for some trade arrangement to stimulate the north-south flow of goods. The shadow of the Anglo-Canadian pact fell heavily here too, inhibiting the negotiators in their efforts to restore some sanity to this economic relationship. Nevertheless, a Canadian-American trade agreement became a reality in 1935, the first successful American attempt to dismantle the imperial system erected at the Ottawa economic conference.

Yet these developments lay in the future. The most immediate opportunity for either intensifying the prevailing attitudes and strengthening the tariff structure or moving in the other direction of cooperative sentiments and facilitating trade within the three-nation bloc was the World Monetary and Economic Conference which assembled in London in 1933.

[49] Norman Davis to Secretary of State, telegram no. 113, May 9, 1933, *Foreign Relations, 1933*, I, 598.

Chapter 2

Tariff Truce and the London Economic Conference: Lost Opportunities

Studies of the World Monetary and Economic Conference of 1933 that have appeared to date follow a similar pattern. They stress the monetary problem raised by desertions from the international gold standard, the search for stability in currency exchanges against the backdrop of rivalry between gold and non-gold nations, and the dramatic repudiation of a stabilization declaration by President Franklin D. Roosevelt. The conference, wounded mortally by his "bombshell" message, limped along for several more weeks, largely due to Cordell Hull's efforts. Unable to do anything until the United States agreed to monetary stabilization, it then recessed. The activities of June and July proved to be the last postwar attempt at the international level to correct economic dislocations, for the conference never reconvened. The emphasis in these accounts on the monetary issue, which dominated the proceedings, is sound. The inability of the major nations to stabilize currencies hampered agreements in other problem areas, such as freeing the world's commerce from the shackles of various trade restrictions. The prevailing view at

London was that a successful plunge into more liberal trade waters depended upon establishing monetary stability.

This chapter does not purport to revise accepted interpretations of the World Monetary and Economic Conference. Historians have given little notice, however, to the trade revival program that was essayed during the first months of the Roosevelt Administration. The following pages focus on the negotiation of the tariff truce of May, 1933, and the abortive attempt at London to lift tariff barriers, giving particular attention to Anglo-American collaboration in the effort.

The governments that sent delegates to London in June of 1933 wanted expansion of trade; the depression had made them extraordinarily anxious to find outlets for surplus goods as a means of fighting domestic hunger, unemployment, and discontent. Some representatives in London—the American Secretary of State is a foremost example—believed that lowering trade barriers took precedence over monetary reform. As long as trade restrictions—whether tariffs, exchange controls, or quotas—remained, a debtor nation would profit little by stabilization. Without trade liberalization, these nations would again lose their gold, and turn to currency devaluation or other action that would precipitate another financial crisis. As expressed by an American delegate before the Subcommission on Commercial Policy, currency stabilization was directed against only a symptom of the foremost problem, the breakdown of international trade. Only reduction of barriers could strike effectively at the basic causes of economic dislocation.[1]

[1] Several secondary accounts of the World Monetary and Economic Conference deserve mention. Pioneer efforts are Basil Rauch, *The History of the New Deal 1933–1938* (New York, 1944), 85–92, and Jeannette P. Nichols, "Roosevelt's Monetary Diplomacy in 1933," *American Historical Review*, LVI (Jan., 1951), 295–317. The most recent are Julius W. Pratt, *Cordell Hull* (2 vols.; New York, 1964), I, 32–70, and Lloyd C. Gardner, *Economic Aspects of New Deal Diplomacy* (Madison,

At London the United States and the United Kingdom had an opportunity to cooperate in the war against economic exclusion. Superficially at least, the chances of success did not appear remote. Admittedly, the tariff walls recently built around the British Isles and the imperial preference system were realities, but they had not become part of a long tradition. Had the nations of the Commonwealth and the United States been willing to bargain with meaningful concessions, duties could have been lowered. The Smoot-Hawley tariff had prevailed since 1930, but a Democratic administration had just assumed control of the American government. Democrats in the past had railed against the high tariffs favored by their opponents, and in the campaign of 1932 they had lost no chance to woo voters with promises of reciprocity agreements. In late April, 1933, the leaders of the two countries had met in Washington and publicly pledged themselves to the "effort to moderate the network of restrictions . . . by which commerce is at present hampered." [2]

Yet even contemporaries, noting the obstacles to a successful conference, made few promises. Nations felt differently about

---

1964), 26–33. Thanks to his inimitable style, the most interesting is Arthur M. Schlesinger, Jr., *The Coming of the New Deal* (Boston, 1959), 203–232. Surprisingly, in spite of his extensive research, Robert Ferrell, *American Diplomacy in the Great Depression* (New Haven, 1957), 255–277, is the least rewarding, because the author neglects completely the developments after July 3. *The United States in World Affairs, 1933* (New York, 1934), 119–158, is helpful, but the most thorough contemporary treatment is in Arnold J. Toynbee, ed., *Survey of International Affairs, 1933* (London, 1934), 35–81. See also the informative article by Raymond Leslie Buell in the New York *Times*, June 18, 1933. Congressman Samuel D. McReynolds' speech can be found in League of Nations, *Journal of the Monetary and Economic Conference* (London, 1933), 110–111.

[2] The Joint Statement by President Roosevelt and the British Prime Minister (MacDonald), April 26, 1933, is printed in *Foreign Relations, 1933,* I, 492–493.

the basic sources of their ills and offered varied prescriptions. The British, doubting the feasibility of solving exchange and tariff problems before the war-debts question was settled, stressed the necessity of raising international price levels. In May, Norman Davis warned the Secretary of State of his findings after talks in London that while the British "recognize the desirability and importance of cooperating as closely as possible with us" in international matters, they "have had only one real preoccupation in their economic and financial relations with us, namely, the war debt issue, until recently when a new element was introduced by the depreciation of the dollar." He felt that the cabinet, with the exception of MacDonald, were interested in the conference only as an opportunity to attack the war-debts and dollar-fluctuation questions. For the moment, they were content with the Ottawa agreements and the bilateral trade treaties then being negotiated by the Board of Trade. MacDonald himself confessed to Davis that "some of his associates" considered it "rather unreasonable" for the United States with its "present high tariff and fluctuating currency to ask them to 'stop now' and do nothing to protect themselves." As Herbert Feis has written, the implication was that the price of British cooperation was American surrender on the debts, agreement to stabilize the dollar, and commitment to leave intact present tariff rates.[3] The United Kingdom delegation—all Cabinet members—was predominantly protariff and inclined toward closer economic unity within the Empire.

While the French, leaders of the gold-bloc powers, gave top priority to currency stabilization, the Roosevelt Administration had not decided what goal to pursue most ambitiously. Men like Raymond Moley and Rexford Tugwell, entertaining few hopes

[3] Davis to Secretary of State, telegram no. 113, May 9, 1933, *Foreign Relations, 1933,* I, 597–600; Herbert Feis, *1933: Characters in Crisis* (Boston, 1966), 171.

for the international approach to be tried at London, wanted the President first to raise domestic prices; they saw both exchange stabilization and lower tariffs as threats to their plans. Others, notably Hull, thought that the United States ought to concentrate on the removal of trade barriers. The American delegation sent to the conference, perhaps the most discordant group ever to represent the country abroad, reflected Roosevelt's indecision regarding, if not disinterest in, the experiment in London. Certainly it would not speak as one voice, and, possibly worse, the President himself neither spoke nor acted consistently during these hectic months. He balanced statements calling for currency stabilization with warnings that the first task of his administration was to raise prices. He endorsed trade revival, while favoring controls to prevent an influx of foreign goods.

Although commentators and some officials thought Anglo-American cooperation to be essential, the two governments failed to exploit the opportunity afforded by the conference. They were unable to reverse the tariff policies of the past few years and, if anything, both contributed to an intensification of economic nationalism. The failure to collaborate economically signaled what lay ahead. When the inevitable political problems appeared, the United States and the United Kingdom were no more able to cope with them than with the challenges presented at London. The reversal—and maybe tragedy would not be too strong—of July left its stamp. When the smoke lifted, the climate in both capitals was hardly conducive to close international cooperation. Inconsistencies in American policy had cooled British hopes, and British recalcitrance had soured Americans. Bitterness became most intense early in July when Roosevelt publicly rejected stabilization. Prime Minister MacDonald was reportedly so upset when he learned of Roosevelt's decision that, like many American conservatives in later years, he could only refer to Roosevelt as "that person." To the President's special emissary he cried, "This doesn't sound like the man I spent so many hours with in Washington. This sounds like a different man." He mellowed little in the ensuing months. In the middle of September, he reviewed the entire episode with Norman Davis. The irritating factor during the days of uncertainty in July, MacDonald related, was Roosevelt's failure to communicate with him "suggesting some modification or explaining just what his difficulty was in order that they might agree on some way of handling the situation so as not to create any serious difficulty." [4] He learned of the presidential decision—which had already been made public—through one of the American delegates.

Bitterness has a tendency to linger. In April, 1936, Secretary of the Treasury Henry Morgenthau, who wanted Roosevelt's permission to begin currency stabilization talks with the British, wrote that he "did not tell the President, because I did not want to irritate him at this time . . . [that] the English definitely feel that he double-crossed them in the summer of 1933 and that is why they have acted so peculiarly about stabilization ever since." [5]

The origins of the London conference date to 1932. European nations had about come to the end of the line with respect to reparations and war debts installments. They could dispose of the reparations torment but needed the cooperation of the

[4] Shepard Stone, "Anglo-American Economic Issues," *Current History,* XXXVIII (July, 1933), 399–405. MacDonald's reference to FDR as "that person" appears in Ernest K. Lindley, *The Roosevelt Revolution: First Phase* (New York, 1933), 211. Raymond Moley records the Prime Minister's reaction in his *After Seven Years* (New York, 1939), 263. For the September exchange, see memorandum of conversation between MacDonald and Davis, Sept. 18, 1933, Davis Papers, Box 9.

[5] Entry of April 29, 1936, Henry Morgenthau, Jr., Diary (Franklin D. Roosevelt Library, Hyde Park), Book 22, pp. 155–156; John Morton Blum, *From the Morgenthau Diaries: Years of Crisis, 1928–1938* (Boston, 1959), 141.

United States to clean the slate completely. At Lausanne, in June, after settling the problem of German default in reparations payments, representatives of these governments studied "the measures necessary to solve the other economic and financial difficulties which are responsible for, and may prolong, the present world crisis." They finally decided that this end could best be served if the League of Nations convened a monetary and economic conference. Acting on their request, the Council of the League in July created a Committee for the Organization of the Conference, and in October, a Preparatory Commission of Experts. American participation in this League-sponsored conference was the outgrowth of diplomatic correspondence between the United Kingdom and the United States. In June, President Hoover had promised the cooperation of his government as long as certain topics—war debts, reparations, and tariff rates—were kept off the agenda.[6]

Charged with the responsibility of drafting an acceptable agenda, the Preparatory Commission of Experts, which included two Americans, met twice in Geneva, in November, 1932, and early January, 1933. On January 19 it submitted the result of its labors, the Draft Annotated Agenda, to the chairman of the Committee for Organization, Sir John Simon, the British Foreign Secretary. By January 26 this body, sitting in London, had made preliminary proposals which the League Council accepted. Prime Minister Ramsay MacDonald thus became the president of the conference, and the participating governments received

[6] For the background of the conference, see the secondary works already cited, and also League of Nations, *Monetary and Economic Conference: Reports Approved by the Conference on July 27, 1933, and Resolutions Adopted by the Bureau and the Executive Committee* (Official No. C.435.M.220.1933.II [Conf. M.E. 22(1)]). Pertinent documents for 1932, including some diplomatic correspondence between the United Kingdom and the United States, appear in *Foreign Relations, 1932*, I, 808–845.

copies of the draft agenda. Because other details remained to be worked out, such as setting the date for the formal opening of the conference, the committee continued to meet intermittently.[7]

Norman Davis, who shuttled across the Atlantic regularly during these years to attend consultations on disarmament or other matters, outlined for MacDonald on one such occasion a positive contribution to commercial sanity which the United Kingdom, Canada, and the United States could make. Like his fellow Tennessean, Cordell Hull, Davis found "the trouble in the world today . . . [to be] the economic warfare . . . [that had] developed into trench warfare as a result of various prohibitions, quotas, exchange controls, excessive tariffs and depreciated currencies." An exponent of the most-favored-nation principle, he believed that "if we try any further to develop bilateral trade instead of multilateral trade we will merely dig the trench deeper."[8] In late March, 1933, replying to a question from the Prime Minister on how best to forward the economic conference, Davis suggested a commercial treaty embracing Great Britain, Canada, and the United States. "No economic group . . . had more extensive trade relations" than the three North Atlantic powers, he remarked, and if they negotiated some agreement "which would really help to stimulate trade, it might serve as a model which other countries could adopt and thus become a step toward the general breaking down of trade restrictions."[9] Although at the time MacDonald and Simon indicated some interest in the suggestion, the British government never formally pursued it. For the remainder of his stay in London, Davis

[7] League of Nations, *Monetary and Economic Conference: Report of the Bureau,* 3.

[8] Davis to William R. Castle, Dec. 20, 1932, Davis Papers, Box 8.

[9] Memorandum of conversation between MacDonald, Simon, and Davis, accompanied by Allen Dulles, March 30, 1933, 4:00 to 5:00 P.M., Davis Papers, Box 9.

devoted his time to preparing the way for MacDonald's visit in April to Washington and to negotiating the tariff truce of May.

Upon taking office the Roosevelt Administration thus found itself committed by its predecessor to an international conference. In spite of the opposition of certain advisers who were unenthusiastic about the prospects, the administration went ahead with plans to attend. Shortly before the inauguration, the British Embassy in Washington wrote a note to the Department of State calling for joint action by the several governments to combat the problems of the depression. Explaining that various avenues would be explored at London, the British outlined as the basis of a cooperative Anglo-American venture the program proposed by the Preparatory Commission of Experts. Since relaxation of trade barriers was one of the principal elements of the program, Whitehall declared in qualified terms its readiness to join the United States in effecting a tariff truce for the duration of the conference and to discuss the possibilities of a tariff agreement. Unfortunately, the British dampened any American enthusiasm by tying the package to positive action on the war-debts question. Citing the Preparatory Commission's reference to this problem as "an insuperable barrier to economic and financial reconstruction," they asserted that "there is no prospect of the World Economic Conference making progress if this barrier cannot be removed." [10]

Washington's reply, not dispatched until March 24, tepidly endorsed cooperation, inviting the British to engage in conversations with departmental officials. As Raymond Moley, a leading economic nationalist in the new administration, recalled the episode, the American memorandum "indicated that the United States did not feel there was any tearing hurry about getting down to business." Consistent with the views of the influential

[10] British Embassy to Department of State, Feb., 1933, *Foreign Relations, 1933,* I, 465–471.

Moley, the memorandum registered opposition to any linking of the debt question with the other problems mentioned in the note. Sir Ronald Lindsay, the United Kingdom's Ambassador in the United States, began talks with the men at State in late March, but the discussion remained general and there were no concrete results.[11]

A tariff truce was not much more popular among planners than were discussions of war debts, but the Roosevelt Administration moved to give the truce form. Varying the draft agenda's suggestion, the President sponsored an agreement that would go into effect before the conference and last until its termination. He thought the United States could best promote the project in the Committee for Organization of the Conference. Accordingly, Norman Davis was instructed to work in the committee for approval of two proposals: (1) inclusion with the invitations to the governments attending the conference the notice of Washington's intention at its outset to introduce a resolution calling upon them to "refrain, during the period of the truce, from creating or making any material upward modification in tariff rates, imposing any new restrictions or enhancing any existing restrictions against the importation of goods" that would inhibit foreign trade; (2) adoption and publication of a draft statement supporting the truce concept and urging all governments "to abstain from all initiatives which might increase the many varieties of difficulties now arresting international commerce."[12]

On April 29, Davis introduced the American proposals. The

---

[11] Department of State to British Embassy, March 24, 1933, *Foreign Relations, 1933*, I, 472–473. On March 30, Hull wired the American Chargé in Great Britain that "the British Government has not yet replied to our memorandum, and while several conversations have been held with Lindsay during the past few days they have been exploratory in scope" (*ibid.*, 474). See also Moley, *After Seven Years*, 197–198.

[12] Secretary of State to the Chargé in Great Britain, telegram no. 83, April 28, 1933, *Foreign Relations, 1933*, I, 578–580.

committee, which at this meeting set June 12 as the date for the opening of the conference, unanimously agreed to send the notification with the invitations, but balked at the second suggestion. Prior to the formal meeting, its chairman, Sir John Simon, had informed Davis of his doubts that the committee had authority to act on the American draft. Simon himself could do nothing until he had consulted with the Cabinet. When the committee actually met, the German representative, supported by other members, challenged the committee's power to implement Washington's proposal. Responding to pressure from Davis, the members finally agreed to ask their superiors for the necessary sanction. After the meeting was adjourned, the League of Nations representative suggested to the American diplomat that the statement in its present form was feared by other delegates because it was too binding. If the wording were changed to read, "[The committee] regards with great sympathy the [American] decision . . . to put forward a proposal for the conclusion of an economic truce and considers that conditions most favorable to the success of the Conference would be created if all governments would in the intervening period before the Conference abstain from any action contrary to the spirit of this proposal," the chances of approval would be better.[13]

Hull lost little time in granting Davis discretionary power to accept a modified statement if that were the only alternative.[14] Even so, Davis encountered delay as he sought a tariff-truce resolution. Simon had been confined to bed, and only he, the chairman of the Committee for Organization, could call it into session. Of greater significance was the Foreign Secretary's reluctance to take any action until Prime Minister MacDonald

[13] Davis to Secretary of State, telegram no. 91, April 29, 1933, *Foreign Relations, 1933*, I, 581–584; New York *Times*, April 30, 1933.

[14] Secretary of State to the Chargé in Great Britain, telegram no. 84, April 30, 1933, *Foreign Relations, 1933*, I, 584.

returned from his conversations with the President in Washington. The bilateral overtones of current British trade policies also inhibited progress. Whitehall had recently concluded agreements with Denmark and Germany and had just finished negotiations with Argentina. The depression convinced many that each nation was forced to fend for itself in its fight to stay alive economically. The British, quite happy with these arrangements granting important privileges to their exporters, wanted nothing to interfere with them. Ray Atherton, the astute American Chargé in London, wired Hull that MacDonald was in a particularly uncomfortable situation with respect to the Argentine agreement "as Runciman [Walter Runciman, President of the Board of Trade] has a strong backing in the Cabinet and has threatened to resign and thus jeopardize the position of the Government unless he is supported." [15]

Reporting on May 3, Davis drew the contrast between the economic policies pursued by the United Kingdom and the program endorsed by MacDonald and Roosevelt in Washington. In their joint statement released on April 26, the two men had contended that "commercial policies have to be set to a new orientation. There should be a constructive effort to moderate the network of restrictions of all sorts by which commerce is at present hampered, such as excessive tariffs, quotas, exchange restrictions, etc." [16] Great Britain meanwhile "has been moving rapidly in the opposite direction by the conclusion of trade agreements containing quota and preferential clauses." MacDonald faced a formidable task if, upon his return to London, he planned to reverse British commercial policy to bring it in line

[15] Davis to Secretary of State, telegram no. 92, May 1, 1933, *Foreign Relations, 1933,* I, 584–586; Atherton to Secretary of State, telegram no. 105, May 7, 1933, 635.4131/83.

[16] Joint Statement by Roosevelt and MacDonald, April 26, 1933, *Foreign Relations, 1933,* I, 492.

with the goal expounded in the communiqué. During his absence support for the bilateral accords had increased. The price
for closer Anglo-American cooperation was, as informed Britishers knew, waiving the immediate profits of bilateralism. Mac-
Donald's opponents could exploit particularly the strong British
dislike of the war-debts issue by arguing that a tariff truce was
unacceptable unless there were also a debt truce. Without this
countermeasure Great Britain, but not the United States, would
forfeit its interests. Much depended upon MacDonald's ability to
carry the Cabinet with him in the face of such opposition.[17]

Davis kept in close contact with the Prime Minister for the
next few days. According to MacDonald, he and Roosevelt had
not discussed specifically the possibility that the Committee for
Organization would initiate the truce resolution. MacDonald
had only supported the principle of a truce; whether a concrete
instrument followed would depend on how it was phrased and
whether it protected adequately quotas on certain agricultural
imports imposed by agreements concluded and negotiations conducted by the British government. Walter Runciman joined the
conversations and reaffirmed that Whitehall favored a truce as
long as it did not interfere with negotiations. The Cabinet was of
similar persuasion, preferring to see the final wording of the
resolution before giving it official sanction. The Prime Minister
replied affirmatively when Davis asked him whether it was necessary that the text not "prohibit further agreements involving
quotas on agricultural products." To the American's interpretation of British policy as opposition to the proposal in its present
form but support for a truce with the proper reservations, Mac-
Donald responded that Davis "was putting it rather bluntly but
he [MacDonald] supposed that was about the truth."

Davis pressed him also about the incompatibility between the public statement issued in Washington and the trade agreements negotiated by the United Kingdom. Of the two approaches, Davis thought, the British would benefit more through a general program. MacDonald admitted in his rejoinder that the Cabinet would not support the proposal unless it allowed the recent agreements and negotiations. The Prime Minister then reached the crux of the question, a consideration that would plague statesmen of the leading countries of the North Atlantic community for the next few years as they grappled with the political problems of an unstable world. Great Britain hesitated to commit itself to anything unless the other principal governments acted accordingly, and it feared that the French would not bind themselves to any truce arrangement.[18] MacDonald and his government wanted a truce, but hesitated to pay the necessary price and feared being isolated if other governments proved to be uncooperative. Any agreement shaped in this atmosphere of suspicion and doubt would be imperfect.

On May 5, William Phillips, the Under Secretary of State, removed any uncertainty that Davis might have had about Hull's sincerity. According to Phillips, the Secretary "very much" wanted a truce. That same day, Hull himself authorized Davis to accept any wording as long as the essential meaning was left intact.[19] The American negotiator predicted that it would take MacDonald at least a week to obtain Cabinet approval of

---

[18] Memorandum of conversation between MacDonald and Davis, to be joined by Runciman, May 4, 1933, Davis Papers, Box 9; memorandum of telephone conversation between Phillips and Davis, May 5, 1933, *ibid.* (a slightly different version appears in *Foreign Relations, 1933*, I, 587–591); memorandum of conversation between MacDonald and Davis, May 5, 1933, Davis Papers, Box 9; Davis to Secretary of State, telegram no. 101, May 5, 1933, *Foreign Relations, 1933*, I, 592–593.

[19] Memorandum of telephone conversation between Phillips and Davis, May 5, 1933, *Foreign Relations, 1933*, I, 587; Secretary of State to the Chargé in Great Britain, telegram no. 92, May 5, 1933, *ibid.*, 591.

any truce. If the British were to agree, the other six governments represented on the Committee for Organization—Germany, Belgium, France, Italy, Japan, and Norway—still had to give their assent.[20] To ease the Prime Minister's burden, Hull specified July 31 as the date on which the arrangement would expire. Hopefully, during that period permanent accords would be negotiated to "relieve international commerce from the present encumbrances." [21]

Three days later, Davis showed a revised draft to Runciman.[22] Favorably disposed himself, the Board of Trade official thought that his department would raise no difficulties as long as it could execute existing agreements. He warned, though, that certain tariffs would be increased to conform with the Ottawa agreements. Runciman promised to discuss the latest draft with Cabinet members, particularly with the Minister of Agriculture, and at Davis' insistence, he agreed to circulate it that same evening. Davis assured Runciman that the new version left Great Britain free to carry out its previous agreements. Actually, the United States was as anxious as Great Britain to protect its rights under the arrangement. A simultaneous development in Washington prompted Davis to say that "the agricultural problem might require special treatment." He had in mind the Agricultural Adjustment Act, which within a matter of days passed the Senate and received the President's signature. The law provided that

[20] Davis to Secretary of State, telegram no. 101, May 5, 1933, *Foreign Relations, 1933*, I, 593.

[21] Secretary of State to the Chargé in Great Britain, telegram no. 97, May 6, 1933, *Foreign Relations, 1933*, I, 593–594.

[22] "The said governments, being further convinced that immediate action is of great importance, themselves agree, and strongly urge all other governments participating in the Conference to agree, to abstain, at least until July 31, 1933, . . . from all new initiatives which might increase the many varieties of difficulties now arresting international commerce" (Davis to Secretary of State, telegram no. 109, May 8, 1933, *Foreign Relations, 1933*, I, 594–595).

if they reduced acreage, American producers of seven basic commodities would be given federal subsidies, to be financed through taxes on processors. Unquestionably, the measure had a vitiating effect on the tariff truce, and thus compromised Davis' efforts in London. The act stipulated that whenever a processing tax was operative, the United States would automatically impose a compensating tax on imports of foreign products processed in whole or in part from that commodity.[23]

On May 9, Davis learned from Runciman and Simon that they could accept the draft if two amendments were added to it: a statement reserving the right of a country to withdraw from the truce at any time after July 31 by giving a month's notice to the Conference, and reference to a section in the Draft Annotated Agenda allowing a nation, in a specific situation, to regulate exports or production. Though he was confident that Hull would accept the modifications, Davis could not speak for the Secretary. Arguing in his report that "we now have a real chance to put over the tariff truce," he requested an immediate reply so that he could finish his part of the job.[24]

That same night, Hull wired Davis his approval of the British version and stated his wish that the Committee for Organization would quickly take action.[25] On May 10, Simon circulated the draft among the other six delegations. Two days later, after a three-hour discussion, the eight nations resolved that they "agree and strongly urge all other governments participating in the Conference to agree that they will not before the 12th of June

[23] *Ibid.* For discussions of the Agricultural Adjustment Act, see Schlesinger, *The Coming of the New Deal,* 36–49, and Rauch, *The History of the New Deal,* 65–71. The key provision of the act is printed in *Foreign Relations, 1933,* I, 687.

[24] Davis to Secretary of State, telegram no. 112, May 9, 1933, *Foreign Relations, 1933,* I, 596.

[25] Secretary of State to the Chargé in Great Britain, telegram no. 101, May 9, 1933, *Foreign Relations, 1933,* I, 600.

nor during the proceedings of the Conference adopt any new initiatives which might increase the many varieties of difficulties now arresting international commerce." At this very important meeting, Simon interpreted the section from the Draft Annotated Agenda as applying to aid that might be granted to agriculture. The Foreign Secretary then suggested that the United States favored the incorporation of that amendment so that it could continue with plans to improve the lot of the American farmer. Davis' concurrence in Simon's statement together with the agreement's injunction against "new initiatives" only, rather than all initiatives, provided Washington officials with quasi-legal authority to enforce the compensating tax feature of the Agricultural Adjustment Act (AAA), which coincidentally also became law on May 12, despite its incompatibility with the truce. The French and German governments attached to this resolution formal "explanations and qualifications" which, in Davis' opinion, weakened it. But he preferred their acceptance to further negotiations and delay.[26]

During this period, supporters of closer Anglo-American cooperation could point with a sense of accomplishment only to the tariff truce. Because of its limited nature and many loopholes, one should be careful not to exaggerate its importance. The United States and the United Kingdom had committed themselves to nothing more than to keep their present tariff levels intact. In practice, they failed to adhere even to this largely symbolic gesture. Great Britain interpreted the truce, in Neville Chamberlain's words, as "not intended to prevent the completion

[26] Davis to Secretary of State, telegram no. 116, May 10, 1933, *Foreign Relations, 1933,* I, 601; Davis to Secretary of State, telegram no. 121, May 12, 1933, *ibid.,* 601–602; Davis to Secretary of State, telegram no. 122, May 12, 1933, *ibid.,* 602–605; Chairman of the American Delegation to the Disarmament Conference (Davis) to Secretary of State, telegram no. 186, May 24, 1933, *ibid.,* 614–615. A copy of the truce is printed in *ibid.,* 605.

of operations already begun" and accordingly raised numerous duties without violating its letter. Following the passage of farm legislation in May and the National Industrial Recovery Act (NIRA) in June, the United States had power to alter its tariff schedules. Shortly afterward, acting under authority granted by the AAA, the President imposed compensatory taxes on certain importations.[27]

Fifty-three governments subsequently subscribed to the tariff truce, which, in spite of its ambiguities, was ostensibly the first step in the direction of liberalizing world trade. Cordell Hull hoped that during this breathing spell the nations at London could take the next step, an attack on the existing barriers. Appointed by Roosevelt to be the chairman of the American delegation at the World Monetary and Economic Conference and instructed to present several resolutions there,[28] Hull placed greatest faith in the resolution appealing to the powers to lower trade barriers. According to Herbert Feis, he "had gone over the resolutions cursorily. Only one really aroused his interest—that which would have obligated all signatories to reduce their trade restrictions and end their exchange controls as fast as circum-

[27] Great Britain, 278 *H. C. Deb.* 5 s., 17. Chamberlain's statement in context was, "The object of the truce is to discourage the starting of new upward initiatives in the adjustment of tariffs and other economic devices, and it is not intended to prevent the completion of operations already begun. Acting in this spirit, the Import Duties Advisory Committee will continue to carry out their statutory obligations, including the receipt and examination of applications for new or altered duties, but the Government will, during the operation of the truce, refrain from making orders for increases of Customs duties in respect of any applications which had not been received by the committee before the 12th May." For the President's action under the new legislation, see New York *Times,* May 23 and 25 and June 28, 1933. Lindley's statement on this topic in *The Roosevelt Revolution,* 186, is somewhat misleading.

[28] Roosevelt to Hull, May 30, 1933, *Foreign Relations, 1933,* I, 620–621. See particularly "Memorandum on Policy for American Delegation," *ibid.,* 622–627.

stances" allowed.[29] Hull believed that he and his government could make a major contribution in the fight to restore economic and political stability to a chaotic world if they vigorously promoted the adoption of that resolution. Shortly before his departure for the United Kingdom, his department began to draft a measure for the President to submit to Congress. If it were passed, the executive would have power to lower tariffs through negotiations of trade agreements with other governments. Armed with this weapon, Hull thought he could convince foreign delegations that the United States was serious about lowering its tariffs.[30]

When the S.S. *President Roosevelt* carrying most of the American delegation departed for London, Hull "did not seem deeply troubled, as a man who was clutching a forlorn cause." Whatever the explanation for his euphoria—"his failure to grasp or his unwillingness to acknowledge the impending difficulties" or "his habitual adaptation to disappointment . . . upheld by a belief that somehow or other the nations would learn that the route which he urged them to follow was the only trail to salvation"—the Secretary of State confidently predicted that "there should be an agreement as to the fundamentals of the situation in a few weeks, that should apply equally to currency stabilization as well as to trade barriers." [31]

Unfortunately, the Secretary's international solution to the depression had to compete in Washington with the economic nationalism of key presidential advisers. Confident that the first priority for the government was to raise deflated domestic prices, these planners were frightened or angered by certain remarks emanating from Washington early in May. Speaking to the

---

[29] Feis, *1933: Characters in Crisis*, 169.

[30] Cordell Hull, *The Memoirs of Cordell Hull* (2 vols.; New York, 1948), I, 248.

[31] Feis, *1933: Characters in Crisis*, 171.

American section of the International Chamber of Commerce, Hull declared that "every nation must supplement its domestic program with a basic international economic program of remedies for business recovery . . . [embracing] the reduction of trade barriers, the stabilization of exchanges and currencies, and monetary standardization." A few days later, in a "fireside chat" to the country, the President asserted that "the domestic situation is inevitably and deeply tied in with the conditions in all of the other nations of the world. . . . [Prosperity] will not be permanent unless we get a return to prosperity all over the world." One of the government's objectives was "the cutting down of the trade barriers" impeding the flow of goods. With an eye on London, he continued, "The international conference . . . must succeed. The future of the world demands it, and we have each of us pledged ourselves to the best joint efforts to this end."

On May 20, Raymond Moley, an assistant secretary of state, corrected erroneous impressions about Roosevelt's intentions entertained by Hull and segments of the populace. Speaking over the Columbia Broadcasting System, he discounted the significance of both the upcoming London Conference and of foreign trade as a factor in American prosperity. It was "overwhelmingly clear" to Moley that "a good part of the ills of each country is domestic. The action of an international conference which attempted to bring about cures for these difficulties solely by concerted international measures would necessarily result in failure. In large part the cures for our difficulties lie within ourselves. Each nation must set its own house in order." Minutes later, the former professor called upon the American people to recognize that "world trade is, after all, only a small percentage of the entire trade of the United States. This means that our domestic policy is of paramount importance." Unknown to Hull,

Roosevelt had read and approved the text before its delivery.[32] By the end of May, then, the economic nationalists had converted the President to their views. There was obviously no place for reciprocity legislation in the package presented to Congress by Roosevelt during the First Hundred Days.

Meanwhile, Hull, still expecting favorable congressional action to strengthen his hand in the fight for lower tariffs, was en route to the English capital. Upon hearing reports that Roosevelt would not ask Congress for authority to negotiate reciprocal trade agreements, he wired the President his judgment that "in addition to most seriously handicapping the mission of our delegation . . . it would be a major error to defer [making the request] until 1934." He averred that "American accomplishments possible [at London] . . . even if only moderately successful at this first session will constitute the most outstanding single achievement of your administration." If the rumors were correct, the American delegation could not implement that part of the instructions Hull had so warmly embraced, reducing the delegation "to a passive role . . . rather than the active role contemplated." In a prompt reply Roosevelt confirmed the reports. To defend his decision, the President cited explosive situations in

[32] Hull's address is printed in United States Department of State, *Press Releases*, VIII (May 6, 1933), no. 188, pp. 310–315. Roosevelt's fireside chat, broadcast over CBS and NBC, appears in *ibid.*, VIII (May 13, 1933), no. 189, pp. 333–339. Just before the quote in the text, the President had said, "Hand in hand with the domestic situation, which, of course, is our first concern." Moley's contribution is in *ibid.*, VIII (May 20, 1933), no. 190, pp. 374–380. According to this Brain Truster's interpretation of Roosevelt's remarks of May, "The President so completely placed his faith and confidence in his domestic program that there was no further question in my mind about his basic reactions." He turned to the radio broadcast because "I saw that the public had been misled into thinking that the main line of recovery was shifting from the United States to London" (*After Seven Years*, 207–209).

Congress that dictated immediate adjournment of that session. "Otherwise, bonus legislation, paper money inflation, etc. may be forced," he wrote, "therefore tariff legislation seems not only highly inadvisable, but impossible of achievement." When he learned of Roosevelt's wish to avoid a fight over reciprocity, the Secretary was "heartbroken" by the "terrific blow." As he related later, "It swept from under me one of the prime reasons for going to London, one of the chief bases I had for hoping that real results could be achieved at the conference to lift the nations, albeit gradually, out of the world depression." [33]

Newspaper reports in Great Britain on the eve of the opening of the conference that the administration in Washington no longer supported tariff reduction as a solution for the world's ills troubled Hull as well; it was rumored that he might resign.[34] At the urging of James M. Cox and William C. Bullitt, two members of the American entourage who thought that a direct communication from the President would buoy his spirits, Roosevelt telegraphed the Secretary of State not to "worry about situation here in regard to tariff reductions and removal of trade obsta-

[33] Hull to Acting Secretary of State, telegram no. 10, June 7, 1933, 550.S 1/906; Acting Secretary of State to Hull, telegram no. 9, June 7, 1933, 550.S 1/916; Hull, *Memoirs*, I, 250–251. On December 28, 1933, William Phillips recorded in his diary that "Senator Harrison had this morning informed Feis that, in his opinion, such legislation [granting the President the authority to negotiate trade agreements] stood a much better chance this winter than it would have if presented last spring. This is the proposal which all of us in the Department were eager to have presented to Congress last spring, but at the last moment the President decided against it. The Secretary of State, who was then on the high seas, bound for the London Conference, was heartbroken when I sent him the news" (William Phillips Diary, Houghton Library, Harvard University; this collection is quoted by permission of the Harvard College Library).

[34] Hull to Secretary of State, telegram no. 19, June 11, 1933, *Foreign Relations, 1933*, I, 631–632. Warren Robbins reported the rumor of Hull's possible resignation (Robbins to Roosevelt, June 15, 1933, Roosevelt Papers).

cles." He reiterated that "the eleventh hour rows in Congress over domestic problems made general tariff debate dangerous to our whole program." But after the death of the reciprocity measure, Hull knew better than to believe his chief's words that "nothing said or done here will hamper your efforts." The President had noted that the Secretary could negotiate trade treaties at London and could subsequently call a special session to deal with them.[35] Hull saw this as patent nonsense. The odds of getting trade treaties through the Senate even under normal conditions were not good. To get treaties approved with the economic chaos at hand, the nationalism rampant in the country, and the absence of prior Senatorial blessing would be nothing less than miraculous. In his state of chagrin, the man was not in the market for miracles.

Nevertheless, upon his arrival in the United Kingdom, the Secretary went through the proper motions. On June 14, after a slight delay, he delivered his opening speech to the delegates assembled at the Geological Museum in Kensington. Although the speech had been toned down by the President before its delivery, it remained a brief for economic internationalism. Hull castigated as fruitless and discredited "the cherished idea of the extreme type of isolationist that each nation singly can, by bootstrap methods, lift itself out of the troubles that surround it" and termed "international cooperation today . . . a fundamental necessity." Giving primary emphasis to "the gradual and careful readjustment of the excesses of tariff and other trade barriers to a moderate level," he challenged listeners in London and Washington that "the first and greatest task at the present juncture is the development here in this hall of a will and a determination

---

[35] Cox and Bullitt to Acting Secretary of State (for the President), telegram no. 1a, June 11, 1933, *Foreign Relations, 1933,* I, 633; Roosevelt to Chairman of the American Delegation, telegram no. 22, June 11, 1933, *ibid.,* 634; Hull, *Memoirs,* I, 252–253.

on the part of nations vigorously to advocate this course." Whatever his expectations, these words, as Julius Pratt has written, "evoked little enthusiasm" among European delegates.[36]

After seven plenary meetings of the conference, two commissions—the Monetary and Financial Commission and the Economic Commission—and various subcommissions were created to deal with the many topics included in the agenda. The Monetary and Financial Commission, with James M. Cox, a former American presidential candidate, as chairman, became the more important. Gold-bloc nations, considering currency stabilization to be a prerequisite to attacks on trade barriers, concentrated their energies on this quest. Hendryk Colijn of the Netherlands headed the Economic Commission, after Hull had refused to serve in that capacity. The Sub-Commission on Commercial Policy, created on June 19 to study means of abolishing the restrictions retarding normal world trade, was its principal affiliate.[37]

The prominence assigned monetary reform and the bickering among the parties stymied real progress by the Sub-Commission on Commercial Policy. The underlying cause of the bickering is easily explained. A contemporary phrased it most succinctly and graphically when he wrote, "It became increasingly evident that in the world's commercial life many blood transfusions would be necessary, but that no nation would be willing to furnish the blood."[38] All countries professed a desire to see trade restrictions removed, as long as this meant removal of restrictions impeding

[36] Hull's speech is printed in *Foreign Relations, 1933*, I, 636–640. See also Hull, *Memoirs*, I, 256–257; Moley, *After Seven Years*, 226–227; and Pratt, *Hull*, I, 44–46. Hull's original draft is Hull to Acting Secretary of State, telegram no. 17, June 10, 1933, 550.S 1/928.

[37] Hull, *Memoirs*, I, 258; Hull to Roosevelt, Aug. 5, 1933, "Summary of Work of Monetary and Economic Conference," *Foreign Relations, 1933*, I, 736–737. Hendryk Colijn was the Dutch Prime Minister.

[38] Stone, "Anglo-American Economic Issues," 399.

the sale of their commodities in foreign markets rather than removal of their own protective devices. Each government, for economic and political reasons, was reluctant to make a concrete concession. In his report on the conference to the President, Hull singled out his candidate for principal villain: "Great Britain was the most insistent on the reduction of quotas [and] 'excessive' tariffs . . . but showed no willingness to make concessions of her own. . . . [Whitehall] led the attack on quotas, reserving her own." Hull directed most of his criticism at the British response to the tariff proposals he had presented just a few days before the recess. As he interpreted it, the United Kingdom "indicated an intention of increasing rather than diminishing her tariff. . . . The British led in the attack on excessive tariffs but took the position that their own tariff structure is still in the making and should be raised while excessive tariffs are being lowered." The basis for this interpretation was Chamberlain's closing remarks to the conference. The Chancellor of the Exchequer, declaring that his country's tariff "was still in the stage of construction," had placed on record that the British delegation "could not accept a position which stereotyped the present differences between the level of protection" in Great Britain and other countries. He "welcomed" Hull's proposals as "proof of his recognition that countries . . . [with] high tariffs should take the lead in reducing them." [39]

The Secretary's campaign for lower tariffs began awkwardly, if not ineptly. He had instructed Herbert Feis, then an important State Department official in London and a foremost proponent of the removal of trade barriers, to formulate proposals that might be considered by the governments at the conference.

[39] Hull to Roosevelt, Aug. 5, 1933, "Summary of Work of Monetary and Economic Conference," *Foreign Relations, 1933*, I, 743–744. Chamberlain's closing address can be found in League of Nations, *Journal of the Monetary and Economic Conference*, 232.

Among these items was the suggestion of a 10 per cent reduction in all tariff rates. Feis, with Hull's approval, submitted them to the secretariat of the conference. On June 17 the press published a four-point program, including a call for a horizontal 10 per cent tariff reduction, which it said the United States hoped to place on the agenda of the Economic Commission. Many reacted as though Washington had actually proposed the 10 per cent cut. Senator Key Pittman, one of the American delegation's protectionists, publicly opposed the plan, and in the confusion that followed Hull had to deny that it was ever a proposal. "We have made no such proposal," the Secretary explained, "but have merely listed various topics on the economic agenda for discussion, which does not in the least constitute a statement of our position." [40] Europeans, suspecting a divided United States delegation, distrusted its actions. One prominent British financial expert expressed the opinion that the conference might as well close shop until the Americans had made up their minds on stabilization and tariffs.[41]

On June 22, at the second meeting of the Sub-Commission on Commercial Policy, the Secretary clarified the picture when, "by the authority of the American delegation and in accordance with instructions of the United States Government," he introduced a more conservative four-point resolution.[42] Altogether this sub-commission held thirteen meetings at which the American

[40] Feis, *1933: Characters in Crisis,* 188–189; Nichols, "Roosevelt's Monetary Diplomacy in 1933," 311; Schlesinger, *The Coming of the New Deal,* 213; New York *Times,* June 18 and 19, 1933; Hull to Acting Secretary of State, telegram no. 42, June 18, 1933, *Foreign Relations, 1933,* I, 648.

[41] A headline in the New York *Times,* June 20, 1933, reads, "American Disunity Baffles London." On the next day, the *Times* quoted criticism of the American attitude from the French press.

[42] League of Nations, *Journal of the Monetary and Economic Conference,* 85–86 (also printed in *Foreign Relations, 1933,* I, 627). See also the New York *Times,* June 23, 1933.

suggestion, as well as others, were discussed, but with no agreement. The United States representative, Congressman Samuel D. McReynolds of Tennessee, contributed little to these discussions, which included mention of possible extension of the truce, the horizontal tariff cut, most-favored-nation clauses, and the like.[43]

By early July, Hull, wanting to avoid making any commitments incompatible with the planning schemes being shaped in Washington, asked whether the executive might exercise the powers granted in the NIRA and AAA to raise duties. With this information, he could promote more effectively the specific provisions of the American resolution introduced in June. Probably the first decision to face the delegation, Hull reported, would be whether to favor extension of the tariff truce beyond July 31. If the United States were to support prolongation, only under well-defined circumstances could it further restrict imports into the country. The Secretary inquired whether the delegation could cooperate with the prolongation effort. Any future quotas imposed by the National Recovery Administration (NRA) would obviously conflict with a related proposal, an agreement embracing the cessation of additional quantitative restrictions and the liberalization of existing ones. Again, Hull sought enlightenment from Washington. At the time, and later in his memoirs, he made known his attitude toward a program of domestic recovery that excluded trade revival. To abandon the campaign against artificially high trade barriers "would enormously strengthen the world-wide forces already making for economic isolationism and would be universally regarded as heralding the adoption by the American government of a policy of national self-containment." He doubted that "long range

[43] League of Nations, *Journal of the Monetary and Economic Conference*, 81, 85–86, 93–95, 100–101, 110–111, 119–121, 124–126, 132–134, 138–139, 144–146, 152, 159, 172.

American interests lie in this direction." For the conference to achieve "permanent benefit," Hull wrote, it must facilitate "an increase of international commerce." [44]

The President's answer, dispatched July 4, settled nothing. As argued by Roosevelt, New Deal policies to that point were not incompatible with the international attempt to restore world prosperity. The programs undertaken by the Administration—raising price levels, managing currency, expanding public works, controlling farm production, and so forth—not only were good for the United States but also would have beneficial effects on other nations. Washington's continued adherence to protection was difficult to defend, but the President accepted the challenge. The intrusion of foreign competition would undermine solutions to American problems. Because such competition was bad for the United States, it would ultimately have adverse effects on the people of the world, who "would have no reason to thank us for entering on such a course." To avert such a disaster, Congress had written into both the National Industrial Recovery and Agricultural Adjustment acts provisions empowering the President either to impose higher duties or processing taxes on imports into the country. In Roosevelt's opinion, "neither of these measures contemplates a change in the present competitive situation." The American government favored both a truce and negotiations for the lowering of tariff barriers, but wanted nothing to interfere with the Administration's national answer to the

---

[44] Chairman of the American Delegation to Acting Secretary of State, telegram no. 91, July 2, 1933, *Foreign Relations, 1933*, I, 676–678. On this occasion, the Secretary also wrote, "I am of the opinion that undue emphasis has been placed . . . on monetary issues. A smoothly operating international monetary system is impossible if conditions do not permit sufficiently easy international movement of goods and capital to effect the easy adjustment of balances of payments between countries. . . . Sufficient scope for movements of goods and capital is the only firm foundation for stable arrangements on the financial side."

economic crisis. Although the two policies were incompatible, the President either refused to admit it or hoped that he could play both games with a minimum of harm. "If the Conference can, through its deliberations, work out the basis for such a program for recovery as is already under way in the United States, the whole trend of international action can be reversed," he concluded, but he also insisted that the American government "has no other recourse than to pursue its present program until a more general international one shall have been worked out" in London.[45]

The following day, first by telephone and then by wire, the Secretary, far from satisfied with Roosevelt's reply, lamented that he and his colleagues were "without sufficient definite instructions to know what to do with respect to tariff truce or any method of lowering trade barriers of any sort except by bilateral bargaining treaty," an unworkable alternative.[46] On July 6 he asked Acting Secretary of State William Phillips just what the delegation was authorized to do in any discussion. Could it support the extension of the truce, or, if not, what reservations were to be attached? Could it agree to no further imposition of quotas and restrictions and to an understanding calling for their gradual removal? Could it adhere to any multilateral agreement designed to lower tariff rates? If the governments at London could not deal with those topics, nothing of any worth would be achieved. Hull ended the telegram by begging again for "clarification." [47]

[45] Acting Secretary of State to Chairman of the American Delegation, telegram no. 102, July 4, 1933, *Foreign Relations, 1933*, I, 685–687.

[46] Memorandum of telephone conversation between Roosevelt, Moley, and Hull, July 5, 1933, *Foreign Relations, 1933*, I, 688–692; Chairman of the American Delegation to Acting Secretary of State, telegram no. 104, July 5, 1933, *ibid.*, 694.

[47] Chairman of the American Delegation to Acting Secretary of State, telegram no. 106, July 6, 1933, *Foreign Relations, 1933*, I, 696–697.

Hull's request for policy guidance was predicated on the assumption that the conference would not break up at that very time. On July 2, President Roosevelt had "torpedoed" a temporary stabilization plan negotiated in the presence of his special emissary to London, Raymond Moley.[48] The incensed gold-bloc nations responded immediately by pressing for termination of the London Conference, satisfied that the presidential message should be its requiem. They were joined by the enraged British Prime Minister. On July 4, before the Steering Committee, MacDonald called for adjournment in a speech characterized by "bitter tone" and "sweeping condemnation." Not wanting the United States to be blamed in this dramatic fashion for the failures at London, Hull fought to keep the conference, even in its crippled state, in session. The tariff truce hung in the balance also, since it would automatically expire with formal adjournment. Hull had unsuccessfully attempted shortly before the Steering Committee meeting to have it deferred until July 5. Only the Canadian Prime Minister, Richard Bennett, was sympathetic. The others were very frigid. Already a committee had drafted a resolution endorsing adjournment and placing responsibility on the United States. Following MacDonald's "terrific speech," the Secretary of State moved for a recess of the Steering Committee until July 5. Fortunately he received support in this request from Bennett and Neville Chamberlain. Chamberlain, who supposedly had the anti-American resolution in his pocket ready for presentation, proposed an amendment to Hull's motion setting July 6 as the date for the Steering Committee's next meeting. The group agreed, and then recessed for two days.

[48] Roosevelt's statement is printed in *Foreign Relations, 1933,* I, 673–674. For discussions of this development, see particularly Nichols, "Roosevelt's Monetary Diplomacy in 1933," 314–317; Ferrell, *American Diplomacy in the Great Depression,* 266–276; Schlesinger, *The Coming of the New Deal,* 216–226; Pratt, *Hull,* I, 50–62. Hull's account appears in *Memoirs,* I, 259–262, while Moley's is in *After Seven Years,* 232–269.

On July 6 the Secretary, aided particularly by the forceful arguments of the Canadian Prime Minister, gained one of his few victories of early 1933 when the Steering Committee unanimously voted that the conference be continued.[49] Hull's efforts had not only saved his government from a diplomatic embarrassment, but had also saved, at least for the moment, the tariff truce.

In its resolution, the Steering Committee requested the various subcommissions to meet again and to report the questions which, under the circumstances at hand, could still be the subjects of conference deliberations. The Sub-Commission on Commercial Policy would thus try again to reach agreement on some proposals. William Phillips finally satisfied Hull's requests for specific information. As the Under Secretary explained, Roosevelt's absence from Washington had made it impossible for him and his associates to answer previously. Following the President's return, Bernard Baruch, Dean Acheson, Norman Davis, Frederick Livesey, and Phillips drafted a document that was sent under Roosevelt's name. It provided that at future meetings Hull could agree to prolong for a year the tariff truce of May, as long as pos-

[49] Hull, *Memoirs*, I, 263–266; Chairman of the American Delegation to Acting Secretary of State, telegram no. 101, July 4, 1933, *Foreign Relations, 1933*, I, 685; Chairman of the American Delegation to Acting Secretary of State, telegram no. 107, July 6, 1933, *ibid.*, 697; Chairman of the American Delegation to Acting Secretary of State, telegram no. 112, July 7, 1933, *ibid.*, 700–701. John MacCormac wrote the following in the New York *Times:* "Second only in force of effect to the speech of Secretary Hull in the meeting of the . . . steering committee . . . were the arguments presented by Prime Minister Bennett . . . in favor of continuance of the economic conference. . . . Mr. Bennett's remarks were a reinforcement of those he made yesterday in warning the gold-bloc countries not to earn the reputation of being wreckers of the conference." His colleague, Frederick Birchall, in addition to praising the efforts of Hull, reported that "Bennett . . . put a climax on the impression Mr. Hull had made. But he was more vehement" (New York *Times*, July 7, 1933).

sible American actions under the AAA and NIRA were made clear. He could endorse Washington's opposition to any further import quotas and support for the gradual removal of those that existed, reporting the reactions of foreign delegates to the American overtures. Although currency fluctuations made the United States dubious about reduction of tariffs through multilateral agreements, Hull could explore this avenue in the hope that he might find some acceptable formula. Roosevelt suggested that his Secretary of State propose an arrangement permitting limited entry of commodities currently prohibited by import duties. At this juncture, Washington was not dogmatically committed to the inclusion in a multilateral pact of a most-favored-nation clause, preferring to await further information from the American delegation before making a definite decision.[50]

Several days later, on July 11, Hull dispatched to the President the draft of a resolution that he wanted to submit to the conference. Hull hoped that the resolution would improve the images of the American delegation and government, and that it might even ease economic tensions. Based on the unanimous conclusion of the governments that the excessively high trade barriers had contributed to the depression, the program called for them to "proceed early and simultaneously to the revision of the whole network of restrictions" undertaken during the past few years. In its resolution, the American delegation proposed a more stringent tariff truce and a plan to reduce tariffs. According to the former, the participating governments would agree not to introduce any "new obstacles direct *or indirect* [italics mine] to the movement of international commerce." To last at least a year, this revised truce would have covered "all governmental actions whether embodied in new legislation or brought into existence

[50] Acting Secretary of State to Chairman of the American Delegation, telegram no. 121, July 7, 1933, *Foreign Relations, 1933,* I, 703–704; Phillips to Hull, June 30, 1933, Hull Papers; Phillips to Hull, July 7, 1933, *ibid.*

by administrative or executive exercise of power under existing legislation." Thanks to the exceptions and reservations attached to make the truce politically palatable, each government still would have had some, if not much, freedom to protect domestic interests. As a positive assault on trade restrictions, Hull proposed a multilateral agreement that hopefully would incorporate two related approaches. For a period of three years, the parties would gradually reduce their tariff rates, subject to certain reservations to screen the economy against a flood of imports resulting from either the lowered schedules or depreciated currencies. Moreover, Hull thought it feasible that, if monetary stabilization were attained during the three years, nontariff restrictions could be removed in the same gradual manner.

To avert any misunderstanding, the Secretary emphasized that the reservations attached to both the proposed truce and the tariff accord constituted the only safeguards against importation at inordinate levels of foreign goods. If the administration "adhered to any such agreement," the NRA subsequently could not restrict their entry. Roosevelt had to determine, therefore, whether American interests were adequately protected. If he thought not, Hull intimated, Washington might as well forget the entire idea.

In presenting this resolution to officials in the capital and requesting authority to submit it, or a modified version, to the conference, the chairman of the American delegation argued that "whether the Economic Committee can continue to operate effectively remains in the balance, and our ability to put forward [a] positive program" could be a decisive factor for the future. Hull felt that the London meeting would recess on or around August 1, which limited the time left his government to provide leadership in easing commercial intercourse.[51]

[51] Chairman of the American Delegation to Acting Secretary of State, telegram no. 121, July 11, 1933, *Foreign Relations, 1933*, I, 706–710;

Roosevelt almost immediately approved the introduction of Hull's proposals, but the Secretary preferred to make no public move until he had received all amendments and suggestions from Washington. It was apparent that Hull had learned some lessons in the past month. With the previous response to American vacillation in mind, he noted that "the slightest change of position on any question by our delegation is magnified out of all reason" and prompts the charge that "we are not stable." [52]

The State Department's major modification of the American delegation's program followed careful study by experts in the State, Treasury, and Commerce departments and the Tariff Commission. Its most telling attempt to stimulate multilateral trade was a proposal that governments reduce tariffs by negotiating bilateral treaties which incorporated the unconditional most-favored-nation principle. Hull welcomed this change which, in his opinion, broke "new ground" and would "be taken here to represent a real contribution by the American Government." The proposal advanced by the Secretary on July 21 went even further. Such bilateral accords "should have [as integral parts] . . . the most-favoured-nation principle in its unconditional and unrestricted form—to be applied to all forms and methods of control of imports, and not only to import duties." The American draft enjoined "upon every power making use of the quota system or other systems for limiting imports, to apply these systems so as to derange as little as possible" the normal flow of goods.[53] Thus, within two weeks, the United States

Chairman of American Delegation to Acting Secretary of State, telegram no. 123, July 11, 1933, *ibid.*, 711.

[52] Acting Secretary of State to Chairman of the American Delegation, telegram no. 134, July 12, 1933, *Foreign Relations, 1933,* I, 711–712; Chairman of the American Delegation to Acting Secretary of State, telegram no. 126, July 13, 1933, *ibid.*, 712–713.

[53] Chairman of the American Delegation to Acting Secretary of State, telegram no. 155, July 20, 1933, *Foreign Relations, 1933,* I, 725–726;

government had done more than just to clarify its attitude toward unconditional most-favored-nation treatment. It had espoused a policy which would form the basis of Hull's trade agreements program and his arguments in favor of commercial equality.

As the Secretary subsequently reported, the proposal "had excellent publicity here and on Continent, as well as keen interest . . . among all delegations here." Unfortunately, time was not its ally, and the conference recessed without taking formal action. Apparently undisturbed, Hull thought that the plan "should afford good basis for program of recess and Conference session following." The World Monetary and Economic Conference never reconvened, and the Secretary's last-minute attempt to reverse economic trends failed to get a fair hearing. In late September, during a session of the Assembly of the League of Nations in Geneva, Hendryk Colijn learned from representatives of several governments that had participated in the proceedings at London that economic and monetary conditions "had not sufficiently developed" to warrant further discussion of the American proposal.[54] To continue his struggle, Hull had to await congressional passage in 1934 of the Reciprocal Trade Agreements Act.

The Sub-Commission on Commercial Policy, then, showed little for its labors. It was the only conference agency that failed

---

Chairman of the American Delegation to the Chairman of the Economic Commission (Colijn), July 21, 1933, *ibid.*, 727–731; Phillips to Roosevelt, July 13, 1933, 550.S 1 Economic Commission/34½.

[54] Chairman of the American Delegation to Acting Secretary of State, telegram no. 160, July 23, 1933, *Foreign Relations, 1933*, I, 732–733; Consul General at Geneva (Prentiss B. Gilbert) to Secretary of State, no. 700, Oct. 19, 1933, *ibid.*, 752–758. The following countries were tapped by Colijn prior to his report to Gilbert: France, Germany, Italy, United Kingdom, Poland, Switzerland, Japan, Hungary, Rumania, and Austria.

to draft even an innocuous resolution to cover its frustrations. Its final report reflected the almost total lack of unanimity among the delegations. All of them admitted that excessive customs duties ought to be reduced quickly and that quantitative restrictions "must disappear as soon as possible." They parted company when they sought the proper means to effect those noble ends. To save some face and also to shift the blame, the authors of the document "stressed at the outset" that their "whole work" was predicated on the premise that currencies would be stabilized. In the absence of stabilization, several countries, prompted by "fluctuations in the exchanges, deemed it necessary to reserve full liberty of action in the matter either of quantitative restrictions, or foreign exchange control, or customs tariffs." [55]

The phrase that stymied statesmen at London—"liberty of action"—paralyzed them later in the decade. After 1935, when political cooperation became urgent, the democracies avoided commitments, preferring the freedom to pursue whatever policy they saw fit when the contingency arose. The inability of these governments to cooperate in economic matters in 1933 portended a similar response when the stakes were political. Hull's internationalism had momentarily met its match. Tariff walls within the North Atlantic Triangle had not been lowered, and there was little hope that in the near future they would be. On July 27, within hours of the recess of the London Conference, the representatives of British Commonwealth countries met and in a formal declaration reaffirmed their adherence to the Ottawa agreements. [56] One perceptive observer of the final proceedings wrote that "the delegates, perspiring and mopping their brows in the hot atmosphere of the Conference Hall listened to an explanation from the President, Mr. Ramsay MacDonald; a justifica-

[55] League of Nations, *Monetary and Economic Conference: Report of Sub-Commission I: Commercial Policy*, 22–24.

[56] New York *Times*, July 28, 1933.

tion from Mr. Hull (United States); a criticism from Señor d'Olwer (Spain); a condemnation from Dr. Schacht (Germany); a gloat from Mr. Maisky (Soviets); together with brief comments from other delegates fitted to the tune of 'Say au revoir, but not good-bye.' " [57]

The fate of the tariff truce is anticlimactic. Technically its life was extended due to the decision at London to recess, rather than terminate, the conference. In actuality this inherently weak instrument, with the many escape hatches for its participating members, lost strength as the year progressed. Consistent with the letter if not with the spirit of the agreement, Great Britain raised schedules on fifty items, having reserved the right to alter levels if applications were made before May 12. In each instance, Whitehall's rationale was that the requests antedated May 12. By late September, the truce, already dead in fact, began to disintegrate formally with the withdrawal of the Netherlands and Sweden. Having thus regained the freedom to determine their own tariff schedules, these two governments defended their decision as being more honest and straightforward than the devious practices employed by other parties to circumvent the agreement.

The United Kingdom for a time resisted pressure from its industrialists and other protectionists to follow the lead of the continental regimes. British officials thought that "wholesale repudiation" of the truce would "be followed by wholesale erection of new tariff barriers throughout Europe." In the circumstances, they preferred an ineffective arrangement "for fear something worse" would replace it.[58] On November 7 even Whitehall dropped the façade. Walter Runciman, who in the spring had reluctantly consented to the truce, informed the House of Com-

[57] Memorandum by Office of Military Attaché in London, July 31, 1933, 550.S 1/1233.
[58] New York *Times,* Sept. 29, 1933.

mons of the Government's decision to withdraw as of December 7. Supposedly influenced by the depreciation of the dollar portending the possible inundation of cheaper American goods into the United Kingdom, Runciman's statement brought cheers from the Tories who for some time had been advocating freedom of action in tariff matters for Great Britain.[59]

On this note the semblance of Anglo-American economic cooperation ended. Hull understandably agreed with the editor of the New York *Times* that "1933 has been a bad year for international collaboration." He wrote to Davis that "the outlook for any sort of international cooperation is seemingly near its lowest ebb," and a few days later to the American Ambassador in Great Britain, "It does seem that at this stage all international relationships are at an astonishingly low ebb, and if anything, sinking lower." [60] Although not solely responsible for this phenomenon, the United States was not blameless. Men indifferent to the solutions sought in London, if not opposed to them, influenced policy in Washington. Repudiation of internationalism further cooled Anglo-American relations, making it almost impossible for the countries to cooperate in other spheres. With economic nationalism dominant in the capital, Hull had to bide his time during the year, unable to pursue the ambition that would become nearly an obsession with him. However, 1934 would be another year, and with the new year came the successes denied him in 1933. Passage of the Reciprocal Trade Agreements Act in June enabled him to war against trade barriers and to strive, in the process, either to remove the causes of the political tensions epitomized in the increasing hostility of

[59] *Ibid.,* Nov. 8, 1933; Great Britain, 281 *H. C. Deb.* 5 s., 14.

[60] New York *Times,* Nov. 12, 1933; Hull to Davis, Sept. 20, 1933, Cordell Hull Papers, Library of Congress; Hull to Bingham, Sept. 30, 1933, *ibid.*

Germany or to thwart German ambitions in the world through a stronger Western community.

Hull's efforts would require friendlier relations with the United Kingdom. Fortunately, an important member of the British family of nations shared a common border with the United States, wanted to draw closer economically to its neighbor, and had given every indication at London that it would be a responsible partner. The groundwork for Canadian-American cooperation was laid in April while preparations were being made for the visits of the heads of government to Washington. On April 12, William Herridge, the Canadian Minister to the United States, told Phillips that certain British officials accompanying Ramsay MacDonald were "defeatists" who would keep the Prime Minister from straying too far from economic nationalism. In Herridge's opinion, Bennett, viewing the situation from a North American perspective, could make a significant contribution. If he were to enter "the picture . . . [he] would fortify the President in his policies." Herridge continued, "the whole program of economic reconstruction" would be stronger if Roosevelt could present to MacDonald and Bennett the charge that "we three represent the leading English-speaking part of the world and must pull together." The implication was, and events in London showed, that Bennett was ready to play his part.[61]

An important observer in London provides additional evidence of Bennett's willingness to cooperate with the United States: "The most striking feature of this Conference thus far [July 8] is Bennett's desire to cooperate with us and I think that if you have any plans for reciprocal tariff negotiations with Canada the time is very propitious." The Prime Minister, he wrote, "told me the other day how much he liked Warren

[61] Memorandum by Phillips, April 12, 1933, *Foreign Relations, 1933,* I, 501–502.

[Robbins] and I am sure that he was talking honestly. . . . I wonder if via Canada we might not make a hole in the Ottawa Agreements." [62]

The London Conference and the events preceding it thus had a salutary effect on Canadian-American relations which partly offset the divisive impact of the conference on Anglo-American diplomacy. Within two years these north-south ties had been strengthened sufficiently for the two governments to negotiate a reciprocity agreement.

[62] Bullitt to Roosevelt, July 8, 1933, Franklin D. Roosevelt Papers, London Economic Conference File.

Chapter 3

The Canadian-American Trade Agreement of 1935: The First Crack in the Wall

On November 15, 1935, Secretary of State Cordell Hull and Canadian Prime Minister Mackenzie King signed a trade agreement that formally marked a return by the two countries to economic sanity. The document's significance, however, extends beyond the termination of the unofficial trade war. The agreement was important both as a product of forces which led to a new era in Canadian-American relations and as a prelude to the close military and political cooperation of the Second World War period. The trade pact, a positive response of Canadian and American leaders to potential world disorders, facilitated in turn the emergence of the joint North American security structure. In the closing of the economic breach between the United States and Canada are the seeds of the Roosevelt-King friendship, from which grew not only the Ogdensburg Agreement and the Hyde Park Declaration, but also the Roosevelt-Churchill understanding. The Canadian Prime Minister later became an important interpreter between these two world figures prior to their own experiments in personal diplomacy. Canadian-American reciprocity had a centripetal effect in yet another way. It confirmed the belief of many Canadians that an American cognizant of their interests and feelings occupied the White House. The military and political collaboration necessitated in later years by German and Japanese aggression was made much more palatable to Canadians by the popularity of Franklin D. Roosevelt in the Dominion. The immediate significance of the pact, however, lies in its effect on economic relations within the triangle. The 1935 accord represented the initial success in the campaign of the United States to undermine the Ottawa system.

The negotiation of this first really important trade agreement reflects a fundamental reality in American diplomatic history—the constant necessity of satisfying conditions imposed by the democratic process. More than any other factor, partisan politics shaped policy decisions during the informal and formal discussions between the two governments. Nor was the pervasive influence of political considerations confined to the United States. Canadian administrations, like American, were careful to avoid antagonizing elements of the voting public and to reap political advantages from skillful use of the negotiations. Organized groups sought not only to create opinion favorable to their special interests, but also applied direct political pressure on the White House, the State Department, the Democratic National Committee, and members of Congress. In numerous communications with these officials, spokesmen of farm, lumber, and cattlemen's organizations predicted that if the trade agreement became a reality, economic chaos would result for their state or region, and warned that the opposition party would accordingly gain ground politically.[1] So successful were the campaigns that

[1] Spokesmen of interest groups wrote directly to the President, applied pressure on congressmen who wrote to Roosevelt, and convinced promi-

even economically feasible concessions were not granted. Quotas on specified Canadian imports were determined with the cooperation of the Department of Agriculture and public support was given the agreement by Secretary of Agriculture Henry A. Wallace in an effort to relieve the pressure. Of course, the maneuvers by Washington to convince American organizations that the accord was advantageous and not detrimental to their interests made more difficult King's political task of persuading the Canadian public that the concessions to the United States had been worth the price. Roosevelt still had fears of repercussions. In November, 1935, he seemed "considerably worried about the kind of publicity he [was] going to get on the Canadian treaty," and in April, 1936, in a letter to the Prime Minister, he referred to taking "our political lives in our hands" by concluding the pact.[2] Although the President showed more political courage than most general works suggest, inchoate disintegration

---

nent Democrats that they should "educate" James Farley, Chairman of the National Committee. See Franklin D. Roosevelt Papers, Official File (hereafter cited as OF), 48–B, Box 14. For a specific example of an overture to the State Department, see F. E. Mollin, Secretary of the American National Live Stock Association, to Cordell Hull, telegram, Sept. 25, 1935, 611.4231/1258.

[2] On November 21, 1935, in a radio broadcast, Wallace assured farmers that the agreement would benefit them, while minimizing the concessions to Canada (Henry A. Wallace, "How the Canadian Trade Agreement Will Affect Farmers," *Vital Speeches*, II [Dec. 2, 1935], 151–152). The Vancouver *Daily Province* (Conservative) of December 1 called its readers' attention to these words, suggesting that the United States would be "the chief beneficiary." Two days later, it predicted "a growing unfavorable trade balance." King, of course, had the power to guide the agreement through Parliament. The November, 1935, quote is in memorandum, Nov. 11, 1935, Morgenthau Diary, Book 11, p. 136. For the Roosevelt correspondence, see Roosevelt to King, April 16, 1936, Roosevelt Papers, President's Secretary's File (hereafter cited as PSF), Canada, 1933–1941 (also printed in Elliott Roosevelt, ed., *F. D. R.: His Personal Letters, 1928–1945* [2 vols.; New York, 1950], I, 578–579).

in Europe gave the negotiations an air of urgency and paved the way for the signature of his Secretary of State.[3]

The immediate results of the economic policies mentioned in Chapter 1 were disastrous for both nations. The collapse of world prices coupled with curtailed sales of Canadian goods in the United States due to the Smoot-Hawley tariff and the Revenue Act of 1932, with its restrictions on the entry of Dominion lumber and copper, set in motion deflationary forces in Canada. Though American prosperity was not so dependent upon world trade, retrenchment in the United States was necessitated in part by losses in the Canadian market. From a peak in 1929 of nearly $1,000,000,000, American sales in Canada had plunged by 1933 to slightly more than $210,000,000. Between 1929 and 1933 the total value of commodity exchanges had shrunk from $1,500,000,000 to $400,000,000.[4] But passage of the Reciprocal Trade Agreements Act of 1934, which granted qualified authority to the President to reduce schedules by negotiating trade agreements with foreign governments,[5] was cause for hope

[3] *Business Week* was one contemporary publication that underscored the political courage of the President. In an editorial of November 23, 1935, it argued that "there has been no more courageous act in all his presidency," particularly when "it would have been easy for him to do nothing, to procrastinate at least until after election" ("So that Nations May Trade," *Business Week,* no. 325 [Nov. 23, 1935], p. 44). On November 26, 1935, Thomas A. Crerar, Canadian Minister of the Interior, wrote to J. W. Dafoe that he had expected a final agreement to be postponed until after the election in the United States. He continued, "I did not think that Roosevelt would display the courage he has—for he has shown real courage" (Dafoe Papers, reel no. M–77).

[4] The trade figures, prepared in the U.S. Department of Commerce by International Economic Analysis Division, Office of International Trade, are quoted from Keenleyside and Brown, *Canada and the United States,* 280.

[5] The President was limited in several ways: no commodity could be transferred from the dutiable to the free list, no duty could be lowered more than 50 per cent, no agreement could be concluded until domestic

that the economic schism with Canada could be healed to the benefit of interests on both sides of the border.

Well before June 12, 1934—the date Roosevelt signed the reciprocity measure—the Conservative Prime Minister of Canada had attempted to revive the bilateral trade. Although other factors were responsible for the continuing depression in the Dominion, the inability of Canadian producers to compensate for losses in the American market through enhanced trade in the Empire was damaging. Certainly Bennett had no political choice but to assume the initiative, since important segments of Cana-

---

economic interests had been notified and given an opportunity to present their arguments for or against change, and the authorization was for only three years. Two interdepartmental agencies, the Committee for Reciprocity Information and the Committee on Foreign Trade Agreements, were created along with a Division of Trade Agreements within the State Department to implement the act. An administrative procedure gradually evolved. The Planning Committee, an affiliate of the Trade Agreements Committee, first studied trade relations with a given country to gauge the immediate prospects of a pact. If its recommendations were favorable, representatives of the two governments held preliminary discussions to determine whether an agreement was possible. If so, a formal announcement by the Department of State of its intention to negotiate together with a list of commodities on which it might grant concessions followed. Interested organizations were invited to express their views, in writing and later orally, to the Committee for Reciprocity Information. A "clearing house" agency, this committee turned the forthcoming data over to subcommittees of the Trade Agreements Committee. Ultimately the Trade Agreements Committee received reports based on intensive research into each concession item. It made recommendations to the Secretary of State and the President, who either accepted or modified them. Actual negotiations began at this point. The Trade Agreements Committee reviewed any subsequent agreement, and when the President accepted the terms, a proclamation brought matters to a close. Grace Beckett, *The Reciprocal Trade Agreements Program* (New York, 1941), 1–20; Henry J. Tasca, *The Reciprocal Trade Policy of the United States* (Philadelphia, 1938), 45–82; Francis Bowes Sayre, *The Way Forward: The American Trade Agreements Program* (New York, 1939), 84–97; Hull, *Memoirs*, I, 366–377.

dian opinion, convinced that salvation lay in greater trade with the United States, were calling for an agreement with the southern neighbor. In February, 1933, the Prime Minister endorsed a Liberal resolution in the House of Commons urging the Canadian government to begin trade negotiations with the United States. In doing this, however, he declared, "In my judgment any trade agreement which creates a channel of trade that may be terminated at the caprice or without notice to the other party, or be terminated by one party without considering the interests of the other, is fatal to the interests of both." With the Taft-Fielding agreement of 1911 in mind, he recalled that "the people of Canada rejected [it] . . . and I believe if they were asked again they would conclude that any arrangement which left us in a position whereby our trade relations could be changed over night for any reason, good or bad, which might occur to the minds of the American congress, would not be a sound or sane venture for a country such as ours. . . . We cannot hope to develop the resources of our country or give it favourable position in the trade of the world if we render it possible for a channel of trade to be dammed up, shut off, diverted or ruined by any action which may be taken by another party without notice or regard for ourselves." Bennett publicly invited Washington to make the initial overture; privately he assured a Legation official that he wanted to negotiate an arrangement of some type. The nation's press, particularly in the Prairies, increasingly supported negotiations, as did resolutions passed by and remarks made in several provincial parliaments.[6]

[6] For pertinent documents reflecting the Canadian desire, see *Foreign Relations, 1933,* II, 44–52. Unfortunately, the public records of Canada are closed, and the Richard B. Bennett Papers are largely unrewarding. The author found little of value in the Robert Manion Papers, the H. H. Stevens Papers, and the C. H. Cahan Papers. These three collections are also housed in the Public Archives of Canada. For the exchange in Parliament, see Can. *H. of C. Debates,* Feb. 20, 1933, II, 2253,

In April, 1933, shortly after the inauguration of Roosevelt, Bennett went to Washington to discuss the forthcoming World Economic Conference with the President. He had preferred not to go, but when belatedly invited by Roosevelt he could not refuse the invitation. During their conversations the two men turned to trade relations between their countries, and the President informed his guest of plans to ask Congress for authority to negotiate commercial agreements. Although the formal trade pact the Prime Minister had hoped for was not concluded at this time, a joint statement issued at the end of the visit committed them to "search" for means to liberalize the flow of goods. Bennett reportedly left the American capital convinced that the foundation for improved trade had been laid, and the New York *Times* suggested that some trade arrangement was imminent. These predictions proved to be illusory, but valuable contacts had been established. The Prime Minister, who before the trip south had already judged favorably Roosevelt's performance as President, remained "well impressed" with the occupant of the White House.[7]

2261–2267. On February 8 the Conservative premier of Saskatchewan declared in the parliament that he was "confident one of the world's troubles today is high tariffs, and the Conservatives in the West have just as many low tariff ideas as have the Liberals" (P. Stewart Heintzleman, Consul General at Winnipeg, Report, May 5, 1933, 611.4231/802). Late in March, 1933, the Legislative Assembly of Prince Edward Island endorsed greater trade with the United States as follows: "This legislature in conjunction with the legislatures of the other Maritime Provinces press upon the Federal Government the advisability of availing itself of any fair and reasonable proposals from the United States of America that would benefit the farming and fishing interests of this province" (Charlottetown *Patriot,* March 31, 1933). The major newspapers in the prairies, the Winnipeg *Tribune* (Conservative) and the Winnipeg *Free Press* (Liberal), consistently supported negotiations.

[7] For an account of Bennett's trip to Washington and the probable topics of discussion, see Boal to Hickerson, April 15, 1933, 611.4231/793½, in which Boal, the Chargé at Ottawa, enclosed a copy

As mentioned earlier, Roosevelt disappointed his internationalist Secretary of State by momentarily dropping reciprocity. The new President was influenced by planners who were wary of an increase in imports that might undermine their domestic solutions to the depression.[8] Thus the inauguration of a Democratic administration did not immediately produce a significant departure from the tariff policies of the Republicans. For the next year, in the absence of any discretionary presidential power, periodic Canadian inquiries about possible trade negotiations were dismissed. The American spokesmen felt that a trade treaty with Canada, facilitating the entry of Dominion farm products, could never muster the necessary majority in the Senate.[9]

---

of a letter to William Phillips, American Under Secretary of State. Boal to Phillips, April 14, 1933, is printed in *Foreign Relations, 1933,* II, 44–49. Memorandum of conversation with the Counselor of the Canadian Legation by Hickerson, July 15, 1933, *ibid.,* 50–51; see also *ibid.,* I, 501–503 and New York *Times,* April 30, 1933. Writing to his son James on April 24, 1933, Robert Manion informed that "R. B. left yesterday for Washington. He has been invited by Roosevelt to go down and discuss matters with him. Confidentially, Roosevelt asked a great many . . . and R. B.'s invitation was late, and he confided to us that he was very glad not to be asked, as he did not wish to go anyway. He was put in an embarrassing position the next day by getting an invitation, and he realized at once that he could not very well refuse." In the same letter, Manion declared that Bennett "has lately admitted to me—what he did not admit at first—that Roosevelt has done well." On May 2, 1933, again to James, he wrote that "the Prime Minister returned today from Washington and seems to be well impressed with Roosevelt, though I have not had any private conversation with him yet, but I have heard him express his feelings in Council and also in caucus" (Manion Papers, G 27, III B 7, Vol. XVI).

[8] See Chapter 2; Hull, *Memoirs,* I, 248–255.

[9] Memorandum of conversation with the Canadian Chargé by Hull, May 26, 1933, memorandum of conversation with Counselor of the Canadian Legation by John D. Hickerson, July 15, 1933, and memorandum of conversation with the Canadian Minister by William Phillips, Nov. 20, 1933, *Foreign Relations, 1933,* II, 49–52; memorandum by Hull, Feb. 8, 1934, *Foreign Relations, 1934,* I, 845.

On August 6, 1934, Major William Herridge, the Canadian Minister to the United States and the man largely responsible for Bennett's conciliatory gesture toward Washington,[10] informed John D. Hickerson, the State Department's leading expert on Canada, of the Prime Minister's desire to negotiate a trade agreement. Fully aware of the New Deal's program for agriculture, Herridge nevertheless stressed that Canada had to increase its trade with the United States. There was more to this overture, however, than the promise of economic advantages. Herridge remarked candidly that 1935 would be an election year in Canada, and failure by the Conservative government to obtain a trade agreement with the United States would hurt its chances at the polls. Although he would be laying the responsibility on Washington, Bennett could neutralize the issue with an announcement that he had informed American officials of his willingness to start negotiations and was waiting for an affirmative response.

Arguing that the guaranteed preferences of the Ottawa agreements presented a major difficulty, Hickerson saw no prospect of negotiations for several months.[11] Actually, domestic political

[10] On May 9, 1934, Herridge wrote to Bennett, "If and when the Tariff Bill becomes law, I think that we should immediately press for the initiation of negotiations leading to the signing of a trade agreement. From every angle, political and economic, and on the basis of either success or failure, I believe that this move will prove to be a wise one" (Bennett Papers, Vol. F–204). Herridge was the architect of Bennett's "New Deal" of 1935. On September 18, 1935, Chester Bloom, Canadian correspondent in Washington, wrote to Dafoe that Herridge "told me for the first time openly that he had written all Mr. Bennett's radio speeches and, moreover, that he had written all of the four recent speeches which Mr. Bennett has delivered" (Dafoe Papers, reel no. M–77). In this same vein, see J. R. H. Wilbur, "H. H. Stevens and the Reconstruction Party," *Canadian Historical Review*, XLV (March, 1964), 1–28.

[11] Memorandum by Hickerson, Aug. 7, 1934, memorandum by Hickerson, August 7, 1934, and memorandum by Hickerson, Aug. 9, 1934, *Foreign Relations, 1934*, I, 845–849.

forces were the principal cause of Washington's reluctance to proceed. The State Department preferred not to push the reciprocity program too rapidly. The program had met considerable opposition in Congress, and many remained suspicious not only of Hull and his low-tariff proclivities but also of a concept which smacked of unconstitutional surrender of legislative power to the executive. Congressional elections were pending, moreover, and the probable political effect in the Middle West of an announcement of greater importation of agricultural products from Canada was not lost in Washington. Certain Canadians were quick to accept such political considerations as the explanation for the impasse. An article in the Ottawa *Citizen* of August 1, quoting "an authoritative source" in the American capital as having said that the divisive effect of the reciprocity issue on Canadian politics prevented negotiations in the near future with the Dominion,[12] prompted the Ottawa *Journal* to ask how American officials had mistakenly concluded that reciprocity was a political issue in Canada. In the *Journal*'s opinion, the United States was forced to soft-pedal its program for the present and chose not to disclose the real reason.[13]

Divided counsel within the administration also contributed to delay. Economic nationalists, led by George N. Peek, the Foreign Trade Adviser to the President, preferred bilateral trade agreements in which benefits would accrue only to the parties. Internationalists, specifically Cordell Hull, supported the most-favored-nation clause as the device by which the effects of a trade pact would be multilateral making possible general improvement of world economic conditions. There was also disagreement whether the over-all purpose of the program was to

[12] Ottawa *Citizen*, Aug. 1, 1934. The American Minister to Canada, Warren Robbins, denied the allegations privately, and the journalist subsequently conceded that his use of terms was unjustified (Robbins to Secretary of State, no. 747, Aug. 10, 1934, 611.4231/874).

[13] Ottawa *Journal*, Aug. 6, 1934.

increase American exports or to strive for greater trade balances.[14] Differences over the provisions of an agreement with Canada brought into focus these conflicts. One group favored an agreement involving a limited number of commodities. An agreement of this type would not only be easier to negotiate, but could be expanded when the Liberals assumed power. It was hoped that such an accord would restore trade between the two countries to the "normal" ratio of exports and imports. The United States would continue to sell appreciably more in Canada than American consumers purchased from Dominion producers.

Another group thought that the trade agreement might balance the import-export ratio or might even stimulate more imports from Canada than American exports to the Dominion. Politically more appealing to the Canadians, this approach would allegedly strengthen the Canadian economy to the long-range benefit of the United States. However, there were discernible obstacles. The Ottawa agreements admittedly immunized certain key commodities against reduction, and, equally as significant, Washington hesitated to freely grant concessions to Canada. Underlying this thinking were two predicted economic trends: limited markets in the future for American farm products because of stabilized population in the major industrial countries, and the tendency of the world's nations to strive for agricultural self-sufficiency. Coupled with this sobering outlook was the government's policy to limit farm production. The admission of foreign competition was not only incompatible, but politically explosive. It was clearly recognized that agreement with the Dominion was basically an agricultural problem.[15]

The most difficult factor to assess is the extent to which

[14] A general discussion of this cleavage appears in Schlesinger, *The Coming of the New Deal*, 253–260. See also Gardner, *Economic Aspects of New Deal Diplomacy*, 41–45.

[15] Memorandum by Division of Western European Affairs, Sept. 21, 1934, 611.4231/887¼; second memorandum by Division of Western European Affairs, Sept. 29, 1934, 611.4231/887¾.

American inaction was due to the feeling that more could be accomplished in negotiations with the Liberals. They had traditionally sought closer trade ties with the United States, were pressing Ottawa to adopt a more conciliatory policy toward Washington, and were almost certain to prevail in the 1935 election. For a time at least, American officials doubted Bennett's sincerity, not altogether convinced that he wanted to bargain in good faith.[16]

While political forces were thus producing a cautious approach in the United States, pressure in Canada for an agreement increased. Public endorsement of negotiations early in September by the Canadian Chamber of Commerce was a development the Tories could hardly ignore. The Canadian government continued to press for an accord, only to be rebuffed.[17] On November 14, following the vote of confidence given the Roosevelt Administration in the recent election, the Canadians climaxed their efforts with a superlative political stroke in a formal note to Secretary Hull. After a comprehensive analysis of economic relations between the two nations, it concluded with a five-point proposal upon which to base the negotiation of a trade agreement. Ottawa suggested that both countries continue to

[16] In a letter of August 23, 1934, to Victor Sifton of the Regina *Leader-Post,* Chester Bloom reported a confidential conversation with Henry F. Grady, the chief of the State Department's Division of Trade Agreements. According to the correspondent, Grady "said that to date the Bennett government exhibits no real enthusiasm for solving the trade problems between the two countries. . . . The State Department simply thinks that there is no real disposition on the part of the Canadian government to show any real, friendly spirit of give and take essential to progress in making any such agreement" (Dafoe Papers, reel no. M–76).

[17] Memorandum by Assistant Secretary of State Francis B. Sayre, Oct. 4, 1934, *Foreign Relations, 1934,* I, 849. Information concerning the action of the Canadian Chamber of Commerce was enclosed in Henry I. Harriman, President of the Chamber of Commerce of the United States, to Hull, Sept. 24, 1934, 611.4231/888.

admit free of duty those commodities currently on the free list; that Canada extend most-favored-nation treatment to American imports and lower its schedules on certain natural and manufactured items; that the United States reduce by half the existing duties on specified farm products and liberalize those on a number of manufactured goods of Canada. Moreover, the Dominion leaders called for a joint Canadian-American declaration that natural products would ultimately flow freely across the border. The proposed reductions would be the first step in that direction.[18] Instrumental in this maneuver was Herridge, who impressed on Bennett the political wisdom of putting the United States formally on the defensive. As early as August, he had argued in favor of a formal communication to Washington, going so far as to outline its contents. The important point was, as the Canadian Minister candidly expressed to his brother-in-law in Ottawa, that the Dominion had to "shock" the Roosevelt Administration into making a decision on its Canadian trade policy. If the United States rejected the overture, the Bennett government had a ready-made issue, "a powerful one," which it would be foolish to discard.[19]

The Dominion timed its note perfectly, for on November 9

[18] Canadian Minister to Secretary of State, note no. 157, Nov. 14, 1934, *Foreign Relations, 1934*, I, 849–857. Extracts of this note are published also in Walter Riddell, ed., *Documents on Canadian Foreign Policy, 1917–1939* (Toronto, 1962), 633–635.

[19] Herridge to Bennett, Aug. 4, 1934, Bennett Papers, Vol. F–242. On November 1, 1934, Herridge wrote Bennett urging "quick action . . . on the suggested note to the Sct. of State." Anticipating an American proposal to discuss a trade agreement, he continued, "I do not believe that anything worth while will result, but such action will succeed in stalling the issue for many months. Failure to get anywhere will simply support the grits' [Liberals] stand that we won't and the U.S. can't do business. If however you jump in ahead with a good bold note, you will have the administration on the defensive—as I have had it for the past year" (*ibid.*, Vol. F–244).

the Trade Agreements Committee had decided to begin study of trade relations with Canada. The procedure contemplated was for the Canadians to do the same, after which the two governments would exchange lists of desired concessions and then determine from this information whether formal negotiations were possible. Although the Canadian Legation had not learned officially of this decision, an American "leak" undoubtedly accounts for the timing of the Dominion note. As a Canadian correspondent wrote privately at the time, "It is no secret that the Canadian Legation has been open house at all times to the New Deal crowd. On many occasions, Mr. Herridge has told me proudly of his closeness to Professor Rexford Guy Tugwell, to . . . Henry A. Wallace, to Mr. Leon Henderson." [20]

The initial reaction to the note in Washington, supported by the reports from the American Minister, Warren Robbins, and his staff in Ottawa, was that its primary target was the Canadian electorate. At the strategic moment, either in Parliament or during the campaign, Bennett would release the text to the press. While it might strengthen the Prime Minister's political hand, publication could complicate future economic relations. Robbins suggested, therefore, that Washington register firm opposition to the release of any correspondence prior to the signing of an agreement.

The general tenor of Canadian thinking particularly bothered the Minister. In his opinion, the note implied a goal of eventual trade equality, which was "entirely out of keeping with practical working economics." The State Department, he urged, should

[20] In Herridge to Bennett, Nov. 1, 1934, the Canadian Minister also wrote, "My information is that the P. is a little worried about the Canadian situation and feels that something should be done, at least by way of gesture, to improve it." The quote in the text is from Bloom to Dafoe, Jan. 14, 1935, Dafoe Papers, reel no. M–77. For the American decision of November 9, see memorandum, Grady to Sayre, Nov. 14, 1934, *Foreign Relations, 1934,* I, 858, and Phillips Diary, Nov. 8, 1934.

declare unequivocally that a trade agreement could not be based on that principle. Robbins thus identified himself with those in Washington who wanted to increase total bilateral trade only within the framework of the traditional import-export patterns. The Legation staff had assessed Canadian strategy correctly. Herridge, in outlining the format for a note, had written Bennett that it should cite remarks by Roosevelt and others that "ideally, trade between any two countries should be in balance. Of course," he added, "this is economic bunk, but at least we have a right to expect them to try to fit facts to their theories." [21] Robbins saw another danger: the Conservatives might instill in the public mind the idea that exports between the United States and Canada must balance. Then if they failed to conclude an agreement while still in power, they had political ammunition with which to attack any subsequent agreement which the Liberals might negotiate that was not based on that principle.

The Canadian suggestion that a joint statement be made favoring free exchange of natural products was especially annoying. A vain hope for Canadians, it would only incur the wrath of the American farmer. "Since the United States is presumably interested in attaining the freest possible exchange of manufactured products with Canada rather than the freest possible exchange of natural products," Robbins thought it more expedient to have no declaration at all. A statement incorporating American desires would arouse vested interests in Canada as much as the Canadian proposal would incite farm groups in the United States.

The American envoy thought furthermore that specific Canadian commitments on several matters prior to actual negotiations might avert misunderstanding. He wanted Ottawa to explain what the status of the valuations system would be if a trade

---

[21] Herridge to Bennett, Aug. 4, 1934, Bennett Papers, Vol. F–242.

agreement became a reality and to send two lists of tariff items: those which could not be lowered because of the Ottawa agreements and those which had to be lowered subsequently to maintain preferences.[22]

These November days found Secretary Hull in "his cautious mood, even in economic affairs." His associates had drafted a reply to the Canadians, but Hull refused to forward it to Herridge even though he had approved it and had called a meeting with the Canadian Minister for that purpose. As a contemporary noted, Hull was "an extremist in his language" when "enunciating general principles," but "when it comes down to brass tacks, he is cautious as any horse trader." [23]

On December 1, the State Department gave the Canadian Minister the first clue to its decision. While desiring an economic accommodation, Washington hesitated to grant the specific Canadian requests. It wanted certain features of the note deleted, particularly the references to agricultural imports, before beginning preliminaries. Otherwise, the official American reply would contain reservations that might be misconstrued in Canada. Herridge was asked whether Bennett would agree to alter the note in line with American wishes. The Canadian Minister declared that Bennett presently had no desire to publish the

[22] Robbins to Secretary of State, telegram no. 110, Nov. 21, 1934, and Robbins to Secretary of State, no. 912, Nov. 22, 1934, *Foreign Relations, 1934*, I, 858–870. Before these analyses were received, Phillips recorded in his diary, "I had a Departmental meeting this afternoon to discuss our reply to the recent Canadian trade note, which we all felt was a political document to be used by Bennett when going before the country" (Phillips Diary, Nov. 20, 1934). With respect to the "equality" overtone of the note, Herridge had written to Bennett that, in the communication, "we would refer to statements of the President and others that ideally, trade between any two countries should be in balance. Of course, this is economic bunk, but at least we have a right to expect them to try to fit facts to their theories" (Herridge to Bennett, Aug. 4, 1934, Bennett Papers, Vol. F–242).

[23] Moffat Diary, Nov. 30, 1934, Moffat Papers, XXXVI.

notes, but admitted that such a contingency might arise during the Parliamentary session. If so, he would want an unexpurgated version. From the Canadian point of view, the paragraphs in question were the "heart" of the communication. In any event, Herridge thought, the two governments could undertake the preliminary studies and have them completed before any possible request for publication. He saw no reason, therefore, to modify the note.[24]

For the moment the positions of the two countries remained fixed. From the American standpoint, any tacit approval of the Canadian proposals might alarm the farm belt at the very outset of the negotiations, a price the State Department could not pay. Economic benefits aside, for Bennett it was imperative politically to promise Canadian producers lower American tariffs. During the month of December the Prime Minister refused to yield, while his political supporters intimated that Canada's unfavorable balance of trade with the United States would be eliminated.[25] On December 20, Herridge informed the Secretary of State that Bennett would not amend the note. Upon learning this, Hull announced that he would send the American reply as originally drafted. The Canadian Minister reaffirmed that no correspondence would be published at the moment, but he reminded Hull that he could not predict developments at the forthcoming session of Parliament.[26]

[24] Memorandum by Phillips, Dec. 1, 1934, *Foreign Relations, 1934,* I, 870–872.

[25] On December 5, Bennett himself declared that he was "perfectly willing to make a bargain on terms fair and just" but was opposed to any agreement in which Canadian interests were forfeited, an obvious allusion to Liberal subservience to Washington (Toronto *Globe*, Dec. 6, 1934). The Montreal *Gazette* echoed the refrain, doubting that a reciprocity treaty that did not correct the unfavorable trade balance would be advantageous to the Dominion (Montreal *Gazette*, Dec. 7, 1934).

[26] Memorandum by Phillips, Dec. 10, 1934, *Foreign Relations, 1934,* I, 872–873. Actually, a different draft was sent; see Phillips Diary, Dec. 26, 1934.

The next day Moffat noted in his diary, "There is such a divergence of opinion as to how to answer the Canadian note that we have now had three or four meetings and have discarded three or four drafts." The problem was that Hull "wishes to protect himself from the charge that he is favoring the lowering of duties on agricultural products from Canada, and yet that is the gist of the Canadian request. How to write into one and the same note paragraphs which will protect the Secretary and yet keep the tone of constructive cordiality that the rest of us want is baffling indeed." [27]

On December 27, 1934, after the Americans had resolved their differences, the United States invited Canada to exchange preliminary views. It stated pointedly, "International balances are settled on many fronts, and it would be a serious setback to world trade if countries undertook to achieve balances with individual countries." Washington refused to commit itself to any reductions proposed in the Canadian note, calling instead for careful analysis of each item in light of existing conditions to be made before any final decision. The Secretary of State suggested also that discussions of valuations procedures be included. Within a few days, the Canadian government accepted Hull's invitation. The formal notice of intention to negotiate an agreement was given several weeks later, and the Committee for Reciprocity Information set March 11 as the deadline for the receipt of both written data from American interest groups and applications to appear at the public hearing scheduled to begin March 18. [28]

The announcement added another dimension to the political

[27] Moffat Diary, Dec. 21, 1934, Moffat Papers, XXXVI.
[28] Secretary of State to Canadian Minister, Dec. 27, 1934, *Foreign Relations, 1934,* I, 873–874; Canadian Minister to Secretary of State, Jan. 4, 1935, *Foreign Relations, 1935,* II, 18; Department of State, *Press Releases,* XII (Jan. 26, 1935), no. 278, pp. 44–54.

debate in Canada that lasted until October, when the electorate returned the Liberals to office.[29] Whereas the Conservatives defended their tariff policies of the past five years as being responsible for the American invitation, the Liberals argued that these measures had hindered Canada's trade with its natural market. In Parliament, Mackenzie King, the Leader of the Opposition, deftly concentrated on Conservative efforts to cooperate economically with the Empire. He upheld the principle underlying imperial preferences, but argued that they should be attained through reductions of tariffs against imperial imports, and not, as advocated by Bennett, through increased schedules against third parties.[30] To the Tories, the courageous and "realistic" Bennett deserved praise for his political about-face on the tariff issue and his retreat from the commitment made in February, 1933, that he would never negotiate a trade agreement with the United States because such an agreement would lack stability. The Opposition construed Bennett's decision as an admission that he had pursued the wrong policies for years and as a vindication of its tariff views. Recalling the Prime Minister's declaration of 1933, the Winnipeg *Free Press* commended his "recantation and change of front." [31]

Conservative papers suggested that if the negotiations failed, the blame would rest on the United States because it had not corrected the trade balance or offered the necessary concessions.[32]

---

[29] For another development which affords the reader the opportunity to view the election in perspective, see Wilbur, "H. H. Stevens and the Reconstruction Party."

[30] Can. *H. of C. Debates,* Jan. 31, 1935, I, 376–392.

[31] For a contrasting view, see the Ottawa *Journal,* Jan. 22, 1935, which considered this a political triumph for the "realistic" Bennett, and the Winnipeg *Free Press,* Jan. 29, 1935, quoted in the text above.

[32] The Montreal *Gazette,* Feb. 15, 1935, reiterated that "no reciprocity treaty can possibly be fair to the Dominion if based upon the present . . . lopsided movement of trade between the two countries." The Winnipeg

The Liberal counterparts felt that the conditions for an agreement in Washington were more favorable than they had been at any time since 1911 and that only Bennett's refusal to grant adequate concessions could prevent a satisfactory result.[33]

The question which party would better promote the vital interests of the Dominion became the focal point of the debate. In the opinion of the Toronto *Mail and Empire,* the Prime Minister would never consent to an arrangement which would leave Canada "holding the short end of the stick, as has generally been the case in the past." [34] The Toronto *Globe* reported the belief of Liberals that they could strike the better bargain with Washington because the American government preferred to negotiate with them.[35] Both Canadian political parties tried to exploit the supposed American preference for a Liberal rather than a Conservative government. According to the Montreal *Gazette,* certain officials in the American capital were deliberately delaying negotiations, hoping for an electoral victory by the Liberals, who would be more generous in their concessions and less demanding in their requests.[36] In normal circumstances the Conservatives might have gained political strength by raising the specter of Washington's indirect attempt to influence a Canadian election. In the midst of depression, the panacea for which seemed to be sales in the American market, the Tories found themselves burdened with an additional liability. Herridge admitted as much when he wrote to Bennett's personal assistant, "I think that in the minds of a good many people . . . there still

---

Tribune, Jan. 22, 1935, stressed that American interests would be consulted before any accord, proof that unlimited reciprocity would not ensue. No informed quarter, it continued, expected the United States to reduce its tariff against Canadian farm and dairy products.

[33] Winnipeg *Free Press,* Jan. 29, 1935.

[34] Toronto *Mail and Empire,* Jan. 24, 1935.

[35] Toronto *Globe,* March 12, 1935.

[36] Montreal *Gazette,* March 12, 1935.

lurks the idea that the Conservative party cannot make a trade treaty, because it will not. That is a very damaging view." [37]

There is no concrete proof that the American government used dilatory tactics as a political weapon. The preliminary studies were still in progress late in July with no prospect of specific commitments for at least two more weeks.[38] Undoubtedly, if only for historical and traditional reasons, American officials preferred a Liberal government, but they remained circumspect in their overt actions. The administrative procedure and structure themselves, with the necessity of interdepartmental agreement, were sufficient to cause delay without any ulterior motive.[39]

Continued political criticism in Canada increased the government's desire to begin formal conversations. In August, the Liberal premier of Ontario, Mitchell Hepburn, particularly touched the nerve center of the Conservatives. Recalling their appeals in 1911 that Canadians should have "no truck or trade with the Yankees," he interpreted current American policy to be "no truck or trade with the Bennett Government." [40] At this point

[37] Herridge to R. K. Finlayson, Oct. 8, 1935, Bennett Papers, Vol. F–242.

[38] Memorandum by Sayre, July 20, 1935, 611.4231/1195.

[39] Phillips thought that "Sayre's set-up for trade conversations is somewhat top heavy" (Phillips Diary, Nov. 15, 1934). Significantly, Herridge remained convinced to the end that there was no deliberate delay by the American negotiators. According to Bloom, Herridge "went on to say that so far as he could tell, the American state department seemed to be proceeding in all seriousness with the intention of completing the agreement at the earliest possible moment" (Bloom to Dafoe, Sept. 18, 1935, Dafoe Papers, reel no. M–77). In October the Canadian Minister himself wrote, "I do in fact believe that we can conclude a trade agreement within the next four or five weeks. The State Department is of the same mind, and has, moreover, impressed upon us the high desirability of getting through with the business well in advance of January 1st" (Herridge to Finlayson, Oct. 8, 1935, Bennett Papers, Vol. F–242).

[40] Quoted from an editorial in the Ottawa *Journal*, Aug. 13, 1935; memorandum by Division of Western European Affairs, Aug. 14, 1935, *Foreign Relations, 1935*, II, 19–20.

the Prime Minister pressed Norman Armour, Robbins' successor as American Minister to Canada, for a decision. Bennett said that the Cabinet had to select a date for the election. Those who opposed a trade agreement favored the end of September rather than the middle of October. In order to insist upon the later date he needed definite assurance from Roosevelt that negotiations were imminent; he doubted that they could continue once the political campaign had formally begun. The Prime Minister then warned that if there were no final instrument, he would have no alternative but to reluctantly make public his efforts to reach an agreement. Because trade talks had become a campaign issue, he could not remain silent indefinitely.[41] Bennett's objective was obvious. American compliance—simply an assurance that negotiations would soon begin, not the conclusion of an accord—would improve his political posture; if the delay continued, he could cancel the proposed discussions and conduct a strongly anti-American campaign.

In Washington progress had been made. On July 31 the question which concessions the United States would offer to Canada had been discussed at the White House. A final decision had not been reached when Armour talked with Bennett because Roosevelt had requested additional information on certain items. Armour anxiously underscored the political implications of further delay. After considering the situation at hand, the State Department and the President decided to grant Bennett's wish. They assumed that the Prime Minister would use this decision to deal with members of the Cabinet and would not issue a statement to the press. The United States wanted to avoid publicity until the adjournment of Congress, which was nearing the end of the Second Hundred Days. Roosevelt wanted nothing to interfere with successful passage of the major legisla-

[41] *Ibid.*; Armour to Secretary of State, no. 12, Aug. 14, 1935, 611.4231/1217.

tion still pending. On August 14, Armour informed Bennett that American negotiators would receive the Canadian representatives on August 26 "to take up negotiations looking to a trade agreement between the United States and Canada." The Prime Minister subsequently set the date October 14 for the election. O. D. Skelton, the Canadian Under Secretary of State for External Affairs, intimated to the American Minister that cancellation of the proposed negotiations by Bennett had been narrowly averted.[42]

The Prime Minister's veiled threat was just one factor that influenced the American decision. By August a formula to allay the fears of affected economic interests had been devised. Quotas placed on the leading Canadian imports—cattle, lumber, seed potatoes, and dairy products—had both economic and political merits: they served as a cushion against the falling prices which would accompany unrestricted entry, and, more important, as a safety valve for political opposition. American farmers, lumbermen, and cattlemen would supposedly accept an agreement that still left them well protected in the domestic market.[43]

The major question was whether to negotiate seriously with the Conservatives, or to wait for the expected victory of the Liberals. Officials in Washington apparently had decided independently to follow the first course, but the Minister in Ottawa took no chances. Norman Armour argued cogently that the

[42] Memorandum of conversation between Roosevelt, Grady, and Sayre, by Sayre, July 31, 1935, 611.4231/1201½; memorandum by Division of Western European Affairs, Aug. 14, 1935, *Foreign Relations, 1935,* II, 19–20; Armour to Secretary of State, no. 18, Aug. 16, 1935, 611.4231/1219.

[43] Hickerson told Armour on August 14 that "unforeseen circumstances" had delayed matters, and that the message which he finally received would have been sent within twenty-four hours regardless of Bennett's expressed concern. For the quotas and the political use that was to be made of them, see memorandum of conversation between Roosevelt, Grady, and Hickerson, by Grady, Aug. 21, 1935, 611.4231/1224.

United States had everything to gain and nothing to lose by bargaining with the Conservatives. He found reinforcement in a letter written to Roosevelt by an American close to Mackenzie King which outlined the Liberals' political strategy. The inform-ant conceded that the Ottawa agreements were troublesome, but predicted that if the United States began negotiations, King would extend the concessions after he became Prime Minister. According to the letter, the British government had unof-ficially authorized King to alter the preferences in the interest of Canadian-American trade. The Liberal leader hoped Ben-nett would commit the Conservative party to the principle of making tariff concessions to the United States. If negotiations broke down, however, there was a danger that Bennett would carry out his previous threat and campaign on the indefinite extension of imperial preferences. Although it was improbable that Bennett would be elected, failure of the Roosevelt Adminis-tration to gain Conservative support of lower tariffs would make it more difficult to reach a trade agreement in the future. It was essential, therefore, not to alienate Bennett during the negotia-tions. Concurring with these confidences, Armour suggested that Washington would be interfering more in the campaign by discontinuing the negotiations than by continuing them in good faith.[44]

Actual negotiations with Canada began on August 26. When American officials transmitted their proposed concessions, a dis-appointed Canadian Minister expressed doubt that they afforded a basis for an agreement. He left for Ottawa that same night for consultations.[45] For political reasons, Bennett could hardly discontinue the negotiations; in fact, on September 9, Armour

[44] Armour to Secretary of State, no. 18, Aug. 16, 1935, 611.4231/1219.

[45] Memorandum, Hickerson to Secretary of State, Aug. 28, 1935, *Foreign Relations, 1935,* II, 20–22.

learned that, in deference to American wishes, the forthcoming official list of articles on which Canada wanted reductions would contain less than had been discussed informally. Ottawa was still studying the concessions which it would grant on American products.[46]

In the meantime, the difficulty of negotiating during an election campaign became apparent. On September 4, King accused Bennett of procrastination, charging that Roosevelt had virtually invited him to discuss reciprocity two years earlier.[47] A few days later the Prime Minister released the diplomatic correspondence, hoping to refute King's latest accusation, as well as the Liberal indictment that the United States would have nothing to do with the Conservatives.[48] The Opposition immediately concluded that the negotiations had collapsed, an impression which Armour corrected through King's private secretary. Armour defended this extraordinary step of taking the Opposition party into his confidence as an effort to remove the negotiations from Canadian politics. By subtly influencing the Liberals to modify their attack, he hoped to prevent alienation of Bennett. Moreover, Armour was almost certain that there would be a new government in Canada and wanted to keep King abreast of developments. The United States would thus be safeguarded from any charges of duplicity later.[49]

Bennett probably revealed his true feeling about the immediate prospects for an agreement when he asked the Canadian electorate late in September for a mandate to conclude negotia-

[46] Armour to Secretary of State, telegram no. 94, Sept. 9, 1935, *Foreign Relations, 1935,* II, 22.

[47] New York *Times,* Sept. 5, 1935.

[48] The notes were released on September 8 and printed in the New York *Times,* Ottawa *Journal,* and Ottawa *Citizen* on September 9, 1935.

[49] Armour to Secretary of State, no. 76, Sept. 13, 1935, 611.4231/1242; enclosed was a memorandum of a conversation with Edward Pickering, King's secretary.

tions with the United States. By implication at least, the Prime Minister had admitted his doubts that an agreement was possible before October 14. To a group of newsmen covering the campaign, he went even further, saying that he was pessimistic about reaching any accord until after the 1936 presidential election in the United States. In response to an American inquiry, the Conservative leader publicly repudiated this interpretation of his remarks. Privately, American officials got the impression that the Prime Minister was upset not by the substance of the article, but rather by the reporter's indiscretion in writing something not meant for print.[50]

While offering reduced tariffs on approximately seven hundred items, the Canadians had continued to press for concessions on commodities which they considered essential—cod, seed potatoes, cream, cattle, and certain lumber products. By late September the American economic experts were prepared to accept the latest Canadian requests on all these items except cod. Although he knew that his decision would probably wreck the negotiations, Roosevelt balked, to the annoyance of the Canadians.[51] The disappointed opinion of Skelton was that failure to

[50] John MacCormac's article in the New York *Times,* Sept. 22, 1935, prompted Washington's inquiry and led to Bennett's public clarification; Baldwin to Secretary of State, no. 90, Sept. 23, 1935, *Foreign Relations, 1935,* II, 22–24. The Ottawa *Citizen,* Sept. 25, 1935, and the New York *Times,* Sept. 26, 1935, reported Bennett's campaign remarks. For the impression that the Prime Minister accepted the substance of MacCormac's article, see Armour to Secretary of State, no. 163, Oct. 23, 1935, 611.4231/1285.

[51] Memorandum by Western European Affairs, Sept. 24, 1935, 611.4231/1254½; memorandum of interview between Roosevelt, Phillips, Grady, Armour, and Sayre, by Sayre, Sept. 26, 1935, 611.4231/1260½. Phillips recorded that Roosevelt "stood firm against giving any substantial concessions on meats, potatoes, and cream" (Phillips Diary, Sept. 26, 1935).

grant concessions on the four or five principal items requested by Canada had made an agreement almost impossible.

The continued activities of special interest groups, rather than the expectation of doing better in later exchanges with the Liberals, influenced most the President's decision not to accede to Canadian wishes. The final draft of November, however, was "vastly" more favorable to American interests than earlier ones had been, or so the American Under Secretary of State confessed to Roosevelt at that time.[52] Skelton sympathized with Armour over the political situation in the United States. He regretted these electoral realities, for he thought the proposed Canadian concessions would have resulted in a mutually beneficial agreement had the State Department moved closer to the Canadian position. Under the circumstances he doubted whether Canada could agree to amend its valuations system or to grant most-favored-nation treatment to American goods. Bennett had nevertheless offered to send the Dominion trade experts back to Washington to continue the discussions. Since time was short, Skelton had little hope that even a limited accord could be reached before the election.[53] The Under Secretary's prediction proved to be correct; on October 3, several days before Bennett's approval of the resumption of talks was known in Washington, the State Department decided to suspend negotiations until after the election. Perhaps then, it was thought, the United States could satisfy Canadian requests and improve its own position as well.[54]

The Liberal victory was an apparent mandate to conclude the

[52] Phillips to Roosevelt, Nov. 7, 1935, Roosevelt Papers, PSF, Canada, 1933–1941.

[53] Armour to Secretary of State, no. 119, Oct. 4, 1935, *Foreign Relations, 1935,* II, 24–27.

[54] Phillips Diary, Oct. 3, 1935.

reciprocity talks, for during the campaign King had promised a successful result within ninety days of his taking office, and on election night he called the outcome "an unmistakable verdict" in favor of making an agreement with the United States.[55] The following day, Skelton told Armour that, although he had not seen King recently, he felt certain that King was firmly committed to the negotiation of a trade agreement and would want to proceed at once. But he also warned of King's probable disappointment at the American offer, and of the possibility that King might terminate the negotiations and explore the Ottawa agreements.

Skelton then turned his attention to the international scene, developments which were destined to play a significant role in the relations between the two countries. The Canadian Under Secretary stressed that of the two alternatives confronting Canada—agreement with the United States or closer union with the Empire—he preferred the former for political as well as economic reasons. To those who knew Skelton, his choice was not surprising. In his memoirs, Sir Vincent Massey, Canada's first minister to Washington, wrote that despite Skelton's "brilliant academic mind," he was not uniformly "objective in outlook." Specifically, the Under Secretary "had a strong and lasting suspicion of British policy and an unchanging coldness towards Great Britain. In other words, to put it bluntly, but I feel not unfairly, he was anti-British. No one who worked with him, or knew him well, could, I think, fail to recognize this."[56] Incipient international disorder, highlighted by the Abyssinian crisis, led Skelton to talk of a "North American mind." The two nations could either erect a closer political community or they could continue

[55] The statement was enclosed in Armour to Secretary of State, no. 144, Oct. 16, 1935, 842.00/483.

[56] Vincent Massey, *What's Past Is Prologue: The Memoirs of the Right Honourable Vincent Massey* (Toronto, 1963), 135.

down independent paths marked by a minimum of cooperation, understanding, and goodwill. A trade agreement resulted because King and Roosevelt saw the need for North American solidarity.

Armour was satisfied that the negotiations would succeed if the United States were willing to make one or two sacrifices pertaining to the list of five commodities considered essential by the Canadians. According to one of the Canadian negotiators, the Dominion would yield on everything if the Americans went along with three of its five principal requests. The American Minister felt that it would be tragic if the United States forfeited this opportunity.[57]

On October 24, Armour discussed the subject with the new Prime Minister for the first time. As expected, King said that he was ready for the two governments to tackle reciprocity. Like Secretary of State Hull, King traced political discord to economic ills. Unless something were done quickly to end economic nationalism, he believed, the world might reap serious consequences. Economic autarchy caused not only "isolation and ruination," but "created bitterness and poisoned good relations between governments." Already the Italo-Ethiopian war had begun, and the prospects for the forthcoming London naval talks were not good because of the apparent disposition of Japan to implement its announcement of 1934 that it would no longer adhere to existing restrictions. These two topics, together with the Canadian-American pact, had monopolized recent Dominion Cabinet meetings. As an example and perhaps a warning to other nations, King wanted to strengthen and solidify relations between the United States and Canada, "to show Canadian-

[57] Memorandum of telephone conversation between Armour and Hickerson, Oct. 17, 1935, 842.00/481; Armour to Phillips, Oct. 22, 1935, Roosevelt Papers, PSF, Canada, 1933–1941; Armour to Secretary of State, no. 149, Oct. 17, 1935, 611.4231/1273.

American solidarity and for the two countries to stand together before the world." Closer trade ties would be the first step, if the United States would make it possible. At the end of the conversation, the Prime Minister suggested that he might go to Washington to confer with Roosevelt. But by the following evening King had decided that a meeting with the President would be useful only if a trade agreement were in sight. He thought that the agreement should be concluded before Canada started negotiations late in the year with Great Britain for a downward revision of the Ottawa agreement.[58]

In order to resume negotiations King made plans to send the two Canadian tariff experts to Washington.[59] On October 31, Skelton reiterated to an American Legation official the concessions desired by Ottawa. The Under Secretary was advised that King would be welcome in Washington, but that if he chose to make the trip, he should not misinterpret its meaning: the negotiations must succeed or fail on their own merits. Although Skelton replied that King understood perfectly, the Prime Minister himself subsequently made it clear that, for psychological reasons particularly, he hoped a major announcement concerning the agreement could be made on Armistice Day. Meanwhile, the Canadian negotiators were working with the appropriate ministers in Ottawa. They began their duties in the American capital on November 4.[60]

[58] Armour to Secretary of State, no. 169, Oct. 25, 1935, *Foreign Relations, 1935,* II, 27–30; memorandum of conversation with King was enclosed. See also Can. *H. of C. Debates,* Feb. 11, 1936, I, 90. For the later conversation, see memorandum, Armour to Phillips, Oct. 25, 1935, Roosevelt Papers, PSF, Canada, 1933–1941; Phillips to Roosevelt, Oct. 26, 1935, *ibid.;* Armour to Secretary of State, no. 173, Oct. 26, 1935, 611.4231/1291; memorandum of telephone conversation with Armour by Phillips, Oct. 26, 1935, 611.4231/1316.

[59] Can. *H. of C. Debates,* Feb. 11, 1936, I, 90. See also Phillips to Roosevelt, Nov. 7, 1935, Roosevelt Papers, PSF, Canada, 1933–1941.

[60] Memorandum by Counselor of Legation, Oct. 31, 1935, 611.4231/1318. A memorandum by Phillips to Sayre, Oct. 30, 1935,

King arrived in Washington on November 7; the conference with Roosevelt was scheduled for the following day. Meanwhile Under Secretary William Phillips informed Roosevelt that for the past few days the American and Canadian representatives had worked unremittingly and, from the American standpoint, had drafted a very promising arrangement, "a far more favorable set-up than with the Bennett government." The President also studied a Department of Commerce report which recommended liberalization of duties. On November 8, Roosevelt called Phillips, and later the American trade experts, to the White House for a final briefing. The Under Secretary warned of possible Canadian extension of the Ottawa treaty if negotiations failed, but pointed out to the President the difficulties of agreeing to the concessions on cattle, seed potatoes, and cream. Although personally pleased with the latest schedules, Roosevelt wanted to check with Secretary of Agriculture Henry A. Wallace, which he did later that day.[61] It was apparent that the President was as interested as King in a speedy conclusion of a trade pact. According to one of its members, he informed the Cabinet at this time that the proposed agreement was definitely advantageous to the United States and that he hoped to get King's signature while the Prime Minister was in the mood.[62] In late November, John Hickerson wrote that working on the trade negotiations "three solid weeks with an average of sixteen hours a day on the job

---

611.4231/1296, reported a telephone conversation with Armour in which the American Minister first relayed King's sentiments to sign an agreement on November 11. The Prime Minister reaffirmed this desire in a personal call to William Phillips (Phillips Diary, Nov. 4, 1935).

[61] Phillips to Roosevelt, Nov. 7, 1935, Roosevelt Papers, PSF, Canada, 1933–1941; Phillips Diary, Nov. 8, 1935. For general coverage, see New York *Times*, Nov. 8 and 9, 1935.

[62] Harold L. Ickes, *The First Thousand Days, 1933–1936*, Vol. I of *The Secret Diary of Harold L. Ickes* (3 vols.; New York, 1953–1959), 465–466.

. . . nearly finished me." In his judgment, the American negotiators had convinced Roosevelt that "despite a temporary howl,
the Canadian agreement is so favorable to us that in six months
it will be recognized generally as a great economic and political
asset." [63]

On the afternoon of November 9, following two King-
Roosevelt meetings of the previous day, the President invited
Hull, Wallace, and Phillips to the White House. There he
decided to proceed with the agreement. While the arguments for
and against it were being reviewed, the Secretary of Agriculture
threw his support behind the pact. As Phillips recorded the
event, "I never saw the President to better advantage, his courage, his decision was [*sic*] splendid." That evening Hull and
King initialed the agreement, and the latter left Washington at
midnight for Ottawa to obtain the consent of his Cabinet.[64]
Because the Prime Minister had announced he would stay at the
Canadian Legation through November 11, the press suspected
that King's postponing a vacation to the South and hurrying
back to Ontario meant that an agreement was imminent.[65]

There was one touch of drama on the morning of November
11. Fearful that the concession on whiskey might interfere with
his plans to prosecute certain Canadian firms for shipments of
liquor to the United States during prohibition, Secretary of the
Treasury Henry Morgenthau had asked for a forty-eight hour
delay to study the matter. King's hope for an announcement on
Armistice Day hung in the balance. At the last minute Roosevelt
persuaded Morgenthau to withdraw his objection. King learned
of this through the Canadian Legation, and, shortly before
eleven o'clock, the Prime Minister called the President to inform

[63] Hickerson to Moffat, Nov. 25, 1935, Moffat Papers, X.

[64] Phillips Diary, Nov. 9, 1935.

[65] New York *Times,* Nov. 11, 1935; Department of State, *Press
Releases,* XIII (Nov. 9, 1935), no. 319, pp. 365–366.

him of his government's consent.[66] At Arlington National Cemetery, Roosevelt told the news to the world. Four days later the American Secretary of State and the Canadian Prime Minister formally signed the trade agreement at the White House. The public remained in suspense as to the actual meaning of the agreement, for its terms were not printed until November 18.[67]

The document was basically conservative, limited in its effects by import quotas, guaranteed preferences, and the American policy that confined concessions to those commodities of which Canada was the principal supplier. Nevertheless, both Canadian and American exporters could anticipate significant improvement in sales of their goods. For the first time in history, the Dominion extended most-favored-nation treatment to the United States, a major concession covering 767 items or subitems in the Canadian tariff. Existing free entry was guaranteed, and duties were reduced, or bound against increase, on 180 additional items, mostly manufactured products. In an accompanying note from the Canadian Legation, Ottawa agreed to alter its valuation system. Unfortunately, the excise tax on American imports was left untouched.

---

[66] Phillips Diary, Nov. 9 and 11, 1935. For a more detailed analysis of Morgenthau's activities, see memorandum, Nov. 9, 1935, Morgenthau Diary, Book 11, pp. 61–62, 117, and Blum, *Years of Crisis*, 110–119. For the later development of the Treasury Department's plans to prosecute, see *Foreign Relations, 1936*, I, 796–825. For an account of prohibition and its effects on the relations between Washington and Ottawa, see Richard N. Kottman, "Volstead Violated: Prohibition as a Factor in Canadian-American Relations," *Canadian Historical Review*, XLIII (June, 1962), 106–126. A general summary of King's actions appears in *Can. H. of C. Debates*, Feb. 11, 1936, I, 91.

[67] Department of State, *Press Releases*, XIII (Nov. 16, 1935), no. 320, pp. 377, 379–380; the agreement is printed in *Press Releases*, XIII (Nov. 23, 1935), no. 321, pp. 388–442. See also U.S. Tariff Commission, "The Trade Agreement with Canada," report no. 111, Second Series (Washington, 1936).

As concessions to Canada, free entry of pulpwood, wood pulp, newsprint paper, unmanufactured wood, and several other commodities would continue for the life of the agreement. There were reductions in duties for specific amounts on cattle, cream, seed potatoes, and Douglas fir and western hemlock. Schedules were lowered without qualification on other exports, including certain kinds of fish (cod excluded), lumber other than Douglas fir and western hemlock, cheddar cheese, maple sugar, and live poultry. Finally, Canadian imports would still enter the American market on a most-favored-nation basis.

The trade agreement was received favorably in Canada with all of the major newspapers expressing approval. The Montreal *Gazette,* which had denounced previous Liberal governments, was happy that the United States was apparently beginning to equate Dominion purchasing power with Canadian sales south of the forty-ninth parallel. In its view, the pact reflected King's desire to aid Canada's basic industries.[68] Because of reductions in the Canadian tariff on automobiles and farm implements, reception of the pact in Toronto was less enthusiastic. Although no great opposition appeared, some cautious observers questioned the temporary feature of the accord.[69]

Reaction in the United States tended to follow lines of sectional economic interest. The Portland *Morning Oregonian* thought it "inconceivable" that Roosevelt would "strike such a blow at work and wages . . . which must inevitably follow reduction of the lumber tariff," while the Minneapolis *Tribune* termed the agreement a flagrant betrayal of the American dairy industry. On the other hand, editors in the manufacturing centers saw it in a different light. "Ohio is to benefit directly,"

[68] Montreal *Gazette,* Nov. 18, 1935.

[69] Toronto *Globe,* Nov. 19, 1935; Toronto *Mail and Empire,* Nov. 18 and 25, 1935.

rejoiced the Cleveland *Plain Dealer*. Certain organizations, notably the National Grange and those representing lumber interests, attacked the terms. Others, spearheaded by the American
Manufacturers Export Association, were laudatory.[70]

In late March and early April, 1936, Parliament approved the
accord without a recorded vote. During the two-month debate,
Bennett had tried to embarrass the Liberals by showing that the
agreement was not a good one for Canada because of the small
number of concessions granted by the United States and that he,
for that reason, had refused to be a party to it. "No man, however
great he may be," declared the former Prime Minister, "can in
twenty-four hours, forty-eight hours, or even seventy-two hours
complete a trade agreement" with the United States. That King
signed one in Washington meant "either the agreement in its
essential terms and details had been done before, or it is an
improvident one." Of these two options Bennett chose the second, claiming that "at any time before October it would have
been possible to arrive at that arrangement, but I would not
make it." Rising to the occasion, he exclaimed, "I stand here
tonight and say that I would not make it. . . . I condemn it. I
believe it to be bad, and . . . [it] will bring disaster to Canada."
Bennett carried the fight to the last day, when he informed
Commons that "those of us who have voted against the agreement certainly have not done so with any joy. . . . I would have
infinitely preferred an agreement which I could have supported
and . . . I know I speak for those about me. But we cannot by
any process of reasoning convince ourselves that what we are
giving is in any way comparable with the benefits we should

---

[70] American press opinion from "Trade Pact Controversy Bubbles,"
Literary Digest, CXX (Nov. 30, 1935), 35–36. The New York *Times*,
between November 15 and 20, carried a number of articles dealing with
reactions of various American special interest groups.

receive. What we are giving is so much greater than any possible benefits that we cannot give the agreement our support." [71] As might be expected, the Conservative leader failed to rally popular opposition to the pact, and King had little trouble guiding it through Parliament.

The major embarrassment for the United States, so serious that John D. Hickerson traveled to Ottawa for trade discussions with Mackenzie King, was the possibility that Canada would raise its intermediate tariff and thus discount a major gain for American exporters. While consistent with the letter of the trade pact, such a ruse, supported particularly by William Euler, Minister of Trade and Commerce, would violate its spirit. The key item being considered for the increased duty was furniture. After pressure was applied from Washington, Ottawa dropped this commodity from the short list of items on which levels were raised.[72]

The favorable action by the Canadian Parliament ends the first chapter in Canadian-American reciprocity. That its economic results fell short of expectations should not be allowed to detract from its significance.[73] Bennett, influenced throughout by

[71] Quotes from Can. *H. of C. Deb.*, Feb. 10, 1936, I, 38, 55–56; *ibid.*, March 23, 1936, II, 1347.

[72] Armour to Secretary of State, telegram no. 22, March 2, 1936, 611.4231/1687; memorandum by Division of Western European Affairs, March 2, 1936, 611.4231/1687½.

[73] American sales in Canada increased, though not spectacularly, and this increase was partly attributable to the general improvement of world economic conditions—particularly the upturn in the United States and Canada. The volume of American imports had risen in 1934 and 1935, both pre–trade agreement years. Nevertheless, statistics confirm that beginning in 1936 exporters of goods covered in the agreement fared better than those selling non-concession items. In 1936 and 1937 the percentage of the increase of their imports was higher, and, when total sales fell off in 1938, they experienced a relatively smaller decline than

Herridge, deserves credit for initiating the conversations.[74] But in the final analysis it was Mackenzie King who made a further friendly gesture to the United States, who accepted less in the negotiations than had his predecessor in the interest of Canadian-American cordiality and North American identity, and who hoped to reorient the world's thinking to freer trade and to peace.

Within the American context, Roosevelt had found himself being both drawn away from an agreement by electoral responsibilities and increasingly attracted to it by the requirements of international order. Canadian-American solidarity was a necessity in a world showing signs of political and moral disintegration. The President, converted to internationalism as a means of improving the economic climate in the United States, might have gambled that more interests would benefit from the pact than be alienated by it and that the administration would be properly rewarded in the 1936 election. Available evidence does not support that interpretation. Rather, it appears that he subor-

---

the exporters of non-concession products. Recovery in Canada remained incomplete, due in part to the partial recovery in the United States; in 1938 Canadian exports declined following the recession of 1937. Canada also had economic problems which were not directly connected with increased sales in the American market. To pursue this further, see Department of State, *Bulletin*, II (Jan. 13, 1940), no. 29, pp. 43–48; A. E. Safarian, "Foreign Trade and the Level of Economic Activity in Canada in the 1930's," *Canadian Journal of Economics and Political Science*, XVIII (Aug., 1952), 336–344; also, Safarian's *The Canadian Economy in the Great Depression*, 66–82, 97–116, 137–145.

[74] Hume Wrong of the Canadian Legation wrote the following to Dafoe: "It is rather bitter for Herridge, who probably did more than anyone to make signature at this time possible, that he will get no public credit and will be condemned in his own party for not getting the agreement through before the election—which could not have been done" (Wrong to Dafoe, Nov. 18, 1935, Dafoe Papers, reel no. M–77).

dinated the possibility of political retaliation to the importance of strengthening the bond between Ottawa and Washington,[75] hoping that this bond would in turn have a salutary effect on the relations between the United Kingdom and the United States.

[75] To carry this point further, on Oct. 15, 1935, Bloom reported a confidential conversation with Wallace in which the Secretary of Agriculture declared that the United States could not make major concessions until after the election of 1936 (Bloom to Dafoe, Oct. 15, 1935, Dafoe Papers, reel no. M–77).

Chapter 4

An Anglo-American Trade Agreement: Preliminaries and Portents

To American officials the Canadian-American trade agreement had significance beyond its immediate effect on relations between the United States and Canada. Now that the first accord with a Commonwealth country had been made, some arrangement with the United Kingdom, the world's foremost trading power, might follow. That hope was tied to certain economic realities. Between 1926 and 1930, Great Britain had been the leading market for American exports, absorbing 17.5 per cent of total American sales abroad. In 1937 this figure was 16 per cent. Moreover, 16.1 per cent of United Kingdom imports in 1929 had been of United States origin. After 1929 this percentage fell appreciably—to 11.2 per cent in 1934, 11 per cent in 1936, and 11.1 per cent in 1937—while the Ottawa agreements had encouraged a substantial increase in the percentage of imperial imports, from 28.7 per cent in 1931 to 39.4 per cent in 1937. By 1934, when the State Department first considered negotiating an Anglo-American agreement, it had already risen to 36.9 per cent.

The American farmer was particularly affected by these changing patterns, for the United Kingdom had always been a major market for his products. Competition from the Dominions would not be welcome at any time, but the depression made his dependence upon this outlet acute.

The reasons for Washington's persistent quest for reciprocity with Great Britain go deeper, however, than the promise of economic rewards for deserving inhabitants of the farm belt. Criticism among farm organizations that to that point the majority of trade agreements had been with agricultural countries, resulting in greater competition for their members, created an electoral problem. While the sales abroad of American industrial products had been stimulated, farmers considered themselves the sacrificial agents making possible that growth. The political fringe benefits that would accompany an agreement with the United Kingdom help to explain why American officials labored many months to persuade Whitehall to modify the preference system. In larger perspective, then, the Hull trade program required for its political and economic health a tonic with a British label.[1]

[1] Percy W. Bidwell, *Our Trade with Britain: Bases for a Reciprocal Tariff Agreement* (New York, 1938), 4–17; Bruce M. Russett, *Community and Contention: Britain and America in the Twentieth Century* (Cambridge, 1963), 49–62, 81–95. One might also profit by reading H. C. Allen, *Great Britain and the United States: A History of Anglo-American Relations (1783–1952)* (New York, 1955), 53–94. For some speculations on motivations, see Kreider, *The Anglo-American Trade Agreement,* 29–34. In Hull, *Memoirs,* I, 520, the Secretary wrote, "It seemed to me that our trade agreements program could not be considered complete until the United Kingdom was inserted as the apex of the arch." A very general account of the negotiations from 1936 to November, 1938, appears in Pratt, *Hull,* I, 123–132. In April, Sayre wrote the following to William Phillips in Rome: "It is important from the standpoint of the situation in this country that we obtain improved export opportunities for American agriculture. As you know, there has been a good deal of criticism in agricultural circles that we have heretofore

The erosion of international order and morality following the rise of Hitler forms the backdrop for Hull's efforts to strengthen the trade program with an Anglo-American pact. The anti-Semitic persecutions inaugurated in 1933 by the German government and the Nazi designs on Austria, punctuated in 1934 by the assassination of Chancellor Engelbert Dollfuss, had mild reverberations compared with the explosions of 1935 and 1936. Mussolini's Ethiopian adventure, which produced only a limited rebuff from the United States and the League of Nations, was followed by German military occupation of the Rhineland in defiance of the Locarno pact. Civil war in Spain, pitting army and church against Republic, ended the importance of the League as an effective agent of collective security. Berlin, Moscow, and Rome engaged men and material in the slaughter, while the Western democracies, wishing to avoid involvement and the possible escalation of the conflict into a general European war, established the Non-Intervention Committee. The democratic governments thus were not equal to the test of collectively resisting aggression. Lacking confidence that the other parties would honor their commitments—the essential ingredient in any joint endeavor—they feared that a future crisis would find them diplomatically isolated.

Nor is the record of the Roosevelt Administration, particularly in its Spanish policy, a proud one. It, too, shirked its political responsibilities. American initiatives in these years were confined to economic proposals. The conflicts in Europe and the possibility that worse conflicts might follow played a prominent role in

negotiated to a disproportionate extent with agricultural countries and, in consequence, that agriculture has been called upon to make sacrifices . . . for the benefit of increased industrial exports. If satisfactory concessions can be obtained for our agricultural exports in the important United Kingdom market, it will make it much easier to go forward with negotiations with agricultural countries" (Sayre to Phillips, April 12, 1937, Francis B. Sayre Papers, Library of Congress, Box 5).

Hull's decision to pressure Great Britain to cooperate economically with the United States. The program of trade revival, Hull's answer to political maladjustment, would either coerce Germany and Italy into cooperating with the democracies or present the example of Anglo-American solidarity to the world as an antidote for contemporary nationalism. The same international disturbances that prompted Hull to look toward Great Britain, however, made British politicians extremely cautious and led to Whitehall's search for an Anglo-German accord.

The attempt to effect an arrangement with the United Kingdom was begun in 1934 when the Canadian-American agreement was in its initial stages. Numerous obstacles and difficulties were encountered, and before long the issue became entangled with a more fundamental problem, the divergent commercial policies of the two governments. The Ethiopian and Rhineland crises, exciting fears of war and enlisting the energies of British statesmen to find grounds for rapprochement with Hitler and Mussolini, prevented much progress for the next two years. With each international development, Hull intensified American efforts to convince Whitehall that future peace depended on joint economic policies, but the efforts went largely unrewarded. There was sometimes agreement on general principles of international economic behavior, but discord accompanied the discussion of how best to implement the generalities. While London was paralyzed by the specter of war, domestic pressure groups were carrying on public education campaigns. The perceptive diplomats could thus see that successful negotiation of an Anglo-American trade agreement would be no easy task.

In the summer of 1934 sentiment in favor of an accord grew in both capitals, finally converging in September with the discussion of a trade pact by Sir Ronald Lindsay, British Ambassador in Washington, and Francis Sayre. During the summer, Lindsay had mentioned the subject to Walter Runciman, the President of the Board of Trade, but the latter had opposed London's taking the initiative, preferring instead to be receptive to any overture that might come from the United States. While he could say nothing officially, Sayre did inform Lindsay that the State Department had recently begun to explore trade agreement possibilities, though as yet it had reached no concrete decisions.[2]

The immediate result of the Department's preliminary inquiry was the creation in the United States of the British Empire Committee. Its primary function was to determine the best means of undermining the imperial preference system: multilateral negotiations with the countries of the Commonwealth, simultaneous bilateral negotiations, or negotiations with Canada alone or with two or three members of the British family. Assuming that discussions with Dominion governments were the choice, the committee was to ascertain also which diplomatic tactic would most effectively attain the goal: granting them one-sided or reciprocal concessions, having them denounce the Ottawa treaties, withholding most-favored-nation treatment, or introducing discriminations. One other possibility, that of seeking trade alternatives outside the bloc, was to receive the committee's attention. Moreover, it was to weigh the political and economic advantages and disadvantages of a permanent treaty, rather than an agreement, with Canada. If the treaty were rejected in favor of working within the framework of the Reciprocal Trade Agreements Act, it had to render a verdict on how the United States should treat the Anglo-Canadian treaty. Washington might negotiate on items not covered by the 1932 pact, thus evading the issue; the State Department might defer to the Ottawa treaty by granting important concessions to the Dominion while asking for nothing protected in the accord; it might offer Canada such major concessions that the Dominion, if it

[2] Memorandum by Sayre, Sept. 14, 1934, *Foreign Relations, 1934,* I, 797–798.

wanted an agreement, would have no practical alternative but to alter the Ottawa arrangement.[3] By the middle of September, then, both governments had given at least some thought to a trade agreement, and the United States was seriously studying the question.

During the next few weeks the British Empire Committee held several meetings in line with its instructions. Because of the Ottawa accords and the protectionist trend in Great Britain, the members saw only a slim chance for an Anglo-American agreement. Nevertheless, they compiled a list of proposed requests and discussed possible concessions. Of the Dominions, Canada seemed to be the only prospect with which Washington could profitably negotiate, and the conclusion of this pact would be difficult. Because there was a possibility, Canada became the center of attention. A comprehensive trade agreement with the senior Dominion, besides liberalizing trade between the two nations, "might well be sufficient gain for Canada to warrant her abandonment of the Ottawa Agreements" with the result that this "would in turn force the issue upon the other countries and might be the opening wedge to secure major modifications elsewhere." [4]

[3] Memorandum "Functions of a British Empire Committee," by Office of Economic Adviser, Sept. 12, 1934, 611.4131/115½.

[4] Memorandum on work of British Empire Committee, Sept. 12, 1934, 611.4131/115½; memorandum of meeting of the special committee on the British Empire, Sept. 15, 1934, 611.4131/115½; memorandum, Treaty Division to Chairman of the British Empire Committee, Sept. 18, 1934, 611.4131/115½; memorandum of meeting of the special committee on the British Empire, Oct. 1, 1934, 611.4131/115½; memorandum of meeting of the special committee on the British Empire, Oct. 4, 1934, 611.4131/115½. William C. Bullitt very early saw the importance of an agreement with Canada. Writing to the President from London in July, 1933, he observed, "To me the most striking feature of this Conference thus far is Bennett's desire to cooperate with us and I think that if you have any plans for reciprocal tariff negotiations with Canada the time is

For the moment, therefore, the United States confined its activities to negotiations with Canada. The British, "not particularly interested in a trade agreement . . . at present," refrained from rushing headlong into discussions with Washington. Protectionism, although a rather late development in Great Britain, was increasing, especially among the Tories, and those interests that had received such benefits were not about to surrender them without a fight. In addition, British officials tied the trade agreement to two scarred remnants of 1933, currency stabilization and war debts, wanting to dispose of these problems before turning to reciprocity. Realizing that war debts was a dead issue and that the United Kingdom no longer considered settlement "as imperative," the United States was only too willing to dispense with it if the subject were broached by Whitehall. On the other hand, since currency stabilization was more closely related to the trade pact, Washington stood ready to talk about this matter. Memories of the World Economic Conference remained a barrier, and not until 1936 did the Treasury Department finally begin actual conversations. The French government joined them, and the three countries, with the stabilization agreement of September, 1936, cleared the path of one obstacle.[5]

---

very propitious. Incidentally, Bennett told me the other day how much he liked Warren, and I am sure that he was talking honestly. [He was referring to Warren Delano Robbins, a cousin of Roosevelt, who was in London for the World Economic Conference. This observation could very well have been one very important factor underlying FDR's appointment in 1933 of Robbins as Minister to Canada.] Bruce of Australia talked to me with violence of the British Government in general and John Simon in particular, and I wonder if via Canada we might not make a hole in the Ottawa Agreements" (Bullitt to Roosevelt, July 8, 1933, Roosevelt Papers, London Economic Conference File).

[5] Memorandum by Alvin Hanson of the Tariff Section, Dec. 18, 1934, *Foreign Relations, 1934,* I, 798–802. For pertinent documents on currency stabilization, see *Foreign Relations, 1936,* I, 535–565. The subject is covered also in Blum, *Years of Crisis,* 159–173.

The most noteworthy development in 1935, besides the Canadian-American pact, was the establishment of a committee to study specific commodities that might be included in an accord. In May, Oscar B. Ryder of the United States Tariff Commission, the American representative to the League of Nations Committee on Clearing, discussed the possibilities of reciprocity with British officials in London. Sir Frederick Leith-Ross, the government's Chief Economic Adviser, subsequently reported the substance of the discussion to H. Owen Chalkley, the Commercial Counselor of the British Embassy. In late June, Chalkley, in the company of Ryder and Henry F. Grady, advised the United States that his government, previously skeptical about trade agreement prospects, wanted now to take a careful and more sympathetic look at the situation. Grady agreed to a preliminary survey by an American committee, but said that it could not be ready before July, when the Commercial Counselor would be leaving Washington for a trip to London. Chalkley suggested that while he was in England he would try to persuade members of the Government to produce a similar study.[6]

Accordingly, on August 20, the Committee on Trade Agreements departed from its usual pattern by establishing a "United Kingdom country committee." Such a body ordinarily came into being after the decision was made to negotiate a trade agreement, but the parent committee felt that the American relationship with Great Britain was exceptional. This report had to be more thorough and comprehensive than similar ones used with other countries. Chalkley returned to Washington in the middle of October to learn that study was underway. Until the various facets had been more exhaustively analyzed, however, informal

[6] Robert Bingham, Ambassador in the United Kingdom, to Secretary of State, telegram no. 190, April 26, 1935, *Foreign Relations, 1935,* II, 2; memorandum by Grady, June 21, 1935, *ibid.,* 2–3.

discussions of structure and substance were not in order. The State Department promised to talk with him when the country committee had made significant progress.[7]

With the advent of 1936, American attention turned increasingly to the British trade agreements program, which Washington considered to be at variance with its own. It will be recalled that Hull had first been introduced to his bête noire during the tariff truce negotiations. The Import Duties Act of 1932 had empowered the British government to conclude trade agreements with foreign countries, and beginning in 1933, Britain had made a number that were quite different in nature from the reciprocity arrangements negotiated by the United States. The former, bilateral pacts that the British hoped would balance trade between the two nations, reduced duties on British exports and contained special favors to stimulate imports from Great Britain. Some dealt with the control of international exchange in such a way that bilateral trade balancing was the net result. With "payments" stipulations, the governments of Argentina, Uruguay, Brazil, Hungary, Italy, Rumania, and Germany agreed to reserve a certain percentage of the foreign exchange received from the sale of exports to Great Britain for trade with and debt payments to the United Kingdom. "Clearing" arrangements, authorized by the Debts Clearing Offices and Import Restrictions Act of 1934, were negotiated with Spain, Italy, Turkey, and Rumania. The two "clearing" parties deposited in special accounts in local banks the exchange intended for the purchase of commodities by their importers. The exporter was paid from the account in his country's bank, and bilateral payments came from the same source. In both cases, with foreign exchange thus committed, American trade suffered the consequences of this subordination of "the

[7] Grady to Louis Domeratzky, chief, Division of Regional Information, Department of Commerce, Aug. 22, 1935, 611.4131/122A; memorandum by Grady, Oct. 16, 1935, *Foreign Relations, 1935,* II, 3–4.

flow of current trade . . . to debt collection."[8] By means of the trade agreements together with the payments and clearing arrangements, Great Britain had improved its trading position through mutual reductions of tariff barriers and the diversion of business from other nations to British exporters—tactics the United States deemed to be in conflict with the principle of equality of treatment.

On January 22, 1936, Hull called Sir Ronald Lindsay to his office and preached the first of several sermons on the importance to prosperity and world peace of the revival of international commerce and the dire results of failure by countries like the United Kingdom to cooperate with the United States in its war on trade barriers. Recent British commercial policy could only retard the recovery program in which Hull had so much faith. Admitting that Great Britain had a "perfect right to engage in bilateral practices," Hull voiced the hope that a nation so dependent upon accelerated multilateral trade as the United Kingdom might abandon these "short-sighted" policies and join with his government in support of the broader program.

Conversations like this one explain and support Herbert Feis's assessment in 1933 that the Secretary "no longer gathers ideas from others, and when confronted with the obstacles and difficulties to his good intentions, does not analyze them and figure out ways and means of licking them; he *preaches* against them."[9] When Lindsay contended that the unfavorable trade balances with other nations had forced London's hand, Hull

---

[8] Henry J. Tasca, *World Trading Systems: A Study of American and British Commercial Policies* (Paris, 1939), 78–126. For an analysis of clearing and payments agreements in general, see Lawrence W. Towle, *International Trade and Commercial Policy* (New York, 1947), 482–493, 497–504. A State Department appraisal can be found in memorandum of Office of Economic Adviser, Jan. 20, 1936, 611.4131/139½.

[9] Feis, *1933: Characters in Crisis,* 99.

replied that the net result was restricted world trade and quickly returned to his general analysis of contemporary economic ills and the probable consequences. European political disintegration would keep the British from enjoying for long the comforts of their program of economic isolation. The Italian maneuver in Ethiopia had forced the government to deploy its naval forces and to increase armaments expenditures, to face not only the threat in the Mediterranean, but also the probability of some military venture by Germany. If Hull's correlation between economic instability and war were correct, this could have been prevented. "If Italy had had even near her pre-panic quantity of exports," he said, "there was a real possibility that her armies would not be on the march today." With Hitler's Reich in mind, he continued, "When people are unemployed, and with their families in more or less economic distress, they fall a ready prey to agitators, revolutionaries and dictators, who in turn are liable to throw them into war." Hull found it incomprehensible how "dictators, overnight almost . . . [can] stand 35 million Italians and 65 million Germans on their heads and so dominate their mental processes that they arise the next morning and insist on being sent to the front-line trenches without delay." On the other hand, employment produced comfortable and contented people with "no disposition to follow agitators and to enthrone dictators." The Secretary still entertained hope that the trend toward war could be reversed to one toward peace. The solution was international trade. Commercial activity, leading to "the reemployment of the chief portion of unemployed and more or less distressed wage earners" in Germany and Italy, with resultant investment opportunities, would be the difference between "war and peace in Europe in the not distant future." The situation called for an element lacking to this point, resourcefulness by governments of countries like the United States and Great Britain.

Throughout this conversation, except for the interjection mentioned, Lindsay remained silent, which Hull construed as sympathy for his ideas.[10] Whether or not his judgment was correct, other British officials were convinced of neither his answer to the current economic plight nor his belief that war was determined by economic conditions.

In subsequent months, Hull, varying his theme little, maintained the pressure for British compliance with a program of equal treatment. He called the attention of the Foreign Office to the urgency of the world situation, Washington's disappointment with British disinterest in trade, and the question how, if Whitehall ceased its bilateral bargaining and joined with the United States in a multilateral effort, the two could constructively combat contemporary trends. The Secretary admitted that other issues, including debts and exchange stabilization, could be discussed, but he wanted to avoid the divisive effects of controversial subjects and to work instead for the "wholehearted, unimpeded cooperation of our two governments in support of the long view program and . . . the abandonment of conflicting trade practices of a purely bilateral nature." [11]

There can be no doubt that, to the Secretary of State, British compliance with the American trade program was the acid test whether the two countries could resolve their outstanding differences and present Anglo-American unity to the world. Hull was not exaggerating when, in an instruction to Ray Atherton, the American Chargé in London, he termed the divergence over trade policy "a matter . . . of the highest importance to us." He instructed Atherton to "spare no effort" to make the American position known to Anthony Eden, Secretary of State for Foreign

[10] Memorandum by Hull, Jan. 22, 1936, *Foreign Relations, 1936,* I, 629–632; Hull, *Memoirs,* I, 520–521.

[11] Memorandum by Hull, Feb. 5, 1936, *Foreign Relations, 1936,* I, 633–635.

Affairs, and to any other Cabinet member whom he chose. Assuming perhaps that verbal pressure alone would suffice, Hull advised the Chargé to present his case verbally rather than in a written communication to the Foreign Office. Atherton could thus informally "ascertain first whether Mr. Eden and Mr. Runciman were aware" of the incompatible trade policies and "if so, whether they could not find some means to lessen our apprehension" so that Great Britain and the United States could do their share to stimulate international trade. The appeal would be most effective if the Chargé, rather than "burdening" Eden with "technical details," related the matter directly to the desirability of closer Anglo-American relations. Bilateral trade balancing jeopardized the entente favored by Eden. An enclosed memorandum, designed only to aid Atherton, detailed the American indictment against British trade policies. Incompatible with the principle of equality favored by the United States, they not only hurt American business abroad but made more formidable the bilateralists and economic nationalists in the United States.[12]

On February 26, the Chargé found Eden to be unaware of the effects of British commercial policy. When the Foreign Secretary suggested that the two governments might discuss related problems, the American representative countered that the primary objective was agreement in principle by London and Washington to "work for the abolition of trade barriers." Eden agreed, saying that "it was vital for the economic welfare of the world" for the United States and Great Britain to link their policies. He added that he would talk shortly with Runciman.[13]

One day after Atherton's conversation with the Foreign Secretary, but before Eden could talk with the President of the Board

[12] Secretary of State to Atherton, Feb. 13, 1936, enclosing memorandum dated Feb. 11, 1936, *Foreign Relations, 1936,* I, 635–643.

[13] Atherton to Secretary of State, telegram no. 79, Feb. 26, 1936, *Foreign Relations, 1936,* I, 644.

of Trade, Runciman publicly defended the British trade agreements and promised "to pursue that policy as long as I am where I am." He shrugged off criticism by pointing out the return to Great Britain of many pounds sterling that ordinarily would have remained frozen. To dim prospects even more, the Foreign Secretary could not see Runciman before his departure to Geneva for a session of the League of Nations. Because of their divergence on the question of League sanctions against Italy, relations between the two men were "not too easy." [14]

At this moment, with the world organization debating whether to embargo oil shipments to Italy, Hitler ordered German troops into the Rhineland, ostensibly in response to ratification of the Franco-Soviet pact by the French Chamber of Deputies. Because of the latest political crisis, Atherton was unable to engage British Cabinet members in discussions on Anglo-American differences. He recommended that the State Department hand a memorandum to Lindsay to remind Whitehall of them.[15] This was subsequently done, and a copy was sent to Atherton with instructions to renew conversations at any opportune time. In its memorandum, the United States requested the British government to issue a formal statement identifying itself with the American program. The document reflected the Secretary's belief that words, even though unsupported for the moment by actions, could be determining factors in international affairs. A British announcement, it emphasized, "would in no sense imply" the immediate reversal of recent policies. The declaration itself was the most important thing. Whitehall's state-

[14] Runciman's speech was given before the Bradford Chambers of Commerce. See Atherton to Secretary of State, telegram no. 81, Feb. 28, 1936, *Foreign Relations, 1936,* I, 644–645. For the relations between Eden and Runciman, see Atherton to Secretary of State, telegram no. 82, Feb. 29, 1936, *ibid.,* 646.

[15] Atherton to Secretary of State, telegram no. 136, March 19, 1936, *Foreign Relations, 1936,* I, 647.

ment would prompt similar announcements, Hull believed, with a moral effect so powerful that much of the political and economic tension in the world would be relieved. This single verbal stroke would deal economic nationalism a lethal blow, and the American trade policies, no longer retarded by British bilateralism, would gain momentum. For that reason, the State Department official who handed the memorandum to Lindsay stressed "the Secretary's particular wish" that London eschew "technical discussions" and support rather a "general declaration of intention and policy." The actions "could be taken up in due time and when some possibility of their solution could be foreseen." [16]

If Hull expected a favorable response to the request, he was frustrated by a government apparently not overly concerned about American sensitivity. Within a few days, Sir Ronald Lindsay told Hull that while he personally was much taken with the proposal, it would be difficult for his government either to reverse recent commercial policies or to outline publicly plans for the future. His superiors were wary of "empty declarations" that might never be implemented, or might be interpreted differently by various people. Certainly they could not depart from a purportedly desirable trade policy.

Another real problem was division within the Cabinet, although Lindsay remained silent about it. Whereas the Foreign Office, or at least Anthony Eden, favored closer Anglo-American economic cooperation, others in the Treasury Department and the Board of Trade apparently thought that Britain could pursue an independent economic course and still expect collaboration with the United States when some political threat arose. The

---

[16] Secretary of State to Atherton, no. 103, March 28, 1936, enclosing memorandum which was handed to Lindsay, *Foreign Relations, 1936,* I, 647–649; memorandum by James Clement Dunn, Special Assistant to the Secretary of State and Chief of the Division of Western European Affairs, March 30, 1936, *ibid.,* 649–650.

tendency in the British Cabinet to divorce politics and trade made it almost impossible for London and Washington to repair the policy breach.[17]

Lindsay's pessimistic forecast prompted Hull to deliver another lecture on the conditions of the world, their cause and solution, and the contrast between the commercial procedures of the two governments. In his discourse the Secretary of State revealed clearly his inability to understand the British point of view and the forces shaping it. To him it was "almost inconceivable" that they failed to discern the rewards that would be theirs if multilateralism and broadened trade channels were restored to the world. Obsessed with his principles and analyses, Hull could not appreciate a nation's balking at their acceptance. He was particularly impatient with the argument that political considerations presented an obstacle. As he noted to the Ambassador, the Roosevelt Administration had risen above conservative opposition in the United States and had converted important businessmen to the cause; the British could do the same. The present was the time for the two countries to battle jointly against economic nationalism and its military consequences and to guide the world back to sanity.[18]

Unfortunately for Hull, developments at Geneva nearly monopolized Eden's time. On April 7, Robert Bingham, the American Ambassador to Great Britain, handed the memorandum to the Foreign Secretary. The busy Eden, apologetic about his not having pursued the matter with fellow Cabinet members, was shortly to leave London again and could not wield much influence with them. From the remarks of a Board of Trade official,

[17] See the following correspondence: Moffat to Davis, June 19, 1936, Davis to Moffat, July 29, 1936, and Moffat to Davis, Oct. 7, 1936, Davis Papers, Box 41.

[18] Memorandum by Hull, April 1, 1936, *Foreign Relations, 1936*, I, 650–655.

Bingham inferred that the prevailing sentiment within the Government was that political conditions in Europe dictated the continuation of its present commercial policy. This assessment, coinciding with those from other sources, shows quite conclusively that the possibility of war dominated British thinking. Even in the absence of this haunting fear, the British would have moved slowly, if at all. They believed that the United States would shun trade agreement negotiations until after the 1936 presidential election.[19]

The Secretary of State, who could detect hopeful signs where others could not—or where none existed—still believed that "fuller consideration" might "produce a change in their [British] present judgment" about a public statement. On April 11 he instructed Bingham to give copies of yet another memorandum to Eden and Runciman, which Bingham did late in the month. Both Cabinet officers adopted what later became standard British procedure. The Foreign Secretary piously received and endorsed the ideas but declared that Whitehall was not yet ready to take action or even to reply to the memorandum. Runciman referred specifically to politically powerful vested interests in Great Britain that had already pressed the Cabinet to jettison its adherence to the most-favored-nation principle. He contended also that the close relationship between payment of foreign debts and the health of the English economy had made it mandatory that

[19] Bingham to Secretary of State, telegram no. 184, April 7, 1936, *Foreign Relations, 1936,* I, 655–656. For an account of the activities which were consuming Eden's time, see Anthony Eden, *The Eden Memoirs: Facing the Dictators* (London, 1962), 315–394. A very important assessment of the European political situation and its effect on British thinking, official and private, is to be found in Chester Davis to Roosevelt, Aug. 3, 1936, in which Davis enclosed a lengthy report of his observations and conversations during a visit in Europe from March 30 to May 21 (Department of Agriculture Records, National Archives, Foreign Trade File).

payment or clearing agreements be negotiated by the British government. The following evening, in Bingham's presence, the President of the Board of Trade again publicly defended the commercial policies of the last few years. They had regained "what we had lost in markets abroad." [20]

On May 26, the British replied formally to American overtures. After a recital of parallel aims and methods, they justified the practices condemned by Hull. "Abnormal conditions" had forced the procedural differences which concerned the United States. These deviations would become neither permanent nor accepted features of British commercial policy, but the United Kingdom could not endure passive trade balances and frozen assets. This factor, together with currently unstable markets for British exports, demanded that London proceed with tariff revision at a deliberate pace. Thus the United Kingdom was only lukewarm about making a public declaration in accordance with Hull's wishes. Feeling that since 1933, at the World Monetary and Economic Conference and at Geneva, its officials had sufficiently supported expanded trade, Whitehall nevertheless agreed to make some further announcement if it "would be regarded by the United States Government as a useful contribution to the attainment of the objects" sought by the Secretary of State. [21]

Roosevelt's sanguine reaction to the memorandum—he termed it "a very useful beginning"—is rather surprising, since the situation had not really changed. Far from abandoning its commercial policies, London in fact had justified them. British

[20] Secretary of State to Bingham, no. 125, April 11, 1936, *Foreign Relations, 1936*, I, 656–659; Bingham to Secretary of State, telegram no. 231, April 28, 1936, *ibid.*, 659–660; Bingham to Secretary of State, telegram no. 234, April 29, 1936, *ibid.*, 660–661; Bingham to Secretary of State, telegram no. 238, May 1, 1936, *ibid.*, 661–662.

[21] Bingham to Secretary of State, telegram no. 281, May 26, 1936, *Foreign Relations, 1936*, I, 663–666.

endorsement of a public statement was unenthusiastic, if not feeble. As reported to the Chargé in London by an Englishman a short time later, Great Britain had been afflicted with the "disease of protection" at an advanced age, and thus "it was all the more violent in its initial stages." To make matters worse, the prevailing political climate strengthened the already formidable protectionist sentiment in the House of Commons.[22]

On June 18, Hull instructed Atherton to express his gratification to the British for acceding to his request and to encourage them to issue the statement soon.[23] When the Chargé carried out his duties, he learned that for the present the British had decided against making a declaration. Whitehall officials, currently negotiating the renewal of certain trade agreements, felt that such an announcement might make them guilty of "inconsistency." This response meant just one thing to Atherton: the Cabinet was determined to stall the United States.[24]

Refusing to accept defeat, the Secretary of State sent Bingham a further appeal to be delivered to members of the government. Hull was extremely disappointed; he thought it was time for the United States and the United Kingdom "either [to] take a courageous lead in the fight to restore conditions of sane and peaceful trade, or themselves be drawn into a maelstrom of conflicting and competitive agreements." Prompt action by Great Britain was

[22] Roosevelt's reaction is printed in a footnote in *Foreign Relations, 1936*, I, 663. Atherton to Secretary of State, no. 2257, June 12, 1936, 611.4131/177. Atherton reported conversations with senior officials of the Board of Trade and Treasury.

[23] Secretary of State to Atherton, no. 214, June 18, 1936, *Foreign Relations, 1936*, I, 668–669.

[24] Atherton to Secretary of State, telegram no. 319, June 19, 1936, *Foreign Relations, 1936*, I, 669; Atherton to Secretary of State, telegram no. 323, June 25, 1936, *ibid.*, 671–672; Atherton to Secretary of State, telegram no. 326, June 26, 1936, *ibid.*, 672.

urgent if the United States was to have any success in its program.[25]

Before the Ambassador could comply, a statement by Runciman in the House of Commons moved the State Department to draft another memorandum for delivery to the Foreign Office. Runciman's speech of July 15, with its references to "equality of opportunity for all nations" and to the need to remove trade barriers, Hull found "excellent and encouraging." His concern was the Board of Trade official's failure to indicate any specific step that Whitehall would take toward adopting a more liberal trade policy.[26] In London, Bingham expressed regret to Eden that the speech had not been stronger. The Foreign Secretary said he felt similarly, but explained that he and Runciman had not had time to amend Runciman's original statement without postponing its presentation in Parliament, which they had chosen not to do.[27]

By September 3, when the revised American memorandum was ready, Hull still saw no evidence that the British planned any announcement concerning trade. To American officials it seemed that London was putting the United States off, while pursuing its trade policy with increased vigor at the expense both of third parties and of hopes of relieving world problems. Nevertheless, Bingham was to try again to "awaken" the British government to the importance of parallel action. On September 19 he gave a copy of the memorandum to Eden, stressing in the process that economic revival was the best, if not the only, way to alleviate tensions and to ward off the threat of war. The Foreign

[25] Secretary of State to Bingham, no. 234, July 3, 1936, *Foreign Relations, 1936*, I, 672–674.

[26] Great Britain, 314 *H. C. Deb.* 5 s., 2079–2083; memorandum by Hull, July 20, 1936, *Foreign Relations, 1936*, I, 675–678.

[27] Bingham to Secretary of State, telegram no. 378, July 28, 1936, *Foreign Relations, 1936*, I, 680.

Secretary agreed in principle, but mentioned political difficulties at home. Bingham tried to allay these apprehensions by referring to the history of trade liberalization in the United States, specifically explaining how the program's successes had undermined the opposition to it. Eden promised to discuss the matter with Runciman and Neville Chamberlain, the Chancellor of the Exchequer, upon his return from an imminent trip to Geneva. The Ambassador doubted, however, "his ability to influence his colleagues sufficiently to modify their views." [28]

At this time, William Phillips encountered the obstacles confronting Eden. The newly appointed Ambassador to Italy, previously the Under Secretary of State, discussed trade relations with Sir Robert Vansittart and Sir Alexander Cadogan of the Foreign Office in London. Early in the conversation with Cadogan, Phillips realized that his host knew little about the subject. As the American official continued his analysis of the Hull program, the contrast of American with British policies, reciprocity as a political question in the United States, and the need for some statement from London, he encountered admissions of ignorance. Cadogan confined his remarks largely to references to past tariff proclivities of the United States, a recitation of the economic advantages that had accrued to Great Britain through its agreements, and the political problems connected with change. Phillips concluded that Cadogan, like most important figures in the United Kingdom, was satisfied with British commercial policy, and "was not particularly concerned" that its "continuation . . . might lead the British and American Governments in opposite directions."

The Ambassador to Rome gained the same impression from Vansittart. The latter responded to the presentation of the Amer-

[28] Secretary of State to Bingham, no. 324, Sept. 3, 1936, *Foreign Relations, 1936*, I, 680–684; Bingham to Secretary of State, telegram no. 439, Sept. 19, 1936, *ibid.*, 648–685.

ican plan by asserting that the solution of political problems in Europe should precede any tariff reductions. The most he would admit was that the two problems might be combated simulatneously. In Phillips' opinion, Vansittart "was not really interested in a closer approach to the American Government in this matter." On the basis of these conversations, the former Under Secretary doubted that the two men would be of any value in the struggle to secure British compliance.[29]

The frustrations experienced by the United States in its attempt to obtain British consent to a public posture of cooperation inhibited, but did not preclude, the launching of trade agreement negotiations. The first steps toward this goal since late 1935 were taken on June 17 when Henry F. Grady advised Owen Chalkley, the British Embassy's Commercial Counselor, that American studies indicated a trade agreement was possible if the United Kingdom would modify some of the imperial preferences. Grady emphasized that the State Department did not intend to press for the abolition of the system, but rather to ascertain whether specific preferences were negotiable. If they were not, the two governments could forget the whole thing. The chief of the Division of Trade Agreements informed Chalkley candidly that if the revised Ottawa pacts, shortly to be negotiated, tied London's hands because of commitments made to the Dominions on certain key commodities, there could be no Anglo-American agreement.

The Commercial Counselor, more skeptical than enthusiastic about prospects, thought that some items on which preferences were guaranteed could well be included in the negotiations. The two authorities could get a clearer view when the imperial accords were published. The next step, Chalkley understood, was for the United States to transmit lists of concessions it would

[29] Bingham to Secretary of State, no. 2525, Sept. 21, 1936, enclosing memorandum by Phillips, Sept. 18, 1936, 611.4131/189.

grant on United Kingdom goods and requests for lowered duties in Great Britain. His government, awaiting the American findings, had undertaken no independent studies. Grady and other American officials present impressed on Chalkley that the State Department could consent to no particular concession prior to the public hearings conducted by the Committee for Reciprocity Information. They agreed, however, to submit tentative lists when the survey had progressed sufficiently.[30]

The first informal discussion of specific items took place one week later when Chalkley presented a tentative list of goods on which Great Britain expected liberalization. With respect to concessions on American products, he expressed doubt that many reductions, as opposed to "bindings," could be granted. The American list had not been completed, but some exports were mentioned, including fruit, lumber, machinery, and ham. The Commercial Counselor minimized the effect of preferences on the sale of American commodities in the United Kingdom, making the Department of State's initial task that of marshaling proof to justify reductions in the schedules. He suggested pointedly that if the United States wanted a reduction in duty on a good which would affect a preference given to Canada, it should deal directly with the Dominion.[31]

From June to September talks about trade agreement negotiations were suspended while the State Department continued its studies and the two governments debated their respective commercial policies. On September 21, Chalkley broke the silence by inquiring whether a basis for negotiations had been found in the intervening months and whether the impending presidential election was the reason why the United States had not commu-

[30] Memorandum by William A. Fowler, Division of Trade Agreements, June 17, 1936, *Foreign Relations, 1936,* I, 666–668.

[31] Memorandum by Richard Eldridge, Division of Trade Agreements, June 24, 1936, *Foreign Relations, 1936,* I, 669–671.

nicated with the British Embassy. If the contest between Roosevelt and Landon were the determining factor, he doubted that an
agreement could be concluded by June, 1937, when the reciprocal trade legislation would expire. Confident that in spite of his
disclaimer Chalkley had been instructed to "casually mention
the subject" because London was ready for more conversations,
the American spokesman replied that, in his personal opinion,
reconciliation of commercial policies by the two governments
would be the best "basis" for negotiations. Yet, reconciliation
apparently was not in the offing. The talk ended with an intimation from the Commercial Counselor that he wanted some concrete answers.[32]

Chalkley's inquiry brought results. On September 29 he was
invited to the office of Harry Hawkins, Grady's successor as chief
of the Division of Trade Agreements, where he learned that the
promised American lists would be ready by November 16. Coincidentally or not, by that time the electorate would have ren-
dered its verdict on the New Deal performance. Before the final
decision concerning a trade agreement could be made, the
United States needed a list of requests from Great Britain.
Regarding the list delivered by Chalkley on June 24 as too
general, it hoped that the British could meet the November 16
date with their expanded proposals. In order for the agreement
to be signed by June, 1937, an ambition entertained in the State
Department, the Americans had to decide shortly after November 16 whether to negotiate. To facilitate British efforts, Chalkley was given detailed trade statistics compiled in Washington.
He thought that aided by this body of facts, the British could
have their list ready by the desired date. Following this exchange, the two governments would determine how many of the
requests they could meet. If both were satisfied with the results,

[32] Memorandum by John R. Minter, Division of Western European
Affairs, Sept. 21, 1936, *Foreign Relations, 1936,* I, 685–686.

negotiations would begin. Hawkins stressed that the present talks were informal, involving no commitments of any kind.[33]

As the technical studies moved forward, Hull continued to press Great Britain to make some public maneuver indicating harmony of British commercial policy with American. Late in October, after a two and a half months' stay in England, Lindsay saw the Secretary of State, and the two returned to the topic that had held much of their attention. Taking the offensive, Hull declared that the United Kingdom had no alternative to its present foreign policy, which he interpreted as defense of its interests through rearmament in order to prepare for a possible "military explosion in central Europe" in the near future. The Secretary espoused once more what he considered to be a practical and practicable alternative, economic rehabilitation through expanded trade. He predicted that domination within a few years by Japan, Germany, and Italy of "nearly every square foot of trade territory" presently under the control of Great Britain and the United States as well as economic stagnation in other countries would result if the two governments did not act. Nothing else could prevent "a few desperado" nations from "meandering up and down the earth taking by force" the requirements of their people. He hoped that even at this late time statesmen in the United Kingdom would rise to the occasion and save Western civilization from an otherwise inevitable war.

Lindsay introduced some obstructive factors. Eden was sympathetic, but European complications had deprived him of the necessary time to study the program properly. Prime Minister Stanley Baldwin, suffering from ill health, was soon to be replaced by Neville Chamberlain. The Ambassador did not expect Chamberlain, whose father had been a great advocate of tariffs within the Empire, to move with any dispatch to dismantle the

[33] Memorandum by Hawkins, Sept. 29, 1936, *Foreign Relations, 1936*, I, 687–688.

structure which seemed the fulfillment of his father's dreams. He could not be certain, however, because Chamberlain had spoken in favor of an Anglo-American trade agreement in Phillips' presence. Attaching little significance to that exchange, Hull apparently agreed with Lindsay's impression that the prospective Prime Minister would not immediately join in a concerted attack on economic nationalism. Neither Hull nor Roosevelt trusted Chamberlain. The Secretary interpreted Lindsay's reference to the Chancellor of the Exchequer's statement to Phillips as an attempt "to lessen my opinion of Chamberlain's reactionaryism and embargo tariff proclivities." In April of the same year, Secretary of the Treasury Morgenthau wrote that "the President, of course, himself thoroughly distrusts the British," and recorded Roosevelt's comment that "we must recognize that fundamentally he [Chamberlain] thoroughly dislikes Americans." Disturbed by prospects, the Secretary of State nevertheless wanted the British Ambassador to urge his government to reconsider the entire world situation and the American program.[34]

Although Lindsay subsequently presented Chamberlain in a more favorable light and Hull still pressed for a public proclamation, nothing had changed by November 16 when the two governments exchanged their lists of requests for concessions.[35] As opposed to the British, the State Department transmitted a tentative "must" list. Chalkley questioned the wisdom of this action, suggesting that the mere presence of the "must" list threatened successful negotiation of an agreement. The American representatives replied emphatically that there would be no

[34] Memorandum by Hull, Oct. 22, 1936, *Foreign Relations, 1936*, I, 688–691; Hull, *Memoirs*, I, 522–523; entry, April 29, 1936, Morgenthau Diary, Book 22, p. 155; Blum, *Years of Crisis*, 141.

[35] Memorandum by Hull, Nov. 3, 1936, *Foreign Relations, 1936*, I, 691–692.

retreat and that more items would be added to it. Thus rebuffed, the Counselor agreed to send the American list to London, and the State Department officials accordingly promised to comment as soon as possible on the British list. Chalkley emphasized that his government could not lower many tariffs, because Dominion consent was required in certain instances. The principal concessions would be to freeze duties at present levels or to guarantee continued free entry. On the other hand, British requests for better treatment included almost the entire list of goods of which Great Britain was the principal supplier.[36] This attitude of "giving little and asking very much" bothered Hull when he learned of the list's contents and of Chalkley's remarks, and was further indication that negotiations would be long, difficult, and possibly unsuccessful.[37]

As 1936 drew to a close, the debate over divergent commercial policies had reached an impasse. On November 20, Eden gave Bingham a formal reply to the American memorandum of September 19. It reasserted that the commercial agreements negotiated by the British government and supporting statements by prominent officials had contributed to the revival of world trade. Significantly, Eden's reply contained no hint of any imminent move by London in Washington's direction.[38] At the heart of this impasse was a difference in interpretation of what was essential

[36] Memorandum by Constant Southworth, Division of Trade Agreements, Nov. 16, 1936, *Foreign Relations, 1936,* I, 692–695; British Board of Trade to Chalkley, Nov. 2, 1936, *ibid.,* 695–699.

[37] Memorandum, Herbert Feis to Hull, Nov. 30, 1936, 611.4131/205, in which Feis wrote, "The position suggested in these preliminary exchanges is not encouraging. The British indicate their attitude . . . that 'there is probably not much we could contribute in the way of positive concessions.' . . . On the other hand, the requests they have in mind cover virtually the whole list of commodities of which they are the principal supplier." See also Hull to Sayre, Dec. 1, 1936, 611.4131/207.

[38] Bingham to Secretary of State, telegram no. 552, Nov. 20, 1936, *Foreign Relations, 1936,* I, 700–702.

to altering world conditions. Hull preferred the trade agreements program and its theoretical by-products. He considered public endorsement by Whitehall to be imperative. As reflected in Eden's report of the September conversation with Bingham, the Foreign Secretary thought Hull underestimated political forces and factors in the world, realities that trade pacts could hardly affect.[39] The issue was not so much that the British disagreed with Hull as that they were not convinced that international order was rooted so deeply in economic discontent.

In March, 1937, the Chancellor of the Exchequer amplified these views. Henry Morgenthau, convinced that expenditures on armaments were leading nations to war and that neither the Secretary of State nor Norman Davis had "guts enough" to fight against the arms race, had tried his hand by appealing to Chamberlain for ideas about how to stop the trend toward militarism. In a memorandum to the Secretary of the Treasury, Chamberlain traced the problems of Europe not to rearmament but to the aggressive political ambitions of Germany, contending that only the presence of a counter military force could thwart its plan to dominate the continent. Thus Great Britain had no choice but to rearm. Admitting that a United States–United Kingdom trade agreement would "have far reaching effects both by its practical advantages to the two countries and by the example it would set to others," he stressed that Washington could make an even more significant contribution to international stability by repealing or modifying its neutrality legislation. The present law, the British felt, encouraged aggressive behavior by a potentially outlaw nation, for victims of its belligerency could not import arms

[39] Dunn to Hull, Dec. 4, 1936, 611.4131/208A, includes the following sentence: "I have just received from one of our officers in the field a letter in which he says that he had an opportunity to see Eden's report of his conversation with Ambassador Bingham on September 19."

from the United States whereas the aggressor could stockpile weapons prior to launching a war. Chamberlain then related the situation in Europe to the Japanese propensity for expansion in East Asia. If Britain had to marshal its resources to protect its threatened interests in the Pacific, Whitehall's ability to resist German demands would be weakened. A political settlement in the Far East would free the British from their dilemma. Suggesting that recent changes in the Japanese government marked the time as a favorable one to pacify the region, Chamberlain endorsed Anglo-American discussions to "put relations between the U.S.A., Japan, and Great Britain on a footing that would ensure harmonious cooperation for the protection and development of their respective interests." In any case, the British recognized that economic troubles added a dimension to the world's problems, but placed primary emphasis on political origins of instability. They sought, therefore, political collaboration from the United States. Of course Washington wanted no part of such entanglements and commitments.[40]

Meanwhile, the two governments were slowly moving toward trade agreement negotiations. In the middle of December, Walter Runciman for the first time expressed his belief that an Anglo-American pact could, and should, be concluded. He was careful to note that Great Britain could not contravene the Ottawa treaties, but there were still areas for trade improvement, and thus a basis for negotiations. Bingham too optimistically interpreted Runciman's statement, "the most definite and con-

---

[40] Memorandum, Feb. 6, 1937, Morgenthau Diary, Book 54, pp. 125–126; Blum, *Years of Crisis*, 457; memorandum, British Chancellor of the Exchequer to Secretary of the Treasury, March 20, 1937, *Foreign Relations, 1937*, I, 98–102. Note the American reply in an informal memorandum from the Department of State to the British Embassy, June 1, 1937, *ibid.*, 102–106.

crete" by any important British official, to be proof that the government had put opposition and hesitation behind it.[41]

In Washington, Sayre was optimistic about the immediate future. As he informed Lindsay, the administration hoped to obtain congressional approval of the extension of the Trade Agreements Act by early winter, 1937. This extension, coupled with the recent landslide election victory, would put the administration in a very strong position to negotiate during the winter months. But the British Ambassador foresaw trouble at the United Kingdom end. Dispatches from London "were not encouraging," for the American list of requests had "hit the Ottawa Agreements in the solar plexus," a problem that could not easily be overcome, even though some modifications in the existing system might admittedly be in order. War fever produced pressure in England to sit tight and not to embark on any radical departures. Sayre regretted this, because he thought the times, dominated as they were by Roosevelt and Hull, presented a golden opportunity to strike a blow for economic cooperation. Another such situation might never arise.[42]

On December 26, Chalkley gave John D. Hickerson and Harry Hawkins London's initial reaction to the American proposals. The United Kingdom felt that in order to negotiate a mutually profitable agreement the two governments must es-

[41] Bingham to Secretary of State, no. 2741, Dec. 30, 1936, enclosing memorandum of conversation with Walter Runciman, Dec. 18, 1936, *Foreign Relations, 1936*, I, 702–703. In a letter to Roosevelt of January 5, 1937, Bingham wrote, "Quite recently . . . [Runciman] for the first time definitely committed himself to the principle of an agreement along the lines of your agreement with Canada. This statement would not have come from Runciman without the approval of the financial and commercial influences in the Government, which had hitherto been holding out on us, so that this marks concrete progress towards some form of trade agreement" (Roosevelt Papers).

[42] Memorandum by Sayre, Dec. 19, 1936, *Foreign Relations, 1936*, I, 703–704.

tablish an understanding prior to the formalities. Certain things were bothering the British. The "must" list touched the Empire relationship directly at a time when the uncertain European political picture dictated avoidance of any divisive influences. Chalkley mentioned particularly the British dependence upon members of the Commonwealth for key commodities in the event of war. American neutrality legislation, precluding export of these strategic items from the United States, left the United Kingdom no alternative but to strengthen, rather than weaken, the imperial tie. Furthermore, unless the Dominions released Great Britain from its commitments under the Ottawa pacts London could not grant the American "must" requests. A few items might lend themselves to direct negotiations between the United States and a Dominion—the preference on Canadian lumber, for example—but most required concurrence by several Dominions. If the United States was to obtain concessions from Whitehall it would have to compensate the Dominions for giving their consent. In short, Washington must take the responsibility for winning Dominion approval. The American request for reduced levels rather than frozen ones made this problem even more difficult. The latter could be granted with little trouble, but reductions flirted with potentially powerful political forces in Great Britain. In conclusion, the British official promised to transmit information shortly on precisely to what extent the United Kingdom could accept the American proposals.[43]

With the dawn of 1937, political tensions in Europe, instead of prompting closer cooperation, had created additional problems for London and Washington as they tried to begin formal trade negotiations. The United States had pressed the British to take some concrete action in harmony with the Hull program of international economic rehabilitation, had criticized the strictly

[43] Memorandum by Hawkins, Dec. 26, 1936, *Foreign Relations, 1936,* I, 704–706.

bilateral nature of British trade agreements and exchange arrangements, and had tried to maneuver Whitehall into negotiations for a comprehensive trade pact. The results were limited at best. Although it professed belief in the general principles and goals enunciated by the American Secretary of State, Great Britain actually viewed neither its commercial policy nor the role of economic revival in the same light. Britain was moving only deliberately toward the trade accord, dubious about the extent of concessions that the United States would grant on its exports and fearful of political repercussions at home. Moreover, the possibility of a general European war militated against any radical economic innovations. During the next few months a new dimension was injected into the situation, as Washington sought to fortify its trade program with an Anglo-American trade agreement.

Chapter 5

Canada, the United States, and the Imperial Conference of 1937

While the British and American dialogue continued with little progress, officials in the Department of State turned to Canada as a possible intermediary. Between the spring of 1936 and the spring of 1937 this idea developed sufficiently that the Canadian Prime Minister was asked to present Washington's case directly to Whitehall. Mackenzie King became the agent of the American attempt to break the diplomatic jam. Fortunately, the coronation of George VI brought the various leaders of the Commonwealth to London, where the Imperial Conference of 1937, held shortly after the royal ceremony, provided the setting for a new American tactic.

Of course the United States had not discarded its direct approach to British statesmen. Washington maintained these contacts, and at this very time Norman Davis was attempting to influence British policy. A month before the coronation, he went to London as the head of the American delegation to the International Sugar Conference, with instructions to work toward an Anglo-American trade agreement as well. On April 9 he and Anthony Eden held the first of several conversations in which the British Foreign Secretary professed to acknowledge the economic and political fruits that would follow from an accord. More important, Eden claimed that Chamberlain "was now inclined to agree with him as to the necessity for agreement between our countries and the importance . . . [economically and politically] of obtaining a common trade agreement." He intimated that if the United States would be "patient and give them some time," they would "get into line with us on economic policies." In the larger matter of settling European political problems, the British refused to take action at present, fearing that Hitler might misconstrue its meaning. The Foreign Secretary wanted the United States to take the initiative "when the time came," but Davis gave him no encouragement, returning instead to the necessity of reconciling the "diametrically opposing" trade policies.

Several weeks later Davis and Chamberlain pursued the same topics. While admitting that "political appeasement and economic collaboration go hand in hand," the Chancellor of the Exchequer declared that "any real progress toward economic stabilization . . . must necessarily be preceded by discussions of a political nature and tentative agreements." Davis deduced from these talks that the British wished neither "to assume the responsibility or initiative of checking the rearmament move," nor to have "anyone else . . . do so unless they can be fully convinced that such a move will mean the establishment of real peace." [1]

[1] On July 16, 1937, Roosevelt wrote to Bingham that "when it was decided that Norman Davis should head the Delegation to the International Sugar Conference . . . I suggested to him . . . [he might] aid you in any way in bringing about an Anglo-American trade agreement" (Roosevelt Papers). For the Davis conversations mentioned in the text, see memorandum of conversation between Eden and Davis, April 9, 1937, Davis to Roosevelt, April 13, 1937, memorandum of conversation between Chamberlain and Davis, April 26, 1937, and paraphase of telegram regarding conversation with Chamberlain, April 26, 1937, Davis Papers, Box 55.

Another development accentuated the drive toward economic rehabilitation by casting the Anglo-American discussions in a more favorable light. The Van Zeeland mission to the United States, though it accomplished little in the long run, momentarily raised hopes that the Hull program might be implemented. This effort at trade liberalization made by Belgium had the blessing of Whitehall which, although reluctant to take initiatives itself, consented to Van Zeeland's trying his hand.[2]

The immediate concern of this chapter, however, is the evolution of the Dominion's role as spokesman for the American government and the degree of success of that experiment. The insights into the interrelationships within the North Atlantic Triangle which are gained by isolating this dimension will dispel the notion that Canada was the "linchpin" between the United States and the United Kingdom.

In May, 1936, John D. Hickerson discussed trade relations between the United States and Canada with Mackenzie King in Ottawa. Hickerson called King's attention to Hull's belief that the American trade program was not receiving sufficient support from other commercial countries, particularly Great Britain. To neutralize the charges of his domestic critics that the United States alone was engaged in the fight, the Secretary hoped that Canada would join forces. When King told his visitor that Anglo-Canadian trade talks would begin in the summer, Hick-

---

[2] The Van Zeeland mission is discussed in Toynbee, ed., *Survey of International Affairs, 1937* (London, 1938), I, 67–78, 86–96. A documented account appears in *Foreign Relations, 1937*, I, 671–696. In London, Davis asked the French Minister of National Economy and Chief French Delegate to the International Sugar Conference "the significance of the announced initiative on the part of Belgium to investigate and report on the possibility of reducing the restrictions on trade. He said the British had not felt like taking the initiative but had consented to having Belgium do so" (Davis to Roosevelt, April 13, 1937, Davis Papers, Box 55).

erson made it clear that Washington would be displeased if London and Ottawa negotiated an arrangement that further penalized foreign business by granting excessive margins of preference. He emphasized that the trade pact of 1935 was intended as a "stepping stone" to a more comprehensive agreement. This plan might go awry if Canada did not adhere to the spirit of the accord. Obviously, a revised Anglo-Canadian treaty could jeopardize the possibility of closer Canadian-American economic relations.

While he was in Ottawa, Hickerson handed copies of memoranda of the conversations between the British Ambassador and the Secretary of State to Norman Armour, who was to brief the Prime Minister on their contents at some opportune time. Hickerson said that the United States had no present plans for any action to be taken by King, but simply wanted him kept informed of developments. Undoubtedly this maneuver had a greater purpose than merely to educate the Canadian Prime Minister. It indicated that some people in both capitals thought he might be useful in presenting American views to officials in London. How widespread this thinking was in the Department cannot be measured accurately, but, at the same time, Moffat wrote from Australia to William R. Castle, Jr., Under Secretary of State during the Hoover Administration, inquiring whether "our relations with Canada [have] become sufficiently cordial for us to influence London via Ottawa." In a letter to Hull, Armour maintained that he had taken the initiative about sharing the contents of the memoranda with King because "he [King] could very possibly be of assistance in supporting your position in any talks which he might have with the British." If this were Washington's plan, King was the logical individual to perform the task, for he had made no secret of his belief that Canada could play an important role in Anglo-American friendship. He felt that his country should stand with the United States on key issues and assist it whenever possible in its dealings with Europe. In October, 1935, shortly after his return to power, the Prime Minister had again expressed this thought to Armour.[3]

The summer passed, with the British and American governments no closer to an understanding. In September, before King's departure for Europe to attend a session of the League of Nations, Norman Armour decided that the Prime Minister might represent Hull's position in London. Through a Canadian close to King, Armour had learned that the Prime Minister shared the Secretary of State's feelings about bilaterally balanced trade agreements. The informant said "he knew Mr. King would not only appreciate being brought up to date on [American] talks with the British but would, he intimated, be glad to support your views in talks which he would have with Mr. Baldwin and other members of the British Cabinet" during a week's stay in the English capital on his return to Ottawa. He thought that "if Mr. King could impress upon Mr. Baldwin" that Canada "shared your views . . . this might be of help to both of us in bringing about the end you have in view." On the basis of this information, Armour gave pertinent memoranda to the Canadians, emphasizing that the United Kingdom had neither indicated any changes in policy nor had they issued the desired public statement.[4]

When informing Hull of his actions, the American Minister

[3] Hickerson's visit to Ottawa is treated in memorandum from Hickerson to Phillips, June 4, 1936, *Foreign Relations, 1936*, I, 783–785; memorandum of conversation with King by Hickerson, May 20, 1936, *ibid.*, 785–786. Moffat to Castle, July 25, 1936, Moffat Papers, X; Armour to Hull, Sept. 14, 1936, 611.4231/1878½. For King's October statement, see memorandum of conversation with Armour by Phillips, Oct. 26, 1935, 611.4231/1316; Phillips to Roosevelt, Oct. 26, 1935, Roosevelt Papers, OF, 48–B, Box 14; memorandum by Armour, Oct. 25, 1935, Roosevelt Papers, PSF, Canada, 1933–1941.
[4] Armour to Hull, Sept. 14, 1936, 611.4231/1878½, 1901.

noted that since November of 1935 the Prime Minister had told him "on several occasions that he thinks it extremely important" that when the United States and Canada "do see eye to eye [on key questions] . . . every opportunity should be taken to make known our common viewpoint." Armour continued that King "has always felt that one of Canada's most important roles should be as a link between us and the British. . . . I feel sure that he will welcome this occasion to be of any assistance possible, particularly in a matter in which he shares so fully your viewpoint and has so often expressed admiration for the work you are doing in trying to break down the international barriers erected since economic nationalism has become rampant." In his reply, the Secretary "most heartily" approved of Armour's decision, expressing "high hopes that Mr. King will prove a valuable ally." Hull wrote that "here is a real opportunity for him to perform an extremely useful service in that role." [5]

While in London, the Prime Minister and O. D. Skelton, the Under Secretary of State for External Affairs, discussed the preliminaries of the prospective Anglo-Canadian trade pact with the Dominion Secretary and the President of the Board of Trade. Although nothing official was said to the American representative in Ottawa, he believed that during these conversations King had presented the North American case.[6] Unaware of this facet, the Canadian press focused its attention on the proposed revision of the Ottawa agreement. When publicly queried by reporters, the Prime Minister admitted that progress had been made but refused to commit himself further.[7] The Montreal *Gazette* read greater meaning into his statements, reporting on December 3 that Canada and the United Kingdom had com-

[5] *Ibid.;* Hull to Armour, Sept. 28, 1936, 611.4231/1901.

[6] Ely Palmer to Secretary of State, no. 1032, Nov. 13, 1936, 641.4231/39. See also *Times* (London), Oct. 27, 1936.

[7] Armour to Secretary of State, no. 1046, Nov. 28, 1936, 641.4231/40.

pleted their work and would announce the terms of the new treaty within a few days.[8] Upon reading this, Armour sought verification from the Canadian Under Secretary. Terming the *Gazette's* account premature, Skelton acknowledged nevertheless that the governments had virtually reached agreement. But nothing had been submitted to the Cabinet yet, and Armour learned that the Canadian government intended to transmit the text of the accord to Washington prior to the official release.[9]

Meanwhile, Hull remained vitally interested in the development of his trade program in general, and of the Anglo-Canadian pact in particular. Aware that a recent bilateral agreement had been made between the Dominion and Germany, he invited the Canadian Minister and the Counselor of the Legation to his office. There the Secretary argued that the American reciprocity program, remarkably successful to this point, faced probable failure unless it were supported by the important trading countries. Following the pattern established in exchanges with Great Britain, Hull stressed the movement of European nations toward "increasingly uneconomic conditions, steadily narrowing economic policy, and rapidly increasing armaments." In his opinion, few statesmen on the continent were considering any alternative to the road on which they were traveling, a road that would lead directly to political, military, and economic suicide. In order for greater international trade to avert either a military or an economic catastrophe, concurring nations had to give immediate aid. Hull thought that friends of the program should endorse the most-favored-nation principle in all trade agreements, seek opportunities to negotiate arrangements, and campaign actively to convince others that successful implementation of the program would result in improved economic conditions and world peace. Bilateral agreements were denounced by the Secretary of State

[8] Montreal *Gazette,* Dec. 3, 1936.
[9] Memorandum by James Bonbright, Dec. 4, 1936, 641.4231/40½.

because they impaired the whole concept and, he predicted, would result ultimately in Italian, Japanese, and German domination of virtually all areas of economic life.

The Canadian Minister assured Hull that Ottawa agreed with the trade program, and that any of its actions that ran counter were only temporary aberrations, due to "extreme exigencies." Taking this assurance as his cue, Hull directed his next remarks against the Dominion's agreement with Germany and, implicitly, against an Anglo-Canadian accord inconsistent with Hull's aims. The Canadian-German pact, he said, represented the "most aggravated form of narrow bilateralism, the opposite of the central policy of equality" on which the American program was based. Particularly annoying to the Secretary of State was the ammunition it supplied the political forces within the United States which still adhered to economic nationalism. Opponents of reciprocity could contend that Canada gave lip service to the program to derive certain benefits from it, but showed its true colors by violating it at the first opportunity. According to this argument, Uncle Sam had been taken in again by shrewd foreigners and naive "do-gooders" in Washington. In Hull's opinion, arrangements like the one under discussion might "tip the scales in favor of the embargo forces" in his country. He wanted Canada to appreciate the strength of the opposition and the danger of exceptions to and violations of the rules laid down in the American program.[10] Hull probably intended his critical fire for the Anglo-Canadian agreement, trying to impress on Canadian minds that the forthcoming pact should reflect liberal trade views.

As this accord became more imminent, the Secretary of State intensified his campaign. On January 17, 1937, in a memorandum handed to Lindsay, he retraced many of his steps, while

[10] Memorandum by Hull, Nov. 3, 1936, *Foreign Relations, 1936,* I, 786–790.

Norman Armour conveyed the same ideas to the Canadian government in Ottawa. The State Department had made it abundantly clear to London that in any negotiations American concessions of value could be granted only if trading within the Empire were made less exclusive. Conclusion of another Canadian-American pact hinged on the same contingency. American exporters must not be denied easier access to British markets by an Anglo-Canadian agreement.[11] In the middle of January the American Minister in Ottawa thus spelled out Hull's intimation of the previous November for King and Skelton.[12]

From Washington's standpoint, the major obstacle to an Anglo-American trade agreement was the preferred treatment accorded Canadian goods in the English market. For political reasons at least, the State Department had to gain entry for American agricultural products. Its officials hoped that Canada, as the interpreter between the United Kingdom and the United States, might make this task less difficult. Assurances from the Canadian Minister late in January that he would do anything he could to further the negotiations were encouraging.[13]

The revised Anglo-Canadian pact partially fulfilled these

[11] Department of State to British Embassy, Jan. 17, 1937, *Foreign Relations, 1937*, II, 1–2; memorandum by Hull, Jan. 18, 1937, *ibid.*, 2–3; Secretary of State to Armour, no. 641, Jan. 19, 1937, *ibid.*, 3–4. The following is from a telephone message to Armour from Secretary of State, January 16, 1937: "Mr. Hull remembers with pleasure that when Mr. King was in Washington [1935] . . . he assured him that he intended to work shoulder to shoulder with them. Mr. Hull is turning to Mr. King as one of the original preachers of the doctrine of more liberal trade between nations" (Davis Papers, Box 24).

[12] There is no record of the memoranda of these conversations in the Department of State files. That Armour did discuss the matter with King and Skelton is reported in Armour to Secretary of State, no. 1119, Jan. 21, 1937, *Foreign Relations, 1937*, II, 4–6.

[13] Memorandum by Sayre, Feb. 1, 1937, *Foreign Relations, 1937*, II, 10.

hopes. Submitted on February 25, 1937, to the House of Commons by Charles Dunning, the Minister of Finance, it was considered an improvement over its predecessor. Duties against third parties were not raised, and, reflecting the Canadian pressure for a liberalization of the preference system, the agreement sharply reduced the number of items (approximately 125) on which the Dominion had to maintain fixed margins. Thus, Canada could negotiate more freely in the future with foreign governments. The real significance was, as the Ottawa correspondent of the Montreal *Gazette* observed, that the Dominion had removed obstacles to a new and broader agreement with the United States. When Dunning released the text, he declared that among the items no longer protected were many "of great value in trade negotiations likely to be entered into with other countries." He was satisfied that the accord more closely reconciled British and Canadian trade policies.[14]

Ottawa had indeed obtained greater freedom to adjust future rates, but London had not done so well. Because of Canadian insistence, the United Kingdom had reduced preferences on very few items. These obligations to Dominion producers remained a formidable barrier to an Anglo-American accord. Nor were prospective Canadian-American negotiations immune from this divisive factor. Washington could hardly relax further the restrictions on Canadian farm imports unless American farmers were substantially compensated within the Empire.[15] In sum, the 1937 Anglo-Canadian agreement was decidedly more liberal than the

[14] Can. *H. of C. Deb.*, Feb. 25, 1937, II, 1241–1247. The pact had been signed two days earlier. See an article by F. C. Mears in the Montreal *Gazette*, Feb. 27, 1937.

[15] See the F. C. Mears article in the Montreal *Gazette*, May 18, 1937, for reference to Canadian pressure. For a discussion in some detail of the Canada–United Kingdom trade agreement, see J. F. Parkinson's section in F. H. Soward *et al.*, *Canada in World Affairs: The Pre-War Years* (Toronto, 1941), 200–208.

1932 accord; the efforts of Hull and Armour, combined with Canada's unique position, had borne fruit. The major problems still lay ahead, however, with little expectation of a breakthrough soon in the protracted Anglo-American trade agreement discussions.

The visit of Walter Runciman to Washington in January revealed anew that the United States and Great Britain were deadlocked on the larger issue of trade policy. President Roosevelt, Secretary of State Hull, and Assistant Secretary of State Sayre met individually with the President of the Board of Trade. Roosevelt, who had formally invited Runciman to the White House to the surprise, if not resentment, of Runciman's fellow ministers Chamberlain and Eden, "got along very well" with his guest, but they made little headway when they turned to trade agreement talks. An American observer traced the absence of progress to Runciman's limited authority and to the difference in intellectual character between the two men, whereas Chamberlain bluntly explained that his colleague "was a fine man but . . . his mind did not reach out very far, as he was sure the President's does." [16] On January 26 the Assistant Secretary explained to Runciman the contrast between bilateral and most-favored-nation arrangements, asserting that they could not coexist. In Sayre's opinion, the British official "seemed to have but a foggy and hazy notion of what I was driving at." Runciman defended his government's recent commercial behavior as truly liberal, claiming that he "had been fighting valiantly for liberal trade policies in the face of severe opposition not only among various elements of the British population but among his own colleagues." When the two discussed the Anglo-American accord specifically, Sayre emphasized the political necessity of obtaining concessions on such commodities as fruits, grain, lumber, to-

[16] Memorandum of conversation between Chamberlain and Davis, April 26, 1937, Davis Papers, Box 55.

bacco, hog products, and rice. There could be no agreement, he said, unless the United Kingdom relaxed these barriers.

Hull predicted to the British visitor that if Whitehall "should take the lead in proclaiming a program of liberal economic relations," other countries would follow suit, with the result that "nearly forty nations would be marching across the Western World proclaiming a broad, concrete basic program to restore international order and promote and preserve peace and the economic well-being of people everywhere." Countries which at first did not cooperate, unable to withstand the moral and economic pressure from such a bloc, would ultimately join ranks, opening wide the "gate" to "a discussion of political problems." Like Sayre, the Secretary of State felt that Runciman "was not with me as fully as I should have liked." Norman Davis told a British acquaintance later that "the choice of Runciman [to visit the United States] had been a bad one." One problem was that Hull "was a religious free trader," whereas Runciman "was vexatiously concrete and would discuss specific commodities." Davis himself had "sat next him [sic] at dinner and he would discuss apples." With little practical help from this Cabinet member, the trade experts continued their studies, knowing that approval by Canada would be necessary before Great Britain could lower certain tariffs. In fairness to Runciman, it must be said that upon his return to London he fought for an Anglo-American agreement, continuing to do so until well into 1938. He pressed Oliver Stanley, his successor as President of the Board of Trade, to support the measure, and talked with the British Trade Delegation in February, 1938, just before its departure to Washington to conduct the formal negotiations. One of Sayre's English friends reported that Runciman "certainly came back immensely pleased with the reception you gave him, and I am sure it gave him a new interest in the problems." [17]

[17] Memorandum by Sayre, Jan. 26, 1937, *Foreign Relations, 1937,* II, 6–8; Atherton to Secretary of State, telegram no. 53, Feb. 9, 1937, *ibid.,*

The State Department went ahead with plans for an Anglo-American pact, still believing that Canada could play a prominent role in bringing it about. On March 2, Sayre handed to the Commercial Counselor of the British Embassy a list of products on which the United States wanted better treatment in Great Britain—items which the United Kingdom could alter only with the consent of the Dominions.[18]

The trade situation prompted in part President Roosevelt's invitation in February to Mackenzie King to visit him in Washington, an invitation the Prime Minister enthusiastically accepted.[19] Early in March, almost a year and a half after the inauguration of their personal diplomacy, the two leaders met formally to discuss a number of important topics, including the political situation in Europe. One of the principal results was agreement on the type of strategy to be employed to further the Anglo- and Canadian-American trade accords. After direct urging from the President, King agreed to be the link between Washington and London. If everything went according to plan, the three great trading powers could place themselves in the strongest economic position in the history of the triangle.

In the presence of Hull, King heard familiar reasoning. The economic causes of the contemporary international problems were stressed, the fears that these conditions would breed war were espoused, and political, economic and social stability was identified with a program of lower tariffs. At the conclusion of

---

11; Secretary of State to Atherton, no. 45, Feb. 12, 1937, *ibid.*, 11–13; Atherton to Secretary of State, telegram no. 88, Feb. 23, 1937, *ibid.*, 14–15; Hull, *Memoirs*, I, 524–526; T. Jones, *A Diary with Letters*, 330; Runciman to Roosevelt, Feb. 18, 1938, Roosevelt Papers; Sir Harold Hartley, Vice-President, London Midland and Scottish Railway Company, London, to Sayre, May 18, 1937, Sayre Papers, Box 1.

[18] Department of State to British Embassy, March 2, 1937, *Foreign Relations, 1937*, II, 16–18.

[19] Bruce Hutchison, *The Incredible Canadian* (New York, 1953), 217.

the discourse the Prime Minister suggested that he "might be of some aid in advancing" the Secretary's plan while attending the coronation in London.

King recorded that "the impression Mr. Hull's conversation left on my mind was that of a man deeply concerned in the European situation, one who believed that war was inevitable within two years, or something about as bad as war." The Prime Minister expressed surprise that a man "so kindly and benevolent in his appearance, so gentle in his way of speaking," could color his presentation with " 'Christ Almighty.' " According to King's interpretation, such profanity reflected "how deeply he was feeling the whole situation." If Norman Davis can be believed, King, who fancied himself "as the negotiator between the States, Canada and England," had "made a poor impression" on the Secretary of State during this visit.[20]

The Prime Minister spent the night at the White House, where he and the President devoted most of their conversation to the "European situation which is giving the President and Mr. Hull a good deal of concern." King suggested that Roosevelt, in cooperation with the League of Nations, initiate a "permanent conference on economic and social problems." Roosevelt apparently was of the persuasion to throw the support and prestige of the United States behind a meeting of the countries of the world to study the economic and social ills thought to be at the root of international discord. A few days later King wrote Lord Tweedsmuir, the Governor General, "I believe there is every probability of the President himself taking action of a kind which will make clear his desire to effect an appeasement of conditions in Europe by lending good offices toward that end."

Before launching such a grandiose plan to promote world

[20] Memorandum by Hull, March 5, 1937, *Foreign Relations, 1937*, I, 641–648; James Eayrs, *In Defense of Canada: Appeasement and Rearmament* (Toronto, 1965), 42; T. Jones, *A Diary with Letters*, 338–339.

prosperity and avert war, Roosevelt sought King's help to bring about an Anglo-American trade agreement which, together with an enlarged Canadian-American pact, would create a North Atlantic bulwark against further economic disintegration, powerful enough hopefully to force other nations to abandon potentially catastrophic economic nationalism.[21] The Canadian Prime Minister was most receptive. Shortly after his departure from Washington, he wrote Roosevelt, "It will mean much to the British government as well as to myself for me to have the North American background so clearly defined in my own mind. I hope and I believe I can be of service in promoting a fuller understanding of interest which have much in common for the British Empire and the United States with the world situation what it is today." He concluded, "It is a high privilege to be able to cooperate in the cause of world peace." Writing to Hull, King noted that he had been reflecting "a good deal upon conditions [which he termed "appalling"] as they continue to disclose themselves in industrial and international relations." Barring a speedy solution, "present day civilization will soon be undermined." He added that his recent talks in Washington had encouraged him to "believe that a way will yet be found of averting . . . impending world disaster." The Prime Minister promised to work for Canadian cooperation with the two North Atlantic partners "in every possible way towards preserving and furthering international and industrial peace."[22] Had he been able to translate

[21] Eayrs, *Appeasement and Rearmament,* 42–43. King to Roosevelt, March 8, 1937, contained the Prime Minister's "Notes on Permanent Conference on Economic and Social Problems," March 6, 1937, Roosevelt Papers, PSF, Canada, 1933–1941 (also printed in Elliott Roosevelt, ed., *F. D. R.: His Personal Letters,* I, 664–668). See the very important article by "Rideau Banks" [Norman MacLeod] entitled "That Washington Talk," in Toronto *Saturday Night,* April 24, 1937.

[22] King to Hull, March 17, 1937, Hull Papers; King to Roosevelt, March 8, 1937, Roosevelt Papers.

these thoughts into concrete deeds, such as sacrifice of some of Canada's preferences, the negotiations would have encountered fewer difficulties. Unfortunately, this was not to be.

The Prime Minister left Washington undoubtedly enthralled with the possibility of making his greatest contribution to his favorite project. Nor did the idea lose its force during the month of April. In a conversation with King, shortly before the Prime Minister's departure for London, Armour conveyed Hull's faith in King as "perhaps the only one who could bring the British and the other members of the British Commonwealth into line" in support of the program to lower tariffs and advance the cause of peace. A public declaration to this effect by the nations represented at the Imperial Conference would have an "electrifying" result; it might "stampede" the world toward economic liberalism. King reiterated his support for the program, considering it a privilege to make the effort at London. He was somewhat wary of Chamberlain, but felt that he had "mellowed" in the last few years and might be agreeable. In any event, the Prime Minister promised "to try to have some statement worked out which might meet the situation." King's cooperative attitude aside, the real test was whether Canada would agree to certain concessions.[23]

The Canadian Prime Minister covered the same ground in a letter to Hull. "The most effective measures that nations can take for the preservation of peace," he wrote, "lie in the field of economic collaboration"; the time was ripe for the world's trading countries to make a supreme effort to open the channels of international trade. He admitted that he had been thinking about how Canada could play an important role at the Imperial Conference. On the same day, King informed Armour that "it was his intention in London to do everything he could do with regard to having some form of statement issued embodying the

[23] Armour to Hull, April 19, 1937, Hull Papers.

doctrines in which he and Mr. Hull believed and for which they were both working." The Minister wrote to Hull that King "referred modestly to some small success he had had in the past in making our common point of view not only known but acceptable to the British, and he seemed determined on this occasion to succeed again." Armour considered him to be "in a very serious and earnest mood" and concluded that the Liberal statesman "realizes how critical the situation is and how great is the opportunity that is offered him." [24]

If his correspondence is an accurate measure, Hull expected a major breakthrough at London. To Armour he wrote, "I imagine Mr. Mackenzie King will state his position early in the Conference," and he inquired of the Minister whether it might be wise for him to go from Ottawa to London to report on "what progress he [King] is making toward the liberalization of the Imperial commercial policy." Emphasizing his interest, the Secretary continued, "I hope that you will realize the great importance I give to the expected developments at the Imperial Conference. It is to my mind a critical turning point on the whole work of trying to establish the basis for peaceful inter-relationship among the nations of the world and I feel that we cannot pay too much attention to the discussions which will be held between the various parts of the British Empire." [25]

Between the Prime Minister's departure from Washington and his arrival at the Imperial Conference, Anglo-American trade discussions had taken another turn. On April 13 the British Embassy rejected the American proposals of March 2, considering them neither politically nor economically feasible in the Dominions or Great Britain. London felt it useless to submit the

[24] King to Hull, April 23, 1937, Hull Papers; memorandum of conversation between King and Armour, April 23, 1937, enclosed in Armour to Hull, April 24, 1937, *ibid.*
[25] Hull to Armour, April 22, 1937, Hull Papers.

requests in their present form to the Dominions, as there was no good way to compensate for the concessions the Dominions would have to make. The United Kingdom could increase preferences to the Dominions on articles not covered in the American list, but this could be done only by raising duties against other countries, which was hardly consistent with the American trade program.[26]

Apparently the State Department had expected a different reply. The day before Whitehall dispatched its answer, Francis Sayre wrote of the progress that had been made and of his belief that the prospects for the future were encouraging. He had been informed by the Embassy in London that the trade experts in Great Britain favored most of the requests. At the same time, Norman Davis, still hopeful, had painted a sanguine picture of how, given a little American patience, Eden and Chamberlain might bring their government into line.[27] This information made the Department reluctant to narrow its proposals. On May 18 it countered with a list substantially the same as that of March 2. To accept the British position, Washington argued, would curtail so severely the concessions that the United States could accord the United Kingdom that negotiation of such a limited agreement would hardly be worth while.[28] The two parties had reached a momentary impasse, one refusing to retract the proposals on its "must" list, the other refusing to grant them.

Into this situation came Mackenzie King, "hopeful that . . . he might be able to contribute something toward the great objec-

[26] Second Secretary of the British Board of Trade to Commercial Counselor of British Embassy, April 13, 1937, *Foreign Relations, 1937*, II, 23–24; British Embassy to Department of State, April 13, 1937, *ibid.*, 24–26.

[27] Sayre to Phillips, April 12, 1937, Sayre Papers, Box 5; Davis to Roosevelt, April 13, 1937, Davis Papers, Box 55.

[28] Department of State to British Embassy, May 18, 1937, *Foreign Relations, 1937*, II, 29–32.

tive the President had in mind." [29] The Prime Minister had
hardly set foot in London when he made a decision that, in
retrospect, signaled what lay ahead. On April 28, a few days
before King's arrival in London, Norman Davis discussed the
Anglo-American trade stalemate and Canada's possible contribution to ending it with Vincent Massey. Massey, who had served
between 1927 and 1930 as the Dominion's first minister in
Washington and who was now the Canadian High Commissioner, volunteered to arrange a meeting between Davis and the
Prime Minister. Hull gave his blessing to "inconspicuous" talks
which would include also Ambassador Bingham, who had had
"satisfactory" conversations with King in 1936. On May 4, Davis
told Massey of the Secretary's suggestion that Bingham be included. The Canadian expected to see King shortly and hoped to
make the appointment at that time. Just when it appeared that a
meeting was imminent, the Prime Minister in effect prevented
it. The cautious King, feeling that Bingham's presence might
give the meeting an official complexion, saw his position as
arbiter of Anglo-American differences or as the watchdog of
Canada's interests being compromised. He spoke favorably of
talking privately with Davis, but the American rejected this. So,
at Davis' suggestion, the idea was dropped altogether. [30] This
footnote to the developments of the spring reveals one of King's
personality traits that weighed heavily in the ensuing months.

On May 14, speaking before the first plenary session of the
Imperial Conference, the Prime Minister declared that "endur-

[29] Memorandum by Armour, April 23, 1937, enclosed in Armour to
Hull, April 24, 1937, Hull Papers.

[30] Norman Davis to Secretary of State, telegram no. 24, April 28,
1937, 611.4131/277; Secretary of State to Davis, telegram no. 19, April
29, 1937, Davis Papers, Box 55; Davis to Secretary of State, telegram,
April 30, 1937, *ibid.*; Davis to Secretary of State, telegram no. 41, May
4, 1937, *ibid.* (a paraphrase of this telegram can be found in the Department files, 600.0031 World Program/103).

ing peace cannot be achieved without economic appeasement," and that "the political tension will not lessen without an abatement of the present policies of economic nationalism and economic imperialism." The nations assembled at this conference, King continued, had "a definite responsibility to join with other countries willing to cooperate in a concerted effort" not to raise trade barriers but to lower them wherever practicable.[31] There could be little doubt that the Prime Minister had made a plea for trade agreements between Commonwealth and non-Commonwealth countries, or that he had spoken unofficially for the United States. As F. C. Mears wrote in the Montreal *Gazette*, "echoes of the White House chats in March between President Roosevelt and Premier Mackenzie King have already been heard" in London. The Prime Minister's words were "meant for consumption by the British Government." This astute journalist pointed out that the essential ingredient in any Anglo-American accord was not King's "persuasive talk," but the release of Great Britain from the preferences guaranteed Canadian products in the English market. Mears detected no intimation that the Prime Minister planned to take this step, concluding that "primary producers in Canada . . . stand in the way of such release unless Premier King decides he can get along without their votes at the next general election." [32]

The *Gazette* reporter had put his finger on the dilemma confronting the Canadian Prime Minister. Though he shared Roosevelt's and Hull's faith in the importance of an Anglo-

[31] Toronto *Globe and Mail*, May 15, 1937. One should also read Allan G. B. Fischer's chapter in Toynbee, ed., *Survey of International Affairs, 1937*, I, 56–99. For an official record, see Maurice Ollivier, ed., *The Colonial and Imperial Conferences from 1887 to 1937* (3 vols.; Ottawa, 1954), III, 459.

[32] Montreal *Gazette*, May 18, 1937.

American trade agreement, King was an overly cautious politician who preferred to avoid strife as much as possible. When the ultimate decision had to be made, would King jeopardize political support at home by sacrificing Canada's favored position in the United Kingdom market? Prior to the conference, Norman Armour had speculated what would be the answer to this question. Certain positive forces were working on King. Sensitive to criticism in general and particularly "thin-skinned" concerning the charge of inconsistency, the Prime Minister could refute the Conservatives' claims that he had, by negotiating the 1937 Anglo-Canadian pact, endorsed a significant plank in the Tory platform, and thus guide his party back to its traditional low-tariff posture. Moreover, he had an isolationist desire to tie Canada more closely to the United States. Affirmative action by Ottawa would solidify relations with Washington at a time when European troubles portended those commitments and involvements that were anathema to King. Besides, the Prime Minister was acutely aware of Canada's forming the link between the United States and the Empire, leading Armour to doubt that he would let pass an opportunity to strengthen the Dominion's unique role.

Nevertheless, King had to face opposition to the contemplated sacrifices of certain internal interests, a situation which his political opponents might successfully exploit. This prospect would have been far less vexatious had a united government supported the Prime Minister. Such was not the case. Before the Imperial Conference had begun, Washington was warned of the views of Charles Dunning, the Finance Minister. Dunning had fought hard in 1936 and 1937 for the retention of Dominion preferences, and he showed little evidence that he now favored their abandonment, at least not without adequate compensation. In making his assessment, Armour also conveyed Skelton's skepticism that Canada would desert its exporters in the interest of an Anglo-American accord. The Under Secretary averred, "We have right here in Canada sufficient concessions that we could give the United States in the form of reduced tariffs to repay any concessions that we might be given in return, without giving up advantages we already enjoy in the United Kingdom market." [33] After weighing these factors, the American Minister concluded that when the showdown came, King would make the required sacrifices.[34]

In any case, with his opening speech, the Prime Minister "emerged as the Empire's leader in the search for greater international trade." The *Times* (London) predicted that the extent to which the conference would go in implementing King's proposals would depend upon the vigor with which he followed up his statement. Grant Dexter, another Canadian journalist in London covering the proceedings, reported that inquiries made among the Canadian delegates had revealed that the Prime Minister would give powerful support to liberalization of the Ottawa guarantees.[35]

For a short time, the Roosevelt plan "prospered." As expected, a few Canadians dissented, notably representatives of the fruit growers and lumber interests, but the majority applauded King's attack on trade barriers. Perhaps to King's surprise, Chamberlain seconded the plea. Unfortunately, the emotional pitch faded, and optimistic forecasts proved to be in error. At a meeting the next day of the conference's committee on trade, Charles Dunning asked what the Dominion would obtain in return for diminished trade within the Empire. He and others doubted that

[33] Armour to Secretary of State, no. 1346, May 3, 1937, 611.4131/283.
[34] Armour to Secretary of State, no. 1354, May 5, 1937, 841.01 Imperial Conference (1937)/28.
[35] Toronto *Globe and Mail*, May 21, 1937.

general commercial expansion following the agreement would suffice as compensation.[36]

The first official indication that Canada might present difficulties was made on May 24. Ambassador Bingham reported that a member of the Embassy had talked with Norman Robertson, the Canadian at the Imperial Conference in charge of trade discussions, and had found him pessimistic about the possibility of an Anglo-American agreement. Dubious of the impending internal changes in the British government, Robertson, like many, considered Stanley Baldwin to be more amenable to reduce tariffs than Neville Chamberlain, who became the Prime Minister of the United Kingdom on May 28. The contemplated removal of Runciman as President of the Board of Trade augured no better. Turning to his own country's situation, Robertson became remarkably candid. Canada could not conceal its sacrifices, doubly awkward politically since during the Parliamentary debate on the Anglo-Canadian pact members of the Government had underscored the value to the Dominion of the very same preferences that they would now have to relinquish. The Canadian leaders were wary also of giving London a "blank check." In other words, they did not want to endorse any British statement supporting negotiations—thus promising modifications in the preference system—until there had been discussion of the Ottawa items that affected the Dominion. Robertson was doubtful, therefore, that Canada could accede to all the requests contained in the American proposals.[37]

Late in May, the British communicated to the various delegations the substance of the Anglo-American exchanges, particularly the specific requests made by the United States, and asked

[36] See the perceptive editorial entitled "When Mr. King Returns: A Bit of Inside History" in Ottawa *Journal*, July 8, 1937.

[37] Bingham to Secretary of State, telegram no. 304, May 24, 1937, *Foreign Relations, 1937*, II, 32–33.

the Dominions to inform them of the concessions they could grant. On June 1, Robertson and Lester Pearson, then attached to Massey's office, discussed the Anglo-American talks with influential British officials. Following the meeting, Robertson hinted to the American Ambassador the possibility of multilateral negotiations in Washington. He admitted that he had opposed Canadian concessions unless they formed part of a "comprehensive pattern," by which he meant that compensation be made for the Dominion elsewhere in the Empire and especially that barriers to Canadian imports into the United States be relaxed. Robertson had frowned on the "simple" argument advanced by the representatives of Whitehall that the Dominions would obtain sufficient benefits from the indirect results of the agreement. For economic as well as political reasons, Ottawa expected tangible compensation.[38]

At about the same time, Chalkley met again in Washington with Sayre and Hawkins. The State Department spokesmen introduced improved estimates of the concessions the United States could grant to the United Kingdom if a *quid pro quo* from London were forthcoming and provided there was no marked change in present economic activity and no well-founded protest by American interests to the Committee for Reciprocity Information. With the fate of previous proposals in mind, Chalkley warned of the probable recalcitrance of the Dominions. Specifically, he cited Canadian attitudes regarding freer access into Great Britain of American lumber and suggested that direct

[38] The *Times* (London), June 1, 1937, reported that "full details of the Anglo-American trade talks were communicated to the principal Empire delegates . . . during the weekend. The Dominion representatives have been asked to study the United States proposals and to inform the United Kingdom Government of the concessions they are willing to make." For the information from Robertson, see Bingham to Secretary of State, telegram no. 335, June 2, 1937, *Foreign Relations, 1937*, II, 34–35.

negotiations be carried out between the United States and Canada to settle the matter.[39]

That the Dominions were being adamant was common knowledge. On June 4, the London *Daily Telegraph* printed an article, the general veracity of which was confirmed by a member of Chamberlain's government, asserting that while the United Kingdom believed the Anglo-American agreement to be very significant, the Dominions' reluctance to make concessions without adequate compensation raised formidable obstacles and could require negotiations between them and the United Kingdom.[40] To complicate the outlook even more, an election was to be held later in the year in Australia. At this moment, Australian–United States trade relations had reached their nadir. Since there was considerable popular support in the "Land Down Under" for the government's trade diversion policy, Prime Minister Joseph A. Lyons had understandable qualms about any act or statement that might be exploited politically by the opposition.[41] An early Anglo-American agreement was obviously not in the offing.

By the middle of June, Prime Minister Neville Chamberlain had thrown his support unequivocally behind the pact. On June 9 he had told Bingham that it was his "firm hope and fixed

[39] Memorandum by Hawkins, June 4, 1937, *Foreign Relations, 1937,* II, 35–37.

[40] Bingham to Secretary of State, telegram no. 344, June 4, 1937, *Foreign Relations, 1937,* II, 38–39; see article by Grant Dexter in Toronto *Globe and Mail,* June 10, 1937. As early as May, Bruce Hutchison, writing for the Vancouver *Daily Province,* reported that "the hard-headed minister of finance, Hon. C. A. Dunning . . . will undoubtedly want a quid pro quo for any losses in the British market. . . . Such negotiations are bound to take time, possibly a year or more, and all the Imperial Conference is likely to do is to discuss the general principle of modifying the Ottawa pacts in order to clear the way for the Anglo-American treaty" (Vancouver *Daily Province,* May 20, 1937).

[41] Esthus, *From Enmity to Alliance,* 37–38.

purpose" to conclude a trade agreement with Washington and that he intended to give his "constant support to that end." [42] On June 15, at the last meeting of the heads of the delegations at the Imperial Conference, Chamberlain had appealed spontaneously and eloquently for the cooperation of the Dominions—and of reluctant members of his own Cabinet—in making possible an accord.[43] Writing privately to Hull the next day, Bingham reported the observation of General J. B. M. Hertzog, from the Union of South Africa, that Chamberlain's attitude had changed in the past ten years and that Chamberlain now sincerely hoped to cooperate with the United States in the conclusion of an agreement.[44]

A similar thought came from another source. By plan, Joseph Davies, the American Ambassador to the Soviet Union, had stopped in London on his way to Moscow. On the basis of his talks there, he concluded that the Cabinet wanted to proceed further with reciprocity but had encountered difficulties with the Dominions. Davies predicted that the conference would produce

[42] Bingham to Secretary of State, telegram no. 367, June 10, 1937, *Foreign Relations, 1937,* II, 39–40.

[43] Bingham to Secretary of State, telegram no. 384, June 15, 1937, *Foreign Relations, 1937,* II, 40–41. On September 11, 1937, Henry Grady wrote from Geneva to Hull about some of the points that had come up in a conversation with Sir Frederick Leith-Ross: "I was told also that at the Empire Conference Chamberlain spoke eloquently and in the highest terms of both the President and you. I think that there is no doubt about the seriousness of the British in regard to the trade agreement" (Hull Papers). In August, Moffat wrote the following: "When Chamberlain made his famous appeal at the Imperial Conference for an Anglo-American agreement, it was directed quite as much at a group in his own Cabinet (notably Hore Belisha, Ormsby-Gore, and even possibly Oliver Stanley) as it was to the Dominions" (Moffat to Davis, Aug. 10, 1937, Davis Papers, Box 41). Moffat's source was Ray Atherton.

[44] Bingham to Hull, June 16, 1937, Hull Papers.

nothing concrete, in spite of the "good will and the general desire" of Great Britain to cooperate.[45]

At the same gathering in which Chamberlain had backed the Anglo-American project, Mackenzie King had stated that "he had dealings direct with the United States and knew best how to handle the question with Washington himself." The British construed this oblique remark to mean that the Prime Minister thought he could obtain enough concessions from the United States to permit him to yield on those items necessary to an Anglo-American agreement.[46] For a brief moment, it appeared that Canada might at least not be overly troublesome.

During these same spring and early summer months there was thoughtful discussion of a meeting between Roosevelt and Chamberlain in Washington. The man who took the initiative in this little-known episode was Norman Davis, who was in London as head of the American delegation to the International Sugar Conference. On April 26, while discussing Runciman's January trip to the American capital with Chamberlain, Davis mentioned that he would like to see a similar meeting take place between the President and the Chancellor of the Exchequer. Chamberlain showed interest, alleging that for some time he had wanted to travel to the United States, though he had never done so. With the added burdens of being Prime Minister impending, he would soon have even greater difficulty leaving London. A few days later, Eden expressed to Davis his own desire to visit the American capital. Eden, too, thought Anglo-American cooperation, essential to the security of both countries, would be promoted significantly by a meeting between himself and Roosevelt. On May 7, as Davis, who was about to depart for the

[45] Joseph Davies to Hull, June 8, 1937, Hull Papers.

[46] Bingham to Secretary of State, telegram no. 384, June 15, 1937, *Foreign Relations, 1937*, II, 40–41.

United States, talked with the Chancellor of the Exchequer, the subject of a Chamberlain-Roosevelt meeting was brought up again. The American volunteered to broach the question with Roosevelt upon his return home. Despite the problems at home, Chamberlain said that he would cross the Atlantic if the President wished it. Davis, who had also seen Eden a few hours earlier, suggested that if Chamberlain could not get away, the Foreign Secretary might make the trip. The prospective Prime Minister left the impression that he preferred to go himself, concluding the conversation by indicating that Davis should pursue it in Washington. If Roosevelt decided affirmatively, Chamberlain wanted the arrangements to be made through a personal communication rather than through diplomatic channels.

Once back in the capital, the peripatetic diplomat—or "peripatetic windbag," as Baldwin once called him [47]—informed the President of both Chamberlain's and Eden's sentiments. Roosevelt was most agreeable, but for political reasons favored a visit by Chamberlain to one from Eden. He thought that his countrymen would express less concern if the visitor were the Prime Minister than if he were the Foreign Secretary. In talks with Chamberlain, the spotlight could be focused on topics other than foreign policy, whereas fear in the United States of making international commitments would accompany discussions with Eden. The President, too, recognized the utility, both to Anglo-American understanding and international stability, of a conference. At the same time, the affair was delicate and might be damaging to the bilateral relations were misunderstandings to arise; therefore Roosevelt wanted an agenda made of the issues to

---

[47] T. Jones, *A Diary with Letters*, 129. Baldwin is quoted on April 28, 1934, as follows: " 'He's [Davis] just a peripatetic windbag, without authority, getting into the way of busy men. I managed to keep him away.' "

be discussed before the talks. In his letter to Chamberlain, Davis inquired how best these preliminaries could be managed. Davis himself suggested that a formal announcement of the intention to negotiate a trade agreement, which was hopefully imminent, could serve as the catalyst for the high-level conversations. On a more specific level, Davis informed Chamberlain that Roosevelt did not want to meet until after the adjournment of Congress, presumably in the middle of September. The tentative plan, then, called for the Prime Minister to visit Washington in late September or early October to discuss "questions of common interest and concern."

On July 8, Chamberlain penned his answer to this invitation. Recognizing the propriety of such a conference, he felt nevertheless that the present was not a propitious time for it to be held. A meeting that could bear no tangible fruit might backfire, and he saw no chance of achieving any major result at the moment. The Prime Minister raised two particular problems: the difficulties underlying Anglo-American trade negotiations, and the political situation in Europe, highlighted by new tensions between Great Britain and Germany resulting from the postponement of Foreign Minister Konstantin von Neurath's trip to London. Although Chamberlain concluded his rejection of Davis' overture by expressing a desire to pursue it at a later date, the more favorable climate they hoped for never descended on the two capitals. On July 28, Roosevelt, not content to let Chamberlain's reply be the last word, personally wrote to the Prime Minister asking what preparatory steps might be taken to expedite his visit to the United States. Chamberlain's absence from London prevented him from answering Roosevelt's letter until September 28. The European political scene, which had improved meanwhile, could no longer justify a cool response to the President's invitation. Instead, Chamberlain mentioned the Far East and noted that the actions of the Western powers probably could not alter the situation there. Fearing some new crisis, the Prime Minister wrote that he could not "suggest any way in which the meeting between us could be expedited." In his opinion, "We must wait a little longer," [48] prompting one scholar to note that "whether things were improving, as in Europe, or deteriorating, as in the Far East, the conclusion was the same—that the concerting of policy with the United States was not a serious objective of British statesmanship." [49]

Thus Roosevelt and Chamberlain, unlike Hoover and MacDonald, never met formally. If personal diplomacy might have hastened the start of negotiations and the conclusion of the agreement, and, as Hull believed, reoriented the world's thinking toward economic rehabilitation and international peace, then Chamberlain's decision had far-reaching consequences. Although there is no record in Hull's papers, the Secretary of State

[48] The only published account of the proposed visit of Chamberlain to Washington with which I am familiar appears in Borg, *The United States and the Far Eastern Crisis of 1933–1938,* 375–377. Memorandum of conversation between Chamberlain and Davis, April 26, 1937, Davis Papers, Box 55; memorandum of conversation between Eden and Davis, May 4, 1937, *ibid.*; memorandum of conversation between Chamberlain and Davis, May 7, 1937, *ibid.*; memorandum of conversation between Eden and Davis, May 7, 1937, *ibid.*; Davis to Chamberlain, June 10, 1937, Hull Papers; Chamberlain to Davis, July 8, 1937, *ibid.*; Davis to Hull, telegram, July 13, 1937, Davis Papers, Box 8; Roosevelt to Chamberlain, July 28, 1937, *Foreign Relations, 1937,* I, 113; Chamberlain to Roosevelt, Sept. 28, 1937, *ibid.,* 131–132. The affair prompted an epistolary exchange between Davis and Bingham, who felt himself undermined by Davis' actions (Davis to Bingham, June 10, 1937, Davis Papers, Box 3; Bingham to Davis, July 1, 1937, *ibid.*; Davis to Bingham, July 14, 1937, *ibid.*). In an effort to soothe the Ambassador's feelings, Davis wrote, as a postscript to his last letter, "The President jokingly remarked the other day that he had received through various channels intimations from so many members of the British Cabinet of a desire to come over here that he was considering asking the Prime Minister to bring the whole Cabinet over for a meeting here."

[49] Herbert Nicholas, *Britain and the U.S.A.* (Baltimore, 1963), 28.

must have been disappointed by the outcome. In retrospect, it can be questioned whether later events would have been greatly altered by a Roosevelt-Chamberlain meeting. Possibly an agreement reflecting the apparent solidarity of the English-speaking world might have forced Hitler to modify his plans for Europe. Unless something tangible had resulted, it is doubtful that the German Chancellor would have paid much attention to the proceedings; if anything, they would have confirmed his preconceptions about the ineffectiveness of the democracies. He certainly would not have been deterred by idle promises, and the complexities of the discussions were such that no mere talking by two heads of government, however important, could bury them. Even if something concrete had resulted, there is no guarantee that it would have had any effect on the political situation of the time. His later actions suggest that Hitler probably would have assigned little, if any, political value to the symbolic gesture of a trade agreement announcement or an accord. He would not at any rate have been dissuaded from his ambitions. A pact made between the United Kingdom and the United States, manifesting closer economic collaboration by two financially advantaged powers, might well have buttressed Hitler's belief in the necessity of German expansion into central and eastern Europe.

Other factors besides Chamberlain's negative reply portended additional delay. On July 2, Leo Pasvolsky, Special Assistant to the Secretary of State, and Sir William Brown, the Permanent Secretary of the Board of Trade, talked about the deadlock. This conversation revealed that the two governments, despite the memoranda, the statements, and the discussions, had not communicated effectively. Brown complained that Washington underestimated the difficulties facing the British, particularly the attitudes of Australia and Canada. Pasvolsky contended that the Board of Trade paid insufficient attention to American arguments. Similarly, the two spokesmen, like their superiors, differed in their evaluation of the Anglo-Canadian agreement. The Permanent Secretary reflected Whitehall's contentment, whereas Hull's assistant conveyed the State Department's disappointments—the celerity with which the agreement was negotiated and signed and Canada's retention of certain preferential margins. In Washington's view, these guarantees materially interfered with the conclusion of an Anglo-American pact, appearing to be an almost deliberate attempt to frustrate the accord. Referring to the "difficult" Canadians, Brown related that during the negotiations Ottawa had been told that because of the releases given the Dominion it would be expected in the future to make concessions in the United Kingdom market which would make possible an Anglo-American arrangement. At the Imperial Conference the Canadians had set as the price tag for this cooperation more liberal trade treatment from the United States. The State Department official inferred that the British wanted Washington to bargain directly with the Dominions. Pasvolsky cautioned against this, doubting that it would win for the United States any more of its "must" requests.[50]

Resistance to the accord from British industrialists, Canada's hesitancy, and the unenthusiastic character of Whitehall's support remained obstacles. Bruce Hutchison has written much too simply that Prime Minister King went to London to "act as an intermediary between the United States and Britain. His mission succeeded. By the reduction of Canada's preferences in the British market and Britain's in Canada, in exchange for a reduction in American tariffs, the three-way trade agreement was slowly negotiated and signed on November 17, 1938."[51] As this

[50] Pasvolsky to Secretary of State, telegram no. 429, July 2, 1937, *Foreign Relations, 1937*, II, 43–46.

[51] Hutchison, *The Incredible Canadian*, 218. For Hull's observations on his March conversations with King and assessment of the Prime Minister's influence in London, see Hull, *Memoirs*, I, 526–529.

chapter has demonstrated, he achieved something less than total victory.

On the other hand, the Imperial Conference had not been a complete failure as a vehicle for Canadian representation of United States policy. It is true that the Dominions had not formally released the United Kingdom from its obligation to maintain tariff preferences. Because of this, an Anglo-American agreement was not imminent. Nor had the official statement of the proceedings explicitly and specifically endorsed Secretary of State Hull's reciprocity program. The Canadians had succeeded in having inserted in its first draft an endorsement to that effect, but opposition from Australia had forced its deletion. Significantly enough, the final statement avoided any seconding of the principle of imperial preference, and recognized the relationship between Commonwealth prosperity and increased international trade, to say nothing of the contribution of economic rehabilitation to world peace.[52] A fair conclusion, then, is that within the bounds of political and economic realities, Mackenzie King had attempted to bring together the two giants of the Atlantic community, only to meet opposition that frustrated achievement of his aims. Australia, for reasons of its own, proved recalcitrant. Unfortunately, too, the political and economic realities in Canada were more confining than Washington had anticipated or hoped, and King perhaps was too sensitive to friction within his own camp. Had he been more decisive—had he committed his government definitely to reduce preferences, for example— Australia might have been isolated and forced to reluctantly accept the inevitable. The alternative to a firm stand was further delay.

The day after the adjournment of the conference, Skelton

[52] Ollivier, *Colonial and Imperial Conferences,* III, 441; Herschel V. Johnson, Counselor of the Embassy in London, to Secretary of State, no. 3203, July 13, 1937, 611.4131/339.

informed Armour that three important Cabinet members—
Ernest Lapointe, Thomas Crerar, and Charles Dunning—had
agreed with King that Canada had to "go the limit" in making
possible an Anglo-American agreement.[53] Of course, the government could not accept all of the British requests, but the Dominion officials felt that they could be of assistance. They planned to
tackle the problem upon their return to Ottawa. The question
was which point of view would prevail in the internal deliberations. Though he favored the principle of an Anglo-American
pact, Dunning was less inclined to make the necessary sacrifices.
British overtures at London had only slightly mellowed him.
Others in the Canadian Cabinet wanted the Dominion to take
the lead in granting releases. This cleavage underlay the in-
decisiveness that for the next few months characterized
developments, reflecting the political difficulty of reconciling internationalism and its demands with national economic interests.
It would be doubly difficult if the Prime Minister had to have a
consensus within the government before he would make the
decision.

[53] Armour to Secretary of State, no. 1482, July 9, 1937, 841.01
Imperial Conference (1937)/62.

Chapter 6

Trilateral Negotiations:
A Reality

Discouraging reports from London and Ottawa of internal problems in Great Britain and reluctance of the Dominions to sacrifice their preferential position in the United Kingdom market conditioned Washington for the British explanation of July. Whitehall advised that upon asking what position the Dominions would take concerning the concessions which the United States deemed essential, it had learned that they would probably insist on compensation for their losses in the British market. The note suggested that Canada, one imperial nation in particular that had no alternative but to expand markets elsewhere, would undoubtedly welcome simultaneous Canadian- and Anglo-American discussions.[1] The implication was clear: the British government felt that it alone could not obtain the cooperation of the Dominions. The United States had to assist in resolving the imperial annoyance.

This explanation was disingenuous, as important State De-

[1] Memorandum by Constant Southworth, Division of Trade Agreements, July 8, 1937, *Foreign Relations, 1937*, II, 48; British Embassy to Department of State, July 8, 1937, *ibid.*, 49–52.

partment officials came to realize. Actually, the British had made no great effort at London to satisfy the Dominions or even to inform them of what compensation Whitehall would grant for their compliance. The easier route, and the one adopted by a government only lukewarm about a trade agreement, was to saddle the Dominions with the responsibility for inaction. Though the tactic fooled many in Washington and London, it did not fool Ray Atherton, the Chargé at Grosvenor Square, and J. Pierrepont Moffat, now chief of the Division of European Affairs. Atherton put the problem in its proper context in late July during a talk with Moffat in Washington. He saw that Great Britain had no present plans to effect a "thorough meeting of minds" with the United States. Unlike some of the other British statesmen, Chamberlain hoped for closer relations, supporting the trade pact as a step toward cleaning the slate of divisive issues. As Atherton noted, the Prime Minister's performance at the closing of the Imperial Conference had been directed as much to members of his own Cabinet as to the Dominions. But even Chamberlain had little faith in the practicability of Anglo-American collaboration. He doubted Roosevelt's ability to guide a predominantly isolationist nation, he faced resistance within the Cabinet, and the Foreign Office, except for Eden, was indifferent to improving ties between London and Washington. Vansittart, the Permanent Under Secretary, was a good example. Like some of his associates, he attacked the appeasement policy of Chamberlain and Baldwin and favored cooperation with countries opposed to German expansion, but dismissed the notion that the United States might be a reliable partner. In his opinion a trade agreement could be weighed only by its economic merits, which were moot. Its political merits were so few that they warranted little serious thought. Chamberlain himself never found the same degree of political significance in the accord as did Cordell Hull, although, as a business man, he saw sound economic reasons for its conclusion. He was no messianic advocate of the theory that political crises were economically determined, and when faced with opposition he had applied minimum pressure on the Dominions to cooperate in negotiation of the trade pact. On July 31, in reply to Armour's question whether the Canadian government had reached any decision about preferences, Skelton noted that London still had not informed him of what compensation Canada could expect from either the United Kingdom or the United States.[2]

To Atherton, Moffat, and Roosevelt when he was apprised of the Chargé's thoughts, the immediate prospect for closer Anglo-American relations, exemplified by a trade agreement, seemed dim. Since Whitehall shared with the Dominions the responsibility for this situation, the United States had to direct its diplomatic efforts eastward as well as northward.[3]

Between July and November the Roosevelt Administration discarded its opposition to trilateral negotiations, the United Kingdom reversed its ambiguous course, Canada overcame its indecision, and the authorities agreed to begin formal bargaining sessions. These developments did not come easily. London's primary goal was political settlement with Germany and Italy, not a trade pact with the United States. Moreover, the diplomats had to contend with the interplay of conflicting political forces. Whatever the economic justification, the Canadian government needed concurrent negotiations with the United States, implying that compensation would be made to the Dominion in return for reduced preferences, to guide it past the political shoals at home. The State Department had the equally challenging task of currying the favor of the American farmer with enlarged markets in

[2] Moffat Diary, July 29, 1937, Moffat Papers, XXXIX; memorandum by Armour, July 31, 1937, *ibid.*, XII.

[3] Moffat Diary, July 31, 1937, *ibid.*, XXXIX; Moffat to Dunn, July 31, 1937, *ibid.*, XII.

the United Kingdom while not losing it by seemingly allowing increased imports from Canada. As a result, it wanted to avoid simultaneous discussions. Resolution of this dilemma underlay Washington's announcement of contemplated negotiations with London and Ottawa, a triumph in Hull's battle to lower imperial and national trade barriers and, hopefully, to reverse contemporary political trends.[4]

On July 15 the British elaborated more thoroughly on the attitudes of the various Dominions, again blaming them for the stalemate and suggesting that the negotiations be made tripartite. In London, Canadian officials had expressed a strong feeling that Canada should either be a party to Anglo-American parleys or, preferably, negotiate simultaneously with the United States.[5] The next day the Foreign Office, through three members of its Embassy, asked for the American reaction to Canadian participation and whether the Department of State would modify the principal-supplier rule to include commodities of major importance to the Dominions. In presenting their latest reply to selected American requests, the three expressed hope that the United States would find the proposals sufficiently acceptable to warrant public announcement of forthcoming negotiations. They advanced London's belief that the absence of an announcement, in light "of all the recent publicity," would be as undesirable as the collapse of negotiations—a subtle form of pressure on Washington to make the desired statement at this favorable moment for the British.[6]

---

[4] For general treatments of Anglo-American discussions in 1937, see Toynbee, ed., *Survey of International Affairs, 1937*, I, 99–109, and *The United States in World Affairs: An Account of American Foreign Relations, 1937* (New York, 1938), 106–114.

[5] British Embassy to Department of State, July 15, 1937, *Foreign Relations, 1937*, II, 52–56.

[6] Memorandum by Henry L. Deimel, Assistant Chief of Division of Trade Agreements, July 16, 1937, *Foreign Relations, 1937*, II, 57–58.

Fortunately, State Department representatives were not taken in. Optimistic about the latest British offer, they immediately briefed Cordell Hull. While still unequal to the minimum American demands, it showed considerable improvement over the April response. A statement to the press would be premature, but the future looked brighter. These men believed that Great Britain, if pushed, would move even closer to Washington's position on the essential items. Moffat reflected this reasoning when he wrote, "In the long run, the success of the Trade Agreements program will depend upon the Anglo-American treaty but if we cannot get something worth while it would be better to go down flags flying than to go down by letting an unsatisfactory agreement gradually disillusion people." Like his colleagues, he doubted that this was "the last British offer," but thought that it was rather "a final attempt to make us pay the Dominions before they start putting pressure themselves."

The Secretary of State learned also of his colleagues' attitudes regarding the inclusion of Ottawa in the negotiations, attitudes expressed orally five days later to Embassy dignitaries.[7] On July 21, Washington rejected dual negotiations as procedurally unsound and politically unwise. Too complicated and lacking precedent, they would indicate an attempt by the American government to obtain benefits in the United Kingdom for its farmers while at the same time negotiating to allow more Canadian farm products into the country. The opponents of reciprocity could hardly find a more alluring spectacle. The State Department would appear to be paying twice for one concession: in return for better treatment in Britain, the United States would have to both lower the restrictions on a British good and compensate Canada for having waived its guarantee. Washington also dismissed the suggestion that it alter the principal-supplier guide-

[7] Memorandum, Deimel to Hull, July 16, 1937, 611.4131/336; Moffat Diary, July 20, 1937, Moffat Papers, XXXIX.

line. Concessions to Canada would have to be embodied in a supplementary Canadian-American trade agreement. Finally, the State Department held that the announcement of contemplated negotiations must await settlement of the "must" list problem. Otherwise, the Dominions would be encouraged in their reluctance to release Great Britain.

The British reiterated that Canada was the principal obstacle to London's acceptance of the American requests. The United States could remove this barrier if it rewarded the senior Dominion for cooperating. The British thought this could best be accomplished through negotiation by the two governments of a new trade pact. They mentioned two items of paramount concern, lumber and apples. Producers of both commodities, with lucrative markets in the United Kingdom, would not tolerate interference with their businesses unless they were accorded more favorable treatment in the United States. Since these interests were politically well organized, the Canadian government feared the ramifications of flouting them. From the British standpoint, this thorny situation was made to order for Canadian-American negotiations.

Accepting the British argument at face value, the Americans throughout professed surprise at Dominion recalcitrance. They had expected Canada, an obvious beneficiary of any stimulation of world trade, to be most cooperative in working out solutions to the differences. The State Department spokesmen argued that enhanced purchasing power in England resulting from an Anglo-American pact would considerably profit Canadian exporters. Compensation for the Dominion, then, should come from the United Kingdom through the lowering of British preferences in Canada, enabling its negotiators to conclude other trade agreements more easily. They reminded their British counterparts of American disappointment with the Ottawa agreements. That guaranteed preferences narrowed the area of negotiation was an imperial problem, one which Washington hesitated to solve. At the end of this conversation, John A. Stirling of the Board of Trade inquired whether the United States would agree to informal and confidential "discussions" with Canada once the basis for Anglo-American negotiations had been determined. The Americans deferred their reply, but promised to answer soon.[8]

On July 23 the Department informed the British that after Anglo-American negotiations were arranged the United States would discuss, informally and confidentially, the possibility of a supplementary trade agreement with Ottawa. These conversations, however, would be confined to commercial relations between the two countries, affecting in no way the proposed Anglo-American arrangement. Concessions would be reciprocal. Although theoretically there would be no double payment for freer entry into the British market, Washington did not want the press to know that it was considering a trade agreement with an agricultural nation.[9]

Early in August, while he was in the American capital, Norman Armour discussed this entire problem with interested State Department officials. As a result, it was finally recognized that Canada was not solely responsible for holding up progress on the United States–United Kingdom trade agreement. Great Britain's hands were not so clean as its statements had suggested. At London, King and Skelton had requested Whitehall to tell them what the "non-Ottawa" proposals of the United States were, what compensation Canada could expect from the British if it acceded to modifications in the preferences, and what American concessions the Dominion could anticipate in return for imperial

[8] Memorandum by Hawkins, July 21, 1937, *Foreign Relations, 1937,* II, 58–62.

[9] Memorandum, Hawkins to Hull, July 23, 1937, 611.4131/352½; memorandum by Hawkins, July 23, 1937, *Foreign Relations, 1937,* II, 62–63.

relaxations. When Armour had left Ottawa, the Canadian government had still heard nothing.[10] At the same time, the British had informed the Americans that they had indicated to the Dominions their willingness to forfeit some of their preferences in order to allow the Dominions greater freedom to negotiate trade agreements with other countries.

This factual discrepancy took on added significance in succeeding weeks as relations between Canada and Great Britain became strained due to the feeling in Ottawa that the Cabinet had not been kept adequately informed of the Anglo-American exchanges. The episode shows that Whitehall had done little to expedite negotiations, expecting the United States to make the major contribution instead.

Upon his return to Ottawa, Armour reported that important members of the Canadian government apparently knew nothing about a British offer to the Dominions of mutual release of guaranteed preferences. Hawkins and Hickerson explored the subject immediately with Chalkley, who verified that the Canadian officials had been ignorant of the "tremendously important" proposal. Norman Robertson had discussed it in London, but he had not passed on the information to his superiors. The situation had now been corrected and the minutes of the meeting at which the offer was made were brought directly to King's attention.

Skelton related a slightly different and more accurate version. When pressed by Ottawa, the British admitted that at the Imperial Conference they had presented a more specific proposal to the South Africans, New Zealanders, and Australians than to the Canadians. Skelton confirmed that a Board of Trade official had indicated in "somewhat vague terms" to Robertson and Pearson "that the British might be disposed to consider favorably and at some future date the idea of giving up certain of the

[10] Moffat Diary, Aug. 3, 1937, Moffat Papers, XXXIX.

margins of preference they now enjoy if this would be of assistance to Canada in negotiations with the United States and other countries." At the time, Robertson, one of the most astute and perceptive individuals in the Department of External Affairs, had attached little significance to the remark, interpreting it as a private, rather than an official, proposal. His feeling was strengthened when, at a later gathering of Canadian and British Ministers, nothing was said about it. The "misunderstanding had now been cleared up," but Skelton "still insisted that the British proposal was hypothetical, would have effect only at some future date and would be virtually useless as a concession of the nature to satisfy public opinion in Canada that it was compensation for what they would be giving up."

The wounded pride and frayed tempers that followed were captured well by Moffat when he wrote to Norman Davis, "Mackenzie King is angry both with the British and with ourselves that the two of us are trying to throw the onus of a failure to reach a meeting of minds on Canada, when the true cause should be found elsewhere." The Canadian Prime Minister, Moffat continued, was fortunately "more angry with the British than with ourselves and [told Armour] . . . henceforth he would insist on the British putting things in writing." On another occasion, Moffat, noting that "the British virtually admitted that they were at fault," interpreted the "whole episode . . . [as] indicative of a lack of seriousness to date." [11]

King was irritated further at this same time by another British maneuver that to him smacked of Anglo-American coercion. In a letter to the Canadian Governor-General, Lindsay had apparently "used fairly strong language" admonishing Canada to do

[11] Memorandum by Armour, Aug. 9, 1937, *ibid.*, XII; Moffat to Dunn, Aug. 7, 1937, *ibid.*; Moffat Diary, Aug. 9, 1937, *ibid.*, XXXIX; Moffat to Davis, Aug. 10, 1937, Davis Papers, Box 41; memorandum by Hickerson, Aug. 6, 1937, *Foreign Relations, 1937*, II, 63–64.

the things necessary for a trade agreement. When shown this letter by Lord Tweedsmuir, King reacted sharply to the "blackmail" he thought it contained.[12]

The channels between London and Ottawa were not yet clear in early August, when the Canadians intensified their efforts to make the negotiations trilateral. In a letter to Armour, King explained that to avoid embarrassing the United States while the Anglo-American discussions were continuing, Ottawa had not pressed trade talks with Washington. A recent communication from Great Britain, however, had urged his government to enter the picture. The British thought the added dimension would "facilitate rather than interfere" with their labors. King stipulated that unless the United States approved, he would not raise the question; but if Washington were agreeable to concurrent parleys, Ottawa was ready to begin studies to ascertain whether formal negotiations were feasible. He left no doubt of his personal inclinations, espousing the belief that the trilateral approach was the proper medium to clarify the Canadian position.[13]

The misunderstanding was glaring. The United States had agreed to informal exchanges with Canada, but they were to begin only after Washington and London had officially launched negotiations. Even then the Canadian-American discussions would ostensibly center on mutual concessions. Perhaps the British had not been forceful enough in their explanations to the Canadians. More likely, King, recognizing the political repercussions that would follow if the Dominion were left out of the negotiations and having seen nothing tangible from Whitehall in the form of compensation, intended to keep as many fences

[12] Armour to Secretary of State, no. 1647, Oct. 1, 1937, 611.4131/382.

[13] King to Armour, Aug. 7, 1937, *Foreign Relations, 1937,* II, 160–161.

mended as he could. He wanted the Canadian voter to believe that Dominion interests would be adequately compensated for any relaxations in the United Kingdom tariff; broadening the negotiations to include Canada might avert a "credibility gap." By King's own admission, his government, not the British, had taken the initiative. Only recently, in fact, had London consented to the bilateral conversations.

Whatever the explanation, the tactic bore fruit. The Anglo-American talks were still stalemated, but on August 12 the United States agreed to begin preliminaries. In order to keep them general, Washington preferred to deal with Skelton and Robertson rather than with the technical experts.[14] The intradepartmental sparring that lay behind this decision throws some light on policy formulation. The group that finally prevailed paid much attention to public sentiment in the Dominion. According to Armour, the Canadians were acutely sensitive over two related matters: the American expectation that the Dominion would cooperate in making possible an agreement with the United Kingdom, and the "distinct feeling that Canada [had] been 'put on the spot' through a somewhat rigid application [to Canadian-American negotiations] of the 'red-green' 'stop-go' system of traffic regulations." Skelton had expressed doubt that the State Department comprehended fully the implications for relations between their two countries that would follow if the United States insisted upon Canadian concessions without adequate compensation in the American market. Privately he told Armour that although he himself questioned the wisdom of King's letter, he hoped very much that Washington would reply favorably to the Prime Minister's suggestion.

Hull, who frowned on King's idea, was "all for continuing to

[14] Armour to Hickerson, Aug. 8, 1937, 611.4231/2025; Secretary of State to Armour, no. 937, Aug. 12, 1937, *Foreign Relations, 1937*, II, 161–164.

deal in generalities and to point out once again [to King] . . .
that ever since the [trade agreement of 1935] . . . we had gone
on making other trade agreements and liberalizing our situation
in spite of protests of industrial and agricultural lobbyists . . .
[while Canada] had only made two further agreements." Hickerson, Hawkins, and Moffat argued against further "preaching"
and finally carried the day with their contention that a trip to
Washington by Skelton and Robertson was "essential." Two
weeks later, King, after "a good deal of talk," consented to a short
and secret visit by Skelton to the American capital. Differences
among the Cabinet members made the Canadian Under Secretary wary, even though no one in Ottawa or the Canadian
Legation would know of it. In spite of the political risk, he
agreed to make the hurried trip on August 27 and 28.[15]

The lack of progress in the talks between the United States
and Britain greatly disturbed Hull, who foresaw more political
turmoil in the world if the trade pact were delayed much longer.
Apparently only this instrument, and others like it that would
assuredly follow, might prevent "70 million hungry Germans
from going on the march when they become sufficiently destitute
. . . [or] an economic collapse and cave-in, beginning in the
German area, within another two years." Speaking to Chalkley
in August before the latter's departure from Washington for a
vacation in England, the Secretary focused on the need for "all
possible speed" in concluding reciprocity. The impending agreement almost acquired an air of omnipotence. Without elab-
orating, Hull argued that had an accord been reached earlier, sym-
bolizing the economic and political solidarity of the two nations,
it "would undoubtedly have had a stabilizing effect" on the
situations in China and Spain. He predicted that Japan would
press on toward economic domination in Asia, an aggression that

[15] Memorandum by Armour, Aug. 9, 1937, Moffat Papers, XII; Moffat
Diary, Aug. 11, 1937, *ibid.*, XXXIX; Moffat Diary, Aug. 25, 1937, *ibid.*

only joint Anglo-American action could check. A trade agreement was essential to greater political collaboration between Washington and London.[16]

The British government, supposedly "most anxious" to conclude the pact, devoted the major part of five Cabinet meetings in late August and early September to the topic. Unfortunately the Dominions, and particularly Canada, could not easily be moved, and Whitehall found this sluggishness to be a convenient excuse. "The discussions of the British representatives in Canada with Mackenzie King were conducted with considerable heat," related one authoritative observer, "and London felt that they would have to give him opportunity to cool off before pressing the matter again."[17]

Stepping up the pace of the discussions was important, but Hull sought also to dispel any British misconceptions concerning their tripartite nature. On September 22 he requested certain members of the Embassy to meet with him. During the talks that followed, the Chargé d'affaires placed the responsibility for initiating further action on the United States. His government was awaiting the conclusion of the Canadian-American "negotiations" as well as the receipt of the promised "non-Ottawa" concessions desired by Washington. The Americans present, unwilling to accept that interpretation, asserted that the British for some time had pointed to the forthcoming election in Australia as the cause of the delay and had never raised the Canadian-American contingency. Furthermore, they reminded the visitors that at the moment there technically were no negotiations with Canada, but rather only exploratory conversations. Hull reaffirmed that the United States would not pay twice for an Anglo-

[16] Memorandum by Hull, Aug. 9, 1937, *Foreign Relations, 1937,* II, 65–66.

[17] Grady to Hull, Sept. 11, 1937, Hull Papers. The source of the remarks was Sir Frederick Leith-Ross.

American agreement. He would lessen the political load of Mackenzie King by discussing a trade pact, but the State Department would not compensate Canada in that arrangement for any releases granted the United Kingdom. The Secretary of State felt that "the countries which made the Ottawa Agreements must themselves be responsible for the relaxing of their provisions." [18]

The debate continued the next day. Talking with Assistant Secretary of State Francis B. Sayre, the Chargé contended that his government could proceed no further until Canada had yielded its preferential rights. Only the United States, through concessions to the Dominion, could make this possible. Sayre stated anew that politically the administration "would be blown higher than a kite" if it negotiated with Canada, or any agricultural nation, before it was assured of a trade agreement with an industrial power. The farm community could be appeased in no other way. The United States, declared Sayre, "could not afford to live in a fool's paradise," but "must be realistic and look facts in the face, that it would be folly to negotiate a trade agreement only to see it blown to pieces by a sufficient political opposition generated by failure to keep political conditions in mind." The problem was "how to get around the difficulty that we could not enter into negotiations with Canada until after we had positive assurances that the Canadians would relinquish their preferential rights in the United Kingdom." According to Sayre, initial talks with Skelton had produced no answer. In any case, the next move was Ottawa's.

When the participants turned to the deadlock in the Anglo-American exchanges, Sayre adhered to the standard line. Hull had predicted in January, obviously to no avail, that a revised

[18] Memorandum by William Butterworth, Second Secretary of Embassy in the United Kingdom, temporarily in the United States, Sept. 22, 1937, *Foreign Relations, 1937*, II, 66–68.

Anglo-Canadian accord would complicate matters. Modifications were now the responsibility of Great Britain and Canada, not of the United States. The Assistant Secretary stressed that the United States wanted complete satisfaction on its "Ottawa" list prior to formal negotiations. The more flexible "non-Ottawa" requests would be ready the following week for study by London.[19] On September 28 the State Department submitted this list of commodities.[20]

Undeniably, the government in Ottawa was an important cause of the delay in both Anglo- and Canadian-American negotiations. Mackenzie King was slow to decide whether to relax Dominion preferences in the English market, to ascertain what compensation to seek if he did so, and to settle on the framework of negotiations with the United States. Sir Francis Floud, the British High Commissioner in Canada, provided Norman Armour with key insights into the Dominion picture. The immediate occasion for his remarks was an international peace broadcast which featured speeches by Hull, Eden, and King.[21] The British Foreign Secretary had stated his "hope that it may be found possible for the United Kingdom . . . before very long to reach

[19] Memorandum by Sayre, Sept. 23, 1937, *Foreign Relations, 1937*, II, 68–71.

[20] Department of State to British Embassy, Sept. 28, 1937, *Foreign Relations, 1937*, II, 72.

[21] This international symposium, sponsored by the National Peace Conference, was broadcast on Sunday, September 19, 1937. One of the major points made by Hull was that "through enlarged trade there can come an equilibrium of peaceful interest more stable than the equilibrium of matched cannon and airplanes." The full text of Hull's remarks, plus reference to other speeches, appears in New York *Times,* Sept. 20, 1937. King's address is reported more completely in Toronto *Globe and Mail,* Sept. 20, 1937. His strongest statement in an otherwise noncommital speech was that "there surely lies an effective means of avoiding further widespread, if not world-wide, civil and international strife. In economic cooperation there also exists a means of bringing into being a world order which holds within itself some promise of an enduring peace."

an agreement with the United States for the reduction of customs duties on a most-favored-nation basis. Such an agreement would surely redound not only to our own advantage but to that of the whole world." Floud took some of the credit for Eden's favorable reference to an Anglo-American arrangement, claiming that he had wired him the advice to include that section in the statement after learning of doubts that were being entertained in London. In his speech King had talked in general terms, expressing Canadian interest in trade expansion and observing that his government employed no quotas, exchange restrictions, or embargoes except on the arms traffic. Terming this address "vague," the British official professed surprise and disappointment that the Prime Minister had omitted any mention of the Anglo-American accord.

Informed people knew that the politically careful Prime Minister preferred to sidestep divisive issues. Unfortunately, he could not so easily dodge contemporary domestic difficulties; thus he had remained undecided in late September and early October. A break between King and Mitchell Hepburn, the Premier of Ontario, and its possible effect on the future of the Liberal party gave him pause. This schism began in October, 1935, when Hepburn recoiled after his counsel for the selection of Cabinet members had not been sought. It grew in intensity throughout 1936 as the two differed over the St. Lawrence Seaway project and culminated in June of 1937 with the Ontario politician's declaration that he was no longer a Mackenzie King Liberal. Henceforth, of even greater concern to Ottawa, Hepburn and Maurice Duplessis, the Union Nationale Premier of Quebec, cooperated more closely. King's attempt to repair this breach through Ian Mackenzie, the Minister of National Defense, had already met an "emphatic rebuff" from Toronto.

Equally important to the Prime Minister was the lack of unity and teamwork within the Cabinet, particularly Dunning's continued opposition to Canadian granting of British requests. The Finance Minister apparently felt strongly enough about the issue that he considered resigning if the result were not to his liking. Late in July he had expressed interest in an appointment to a prospective Royal Commission. He wrote to King, "It is more than normally difficult in these times for a Minister of Finance to do what he deems to be his duty & at the same time to continue to be a political asset to his party." Dunning continued, "[I] tried to do my duty as I see it & am not blind to the many evidences that my value to the party in a political sense has lessened. . . . It may well be that your difficulties in supporting me may become insurmountable." [22] Rivalry between the Department of Finance and the Department of Trade and Commerce strengthened King's inclination to do nothing and thus avoid greater trouble within the government.

The Cabinet did appoint a committee to study and then report on possible changes in the trade agreements with the United Kingdom and the United States. The entire Cabinet had to approve this report, which afforded the dissident elements another opportunity to delay matters. If final action were deferred until after the return from Geneva of the more cooperative J. L. Ilsley, the Minister of National Revenue, additional time would be lost. Given the various factors, Floud doubted that King would do much, but promised to press the Prime Minister in subsequent meetings to expedite the decisions.

On October 1, a week later, Floud related to Armour the contents of the previous day's conversation with King. The committee appointed by the Cabinet—Dana Wilgress, Hector McKinnon, and Norman Robertson—had completed enough work that they could go to Washington to meet State Department officials. The United States had wanted just Robertson to

[22] Dunning to King, July 21, 1937, Charles A. Dunning Papers, Queen's University.

engage in these preliminaries, but King found that course difficult, intimating clashes between Charles Dunning's and William Euler's departments in the Cabinet. Floud concluded that
King, who placed party unity above all, seemed increasingly
unable to take affirmative action on the controversial trade pacts.
Apparently the Prime Minister was lukewarm even about Robertson's going to Washington, preferring Wilgress of the Department of Trade and Commerce and McKinnon of Finance to
handle the exploratory talks. He yielded on that point but still
remained reluctant to make the larger decision.

The British High Commissioner turned again to Dunning's
role. Since Floud and Dunning were good friends, he probably
presented the Finance Minister's case conservatively. At any
rate, Floud indicated quite clearly that Dunning was the "stumbling block" who rebelled at Canada's relinquishing the "substance" of a lucrative market for Canadian exports to Great
Britain in favor of the "shadow" of possible concessions by the
United States. In his arguments, Dunning emphasized that a
subsequent administration in Washington might scuttle the entire American reciprocity program.[23]

Despite such gloomy predictions, the American Minister in
Ottawa was somewhat hopeful. As he interpreted public opinion
in Canada, the government would receive considerable support
if it acceded to the release of its preferences. Canadians were
increasingly aware of the long-range benefits to their country of
an Anglo-American agreement, as well as of other accords be-

---

[23] For a discussion of the King-Hepburn schism, as it affected the
Seaway struggle, and particularly for the development of the Hepburn-
Duplessis "axis," see William R. Willoughby, *The St. Lawrence Waterway: A Study in Politics and Diplomacy* (Madison, Wisc., 1961),
165–180, and Hutchison, *The Incredible Canadian,* 236. For the conversations with Floud, see Armour to Secretary of State, no. 1634, Sept. 24,
1937, 611.4131/378, and Armour to Secretary of State, no. 1647, Oct. 1,
1937, 611.4131/382.

tween Commonwealth nations and the United States. They were confident also that Canada would be compensated immediately by Great Britain and eventually by a revised Canadian-American pact. Given King's inclinations and abilities to gauge public sentiment before making major decisions, Armour thought that progress might yet be made.[24] Despite the divergent pressures on the Prime Minister and his natural disposition to procrastinate, he could delay a decision only so long. Time was running out.

On October 14, King told the American Minister that the Canadian government was ready to send its representatives to Washington for the informal exchanges. More outgoing than he had been when Armour had seen him recently, the Prime Minister professed his desire to further the conclusion of an Anglo-American agreement and his confidence in the good faith of State Department officials to carry him past political difficulties at home. Later in the day, Norman Robertson announced that he planned to arrive in the American capital with Dana Wilgress and Hector McKinnon on October 18.[25]

Washington's acceptance constituted another concession to King's political foibles and British disinterest. By including the technical experts the Prime Minister hoped to assure Dunning and other dissidents that Canada would not abandon precipitately a lucrative market. Their presence also meant that discussions would be much broader in scope than originally envisaged by the State Department. The talks covered a wide range of topics, including the items on the "Ottawa" list sent by the United States to the United Kingdom. Within a few days, the Canadians were back in Ottawa, where Robertson reported that

[24] Armour to Secretary of State, no. 1634, Sept. 24, 1937, 611.4131/378.

[25] Armour to Secretary of State, no. 1662, Oct. 14, 1937, *Foreign Relations, 1937*, II, 164–166.

nothing more could be accomplished for three or four weeks, pending analysis of the information left in Washington. In Great Britain forces friendly to an Anglo-American arrangement worried that the broadened range of the Canadian-American discussions might produce further Cabinet delays. Their fear was that opponents of a pact would regard the talks between Washington and Ottawa as evidence that the two parties themselves were tackling the difficulties.[26]

Apparently willing to entertain any proposal that conceivably would launch negotiations with Whitehall, State Department officials momentarily flirted with their most radical scheme. They suggested bringing representatives of all the Dominions to Washington, where the United States and the Commonwealth countries collectively could attack, and hopefully settle, their annoying problems. What might happen at an "Ottawa Conference in Washington" horrified the British. With the spectacle of 1932 in mind, they had visions of logrolling by the Dominions which would ultimately force the United Kingdom to accept concessions that threatened its preferential position in Dominion markets. To avoid this collusion, the members of the Empire must be kept out of the American capital. Because of their special relations, Britain had accepted, albeit under pressure, the concurrent negotiations between the United States and Canada. The frightening plan calling for simultaneous multilateral negotiations was an entirely different proposition. Two days later the British grudgingly agreed to yield if the Secretary of State felt strongly enough about it. The best way to kill the American suggestion, however, was to present an attractive substitute—new proposals that would provide the basis for formal negotiations. With this knowledge, the United States viewed

[26] Bingham to Secretary of State, telegram no. 671, Oct. 27, 1937, *Foreign Relations, 1937*, II, 73–74; Hickerson to Moffat, Nov. 2, 1937, Moffat Papers, XII.

multilateral discussions less favorably. To the relief of White-hall, it let the idea die.[27]

In the meantime, Chamberlain had informed each Dominion Prime Minister personally of the latest offers which the United Kingdom planned to make to the State Department and added that he expected cooperation from the Dominion. In London, Robert Bingham had learned of this development directly from Sir William Brown, the Permanent Under Secretary of the Board of Trade, along with the prediction that the British position would still lack what Washington had stipulated as the basis for negotiation. While defending the proposed concessions as the best that they could grant at the moment, Brown intimated that the formal negotiations might be more productive. Certain members of the Cabinet, fearing political reprisals from special interests, had balked at even these proposals.[28]

As the preliminaries dragged on without any perceptible change, both Hull and Sayre had become, in the words of one observer, "rather discouraged." In the words of another, the Secretary was "in a positively savage frame of mind about the dilatory tactics of the British. He said that he was not at all sure that the time was not about ripe to say [to them] . . . that if they did not want to play the game our way they could go to hell." At this point, "events took place with rather dramatic suddenness."[29] On November 5 the British Embassy submitted the proposals to the State Department, urging Washington to accept them so that negotiations could begin. The offers were provisional; Dominion authorities had to concur. When announcing that it would abolish the tariff on wheat, an export of

[27] *Ibid.;* Bingham to Secretary of State, telegram no. 678, Oct. 29, 1937, *Foreign Relations, 1937,* II, 76–77.

[28] Bingham to Secretary of State, telegram no. 678, Oct. 29, 1937, *Foreign Relations, 1937,* II, 76–77.

[29] Sayre to Phillips, Dec. 2, 1937, Sayre Papers, Box 5; Hickerson to Moffat, Nov. 2, 1937, Moffat Papers, XII.

which the United States was not the principal supplier, the United Kingdom stated that it expected Washington to reciprocate on reasonable requests of benefit to some other part of the Empire.

Taking everything into account, London felt that it had "gone to the extreme limit on these items," since it faced serious enough political problems as it was. On the same day, the President of the Board of Trade emphasized to Bingham that all members of the British Cabinet hoped the proposals would be accepted as a basis for negotiations by Washington. He wanted the American Ambassador to know that the government greatly desired a trade agreement and had done everything possible to arrange one. Brown reiterated this theme several days later. He also volunteered that in a reply to Chamberlain's recent letter, Mackenzie King had indicated that Canada would not be recalcitrant. The Dominion was the key. If the United States could satisfy Ottawa in discussions so that it would waive its preferences, Great Britain, still haunted by the specter of an imperial gathering, would "bear the responsibility of exerting the pressure" on the other members of the Commonwealth. A posture of unity among the United States, Canada, and the United Kingdom would leave Australia no alternative but to cooperate.[30]

Thus, in mid-November it was Washington's turn to make a major decision. Although they had given explicit assurance that additional concessions could be anticipated, the British had not accepted all of the American "must" requests. The Dominions had not released them from prior commitments; to accommodate Canada, the United States would have to engage in three-way bargaining. These considerations were offset by the increased

[30] British Embassy to Department of State, Nov. 5, 1937, *Foreign Relations, 1937,* II, 78–80; Bingham to Secretary of State, telegram no. 700, Nov. 5, 1937, *ibid.,* 81; Bingham to Secretary of State, telegram no. 711, Nov. 11, 1937, *ibid.,* 81–83.

political and economic urgency of an agreement. United Kingdom markets were beckoning, and the British in the past few months had indicated that they would modify substantially the preference system, the principal obstacle to the enhanced sale of goods to "cousins Jonathan." Influenced particularly by the recession in the United States, London had pressed for immediate announcement of negotiations. If too much time passed and the economic setback worsened, London would have greater political difficulty in making attractive to the English people the prospect of negotiating with a country whose purchasing power was declining.[31]

Hardest to assess is the role of the disorder then overtaking Europe and the Far East. The Japanese thrust into China proper, begun in earnest in July, continued with no signs of abatement. The Brussels Conference, called to deal with the China Incident, was in session when the announcements regarding the trade agreements were made. On November 6, Italy adhered to the Anti-Comintern Pact, marking closer cooperation with Germany and Japan. Hull felt that delay could only cause more trouble for the entire world, whereas disaster might yet be averted if significant economic steps were taken. At least the United States and Great Britain would be more closely aligned to meet further threats. The Secretary later told the British Ambassador that the world was "on fire" and unless those who shared common desires to protect "the precious things of our civilization" supported something practical like the trade revival program, "we may be too late." [32] Neville Chamberlain gave this political motivation at least recognition when in November he wrote, "The reason why I have been prepared (*pace* Amery and Page Croft) to go a long way to get this treaty is precisely

[31] Hull to Roosevelt, Nov. 15, 1937, 611.4131/418.
[32] Memorandum by Sayre, Nov. 16, 1937, *Foreign Relations, 1937*, II, 83–85.

because I reckoned it would help to educate American opinion to act more and more with us, and because I felt sure it would frighten the totalitarians. Coming at this moment, it looks just like an answer to the Berlin-Rome-Tokyo axis." At approximately the same time the Prime Minister revealed to Runciman his aspiration to conclude an agreement: "There is nothing in the world I so much desire as a closer understanding with the United States and the President." [33]

Journalists read greater political meaning into the announcement than it deserved. A case in point was the observation that it coincided with Lord Halifax's trip to Germany for talks with Hitler. The record shows clearly that trade agreement negotiations played no role whatsoever in either the origins of this meeting or the subsequent conversations. Halifax, if less enthusiastically than Chamberlain, favored political rapprochement with Germany, and he went to Berchtesgaden to ascertain the conditions necessary to such a settlement. In his apologia, published in 1957, Halifax wrote that the immediate origin of his trip was an invitation from Hermann Goering "to attend a hunting exhibition in Berlin," and to shoot foxes following its closing. Halifax forwarded this invitation to Eden, informing the Foreign Secretary of his intention to accept. A short time later, Eden told Halifax "quite sincerely that he was not sure whether it might not be of some advantage for [Halifax] to go to Germany under this cover." The meeting of Halifax, Eden, and Chamberlain which followed resulted in the future Foreign Secretary's political discussions with der Fuehrer. [34]

Eden's account of the origins of the visit differs only slightly.

[33] Feiling, *Chamberlain*, 308; Runciman to Roosevelt, Feb. 18, 1938, Roosevelt Papers.

[34] For the Halifax-Hitler talks and their supposed relationship to the announcement of November 17, see New York *Times*, Nov. 20, 1937. For the Halifax explanation, see his *Fullness of Days* (New York, 1957), 185–193.

As he recalled the affair, when he learned of the invitation from the German Hunting Association for Halifax to attend the International Sporting Exhibition and his colleague's decision to accept, he "was not eager, but saw no sufficient reason to oppose it." He believed that Halifax wanted to go to Germany and that Chamberlain was similarly disposed. His analysis of subsequent developments, however, is more complete and meaningful. Eden wanted the British government to avoid the impression that the initiative for the visit had come from London, fearing that "we shall appear to be running" after Hitler. On November 6 he learned that Hitler would see Halifax not in Berlin, but at Berchtesgaden. On this same day, Italy, Japan, and Germany announced the enlarged Anti-Comintern Pact, prompting Eden's telegram to London: "From point of view of our position in Europe and public opinion at home it is essential to avoid giving the impression of our being in pursuit of German Chancellor." Following a telephone conversation with the Foreign Secretary, Lord Cranborne relayed these same views to Chamberlain, but to no avail. In Eden's words, "The Prime Minister, however, clearly had great expectations of the visit and said he was most anxious that it should take place. I think he had the idea that the Foreign Office was unduly hostile to Hitler's Germany. . . . He hoped for better results from personal contacts." [35]

One conclusion is inescapable. Halifax's visit with Hitler was not an attempt to impress upon him strong British opposition to his plans, an opposition that would be made more formidable by the announcement of forthcoming Anglo-American trade negotiations, signalling political solidarity between the two countries. Anglo-American reciprocity never entered into the actual talks. [36]

[35] Eden, *Facing the Dictators*, 576–585.

[36] For the content of the actual talks, see Halifax, *Fullness of Days*, 186–192, and *Foreign Relations, 1937*, I, 196–202. The most recent discussion is Harold Macmillan, *Winds of Change, 1914–1939* (New York, 1966), 477–478.

As they sought to avert a calamitous war, Chamberlain and his followers placed greater faith in appeasement of Germany than in closer political relations with the United States. The notion that Anglo-American trade negotiations were conscious attempts to build a barrier to Axis expansion was largely the creation of journalists. Secretary of State Hull certainly entertained this ambition, but London did not reciprocate. Chamberlain wanted the accord and saw political overtones in it. These advantages were so limited, however, that a trade pact was thought to be no substitute for a European policy designed to placate Hitler and preserve the peace.

On November 16, Hull told Sir Ronald Lindsay that the United States accepted the proposals and would make immediate announcement of contemplated negotiations. He recorded that the Ambassador "was visibly moved—immense relief and satisfaction was written all over his face." The Secretary emphasized that the list fell short of American requests and that substantial revision in this respect must precede a final instrument. The two governments could afford no further delay, however, for as Hull remarked, "Unless negotiations are promptly initiated, various circumstances will make difficult, if not impossible, the conclusion of any agreement." The United States was also ready, if Canada agreed, to make public within two weeks of the Anglo-American statement the prospective negotiation of a new trade arrangement with the Dominion.[37]

The next day the British formally concurred, and the Secretary of State briefed the American Minister in Ottawa. Hull instructed Armour to tell King of American wishes to announce plans for Canadian-American trade negotiations. The State Department was studying the Canadian proposals which had been

[37] Memorandum by Sayre, Nov. 16, 1937, *Foreign Relations, 1937*, II, 83–85; Department of State to British Embassy, Nov. 16, 1937, *ibid.*, 85.

left in Washington, and although they presented some problems, efforts would be made to conclude as comprehensive an agreement as was politically feasible. The American accords with the United Kingdom and Canada, when reached, could be signed the same day.[38]

For political reasons the Canadian government wanted the shortest interval possible to lapse between the two announcements.[39] On November 18 the State Department disclosed its project to negotiate an Anglo-American agreement, and on the following day the public learned of the contemplated Canadian-American negotiations.[40] Chamberlain had the most dramatic opportunity of anyone to announce the diplomatic coup. Questioned in Parliament by Clement Attlee about the progress of the discussions, the Prime Minister replied that he was "very happy to be able to inform the House that the informal and exploratory

[38] Memorandum by Hawkins, Nov. 17, 1937, *Foreign Relations, 1937*, II, 86–87; Secretary of State to Armour, no. 114, Nov. 17, 1937, *ibid.*, 166–167.

[39] Armour to Secretary of State, no. 1735, Nov. 19, 1937, 611.4231/2071. He wrote, "Robertson's other point was that the interval between the announcement of our negotiations with the United Kingdom and those with Canada should be as short as possible, as otherwise he was afraid that a hue-and-cry would be raised here, both by the opposition press and by those interests opposed to any giving up of United Kingdom preferences. . . . Mr. King also mentioned the importance of having as little time as possible elapse. . . . If a week elapsed and then announcement were made of negotiations with Canada, the opposition and critics of the Government might then attempt to put forward the argument that this announcement had been decided upon only as a result of this outcry."

[40] The Anglo-American announcement is in Department of State, *Press Releases*, XVIII (Nov. 20, 1937), no. 425, pp. 383–388; the Canadian-American one is in *ibid.*, 388–393. For King's statement in Ottawa, see Armour to Secretary of State, telegram no. 103, Nov. 18, 1937, *Foreign Relations, 1937*, II, 167.

discussions . . . have now reached a point at which . . . [the two governments] feel able to announce that negotiations for such an agreement are contemplated." [41]

Most Canadians welcomed the news. Liberal papers particularly applauded the proposed negotiations, arguing that the benefits that would accrue to the Dominion would more than offset the losses sustained in the English market. The Winnipeg *Free Press* insisted, "Mr. Mackenzie King deserves every credit" for the development, and "The importance of such an agreement is one which transcends all considerations of petty, sectional interests which superficially might be regarded as being injured by the wider scope of the larger plan." [42] Nor did the political implications slip by unnoticed. According to the interpretation of the Toronto *Globe and Mail*, "An agreement that could have the effect of lowering tariff walls and eliminating at least the extremes of economic nationalism is certain to have some influence on the political relations of the nations. It is the collaboration that can be had in this field that encourages, or should encourage, all parties to give the most that it is reasonable and practical to ask." [43]

The papers in British Columbia and the Maritimes, reflecting lumber and fruit growers' interests, lamented the loss of a dependable market for an undependable one. In its editorials the Vancouver *Daily Province* contended, "British Columbia can only oppose, with every means at her command, the suggestion that she should be made a sacrificial goat in the interests of an international betterment," and "There is something mighty difficult for British Columbia to understand in the idea . . . that we

[41] Great Britain, 329 *H. C. Deb.* 5 s., 579.

[42] The favorable press comment is discussed in Armour to Secretary of State, no. 1766, Dec. 10, 1937, 611.4131/566. For the quote in the text, see Winnipeg *Free Press*, Nov. 20, 1937.

[43] Toronto *Globe and Mail*, Nov. 19, 1937.

shall stop selling our lumber in London so that the State of Washington can sell hers there, and then, to make up for what we have lost, sell our lumber instead to the United States." [44] Others, reflecting a certain anti-American bias, frowned at the weakening of the Empire preference system. The Ottawa *Journal* feared that Washington's proposed cooperation with Great Britain, by providing ammunition to "isolationists" in the United States, might enervate rather than strengthen Anglo-American unity.[45] Richard B. Bennett, sensing perhaps that this issue might be the answer to his party's flagging political fortunes, called upon Canadians to "bring all the pressure in [their] power" to prevent the loss of British preferences. They "cannot be lost," he continued, "unless the Prime Minister agrees." [46] Some Conservative papers, notably the Montreal *Gazette,* approved the announcement, preferring to reserve final judgment until further information was known.[47]

In Great Britain the public reports were very well received. Most of the influential sheets—the *Times,* the *Daily Telegraph,* the *Daily Herald,* and the *Economist*—supported the planned negotiations. Newspaper editors, however, generally played down the political motivation behind the decisions. The Canadian journalist, Grant Dexter, writing from London, was an exception. He asserted, quite erroneously, "Undoubtedly the driving force in Britain behind today's announcement . . . is political rather than economic. Nothing is more deeply desired by the British Government in the present perilous conditions in Europe and the Far East than an Anglo-Saxon world front against aggressive dictatorships. It is realized that public opinion

[44] Vancouver *Daily Province,* Nov. 20 and 22, 1937.

[45] Ottawa *Journal,* Nov. 20, 1937.

[46] *Ibid.;* the address was made in Halifax, Nova Scotia, on November 19.

[47] Armour to Secretary of State, no. 1766, Dec. 10, 1937, 611.4131/566.

in the United States is not ready for such a common front, and every effort is being made to discourage comments at this end which would be deemed likely to alarm the United States people." It would be left to the American government to determine whether a "common front" would ensue. "From the British viewpoint," he concluded, "nothing could be more desirable. Indeed it is agreed that the present world trend would be entirely altered by such an event." [48] The *Sunday Times* went so far as to say, "[The] political value strikes us as so considerable that for its sake Great Britain might be justified in driving a less favorable bargain than economic calculations alone would warrant." [49] But most papers went no further than to acknowledge that the United Kingdom and the United States had made an important cooperative gesture.

Privately, Britishers were less reticent. Some were reported by the American Chargé in London to have said, "America's isolation is now a thing of the past; the trade agreement is the thin end of the wedge; the United States will be led to cooperate with the United Kingdom not only in the economic and financial field but eventually in policing the world." At the very least, it was quite common to regard the proposed trade pacts as the democracies' answer to the Axis threat to western Europe. [50] In December the Gallup pollsters in Great Britain found that of those people interviewed, 68 per cent "would like to see a trade agreement with the United States," whereas 2 per cent would not, and 30 per cent were indifferent. [51] The leading dissenter was Leopold S.

[48] For quotes from London papers, see *Literary Digest*, CXXIV (Dec. 4, 1937), 8. Grant Dexter's article appeared in the Toronto *Globe and Mail*, Nov. 19, 1937.

[49] *Sunday Times* (London), Nov. 21, 1937.

[50] Herschel V. Johnson to Secretary of State, no. 3610, Nov. 24, 1937, 611.4131/521.

[51] George Gallup and Claude Robinson, "American Institute of Public Opinion—Surveys, 1935–38," *Public Opinion Quarterly*, II (July, 1938), 395.

Amery, one of the architects of the Ottawa agreements. Several days after the announcement, the Imperial Economic Union, an organization that he headed, published a report entitled "The Fiscal Situation Today." Through this publication the group declared its opposition to any relaxation of imperial trade preferences and demanded that "British agriculture be safeguarded from undue competition" which would follow revision of the Ottawa treaties. The report warned, "Renewed efforts are being made in some quarters to use the discussions now in progress for an Anglo-American trade agreement as an excuse for an indirect attempt to discredit and weaken the tried and proved national Imperial policy." [52] Amery's pleas, it must be stressed, represented a minority.

Newspapers like the New York *Times* and the Washington *Post* [53] endorsed the proposed accords, and a few months later the American Institute of Public Opinion showed that 73 per cent of Americans polled approved "Secretary Hull's policy in seeking a reciprocal trade agreement with Great Britain." An identical number responded positively to the question, "If Great Britain reduced tariffs on American goods, should we reduce tariffs on British goods?" [54] Not surprisingly, however, dissenting voices in the United States were also raised. Spokesmen in New England, fearing competition from textile companies in Great Britain, were the most vocal. Senator Henry Cabot Lodge even announced his plan to ask Congress to halt the reciprocal trade

[52] Ottawa *Journal,* Nov. 22, 1937; *Times* (London), Nov. 22, 1937.

[53] The New York *Times,* Nov. 19, 1937, referred to the announcement of negotiations between the United Kingdom and the United States as "important news and good news. There is a large amount of trade at stake. But, more than this, it seems certain that any step which strengthened the economic ties between the two most powerful democracies would have a stabilizing influence in all parts of the world." The *Post*'s editorial position was noted in *Literary Digest,* CXXIV (Dec. 4, 1937), 8.

[54] Gallup and Robinson, "American Institute of Public Opinion—Surveys, 1935–38," 386.

program pending an inquiry into its effects on the American economy.[55] But the threat of competition alone does not explain this opposition. Certain papers hit a responsive chord among Anglophobic Americans when they noted the political ramifications of the proposed agreement. Referring to the First World War period, the New York *Daily Mirror* contended that "we opened a friendly ear to English propaganda. This country drifted into war. It is happening again." The Springfield (Mass.) *Republican* was of the opinion that "there is a special danger to be avoided if the treaty is to have the backing" of the American people. "It will be most unfortunate," continued the *Republican*'s editor, "if the impression should prevail that part of the bargain is political support of British diplomacy and British political undertakings in various parts of the world." [56]

Thus, after many months of effort, another plateau had been reached in the drive for the trade program's most important agreement. Although Chamberlain doubted that the pact would markedly change the political situation in the world, he and Eden had overcome internal opposition or indifference, the resistance of vested economic interests in Great Britain, and the reluctance of the Dominions to relinquish their favorable positions in the United Kingdom market. The presentation of a "must" list of concessions by the United States had made their task no easier.[57] Mackenzie King had overcome dissension within

[55] An Associated Press dispatch carried the story about Lodge, who made his statement on November 18 (see Ottawa *Journal*, Nov. 19, 1937). A similar resolution was introduced in the House of Representatives, but was buried in committee.

[56] *Literary Digest*, CXXIV (Dec. 4, 1937), 8.

[57] Norman Davis in Brussels to Secretary of State, telegram no. 27, Nov. 11, 1937, 611.4131/414. In the course of a talk with Davis, Eden "said that one reason that has caused the delay was that we had insisted on an agreement to make various concessions as a sine qua non to the actual beginning of the negotiations on such a treaty. . . . It had caused some difficulty and delay with them."

the party and within his Cabinet, opposition of affected economic interests, particularly vocal in British Columbia, and, perhaps most important of all, his own personality traits. The United States government had accepted the reality that to ease Britain's imperial problem it had to negotiate simultaneously with Canada, in spite of the risk of political repercussions. Regardless, Canadian-American negotiations were the *sine qua non* underlying any arrangement.

Hull hoped that the decision in Washington to launch tripartite negotiations would open the door to a possible foreign policy breakthrough. At any rate, the three governments could now move into the final stage—actual negotiations for Anglo- and Canadian-American trade agreements.

Chapter 7

The Trade Agreements of 1938

The trilateral decision to negotiate trade agreements was no mean accomplishment, but the arduous task of working out specific provisions remained. There were officials in all three countries who were sensitive to the political influence that protected industries could wield. In the United States textile and lumber organizations carried on the expected campaign against greater foreign competition. The attitudes of the American farmer were more nebulous, forcing the Department of Agriculture to measure them carefully before granting certain concessions. On occasion Cordell Hull was even more cautious than Henry Wallace. The Secretary of State forfeited few opportunities to admonish nations in very general terms to lower tariff barriers, but when faced with practical decisions he often hedged. In June, 1938, the question whether to begin trade discussions with Australia presented a dilemma because of the probability of reductions in the American tariff on wool. If talks were begun, frightened and unhappy farmers might convert their fears into votes for Republican candidates. If they were deferred, the Grand Old Party might exploit the same apprehensions by contending that once the election was safely behind, the Administration would negotiate a trade agreement lowering the wool duty drastically. Wallace was willing to proceed, but Hull postponed his decision until after an analysis of the June primary in Iowa. On June 8, the Secretary of Agriculture assured him that the reciprocity program had not been a major issue in the Iowa campaign and reaffirmed his readiness to support negotiations. But negotiations still did not begin, while studies of opinion within the farm community continued.[1]

The first important poll came into Wallace's possession in December, 1937, or early January, 1938. The Gallup organization, in addition to the findings cited in the previous chapter, filed with the Department of Agriculture an unpublished report of the opinions of farmers only. That Wallace took seriously the American Institute of Public Opinion and its reports was evident when he shared the results with the Secretary of State. "Our experience with the Gallup Polls," he wrote, "indicates that while they may have a margin of error of sometimes as much as 7 percent on the conservative side, they are conducted honestly and are of real value." To the question, "Have the government's foreign trade agreements helped or hurt farmers in your community?" only 19 per cent of the farmers polled answered that the agreements had helped, while 49 per cent replied that they had hurt, and 32 per cent had no opinion. Only in the South—Democratic country anyway—did more farmers feel that the agreements had helped them, and then with the smallest of margins, 34 to 33 per cent. In the Far West and New England, where Democrats had to work for votes, support was almost nonexistent. The Gallup figures showed only 9 to 17 per cent favorable in the corn and dairy states of the Midwest. The Department of Agriculture's survey in this politically marginal area found 33 to 35 per cent of the farmers favorably disposed,

[1] Moffat Diary, June 7 and 8, 1938, Moffat Papers, XL. For a more complete account of trade discussions between Australia and the United States, see Esthus, *From Enmity to Alliance*, 49–61.

39 to 42 per cent unfavorable, and 25 to 26 per cent undecided. However, the Department had asked a different question, concerning future expectations of the program rather than present gains, which, Wallace admitted, might account for the higher percentage.

These studies did more than make Wallace and Hull cautious. They showed that conclusion of a trade agreement with the United Kingdom, with its benefits for the farm population, was imperative. A concerted effort to educate farmers to the advantages of the reciprocity program in general and the Anglo-American pact in particular naturally followed. In late May, Wallace forwarded to Hull the latest results of a survey of some 2,000 farmers. They showed a high percentage of rural opposition, particularly among the more poorly educated, to reciprocity. That nearly one-third of those polled remained undecided presented to Hull "a compelling task . . . of bringing opinion . . . up toward the level already prevailing among the better educated and better informed farmers." [2]

Of course the solution was not so simple, because the Republicans countered with an educational campaign of their own. In June, bearing in mind both the Gallup and the Department findings, the Assistant Administrator of the Agricultural Adjustment Administration notified Wallace that the average farmer "has strong hopes of benefit from the British trade agreement." Wallace in turn averred to an officer in a private organization that he had "no doubt that the farmers would vote in a very much more friendly way with regard to the British Trade Agreement than with regard to the trade agreement program in general. Unfortunately Republican politicians have done a lot of

[2] Wallace to Hull, Jan. 28 and May 27, 1938, and Hull to Wallace, June 11, 1938, Department of Agriculture Records, National Archives, Foreign Trade File.

poisoning of farm minds. . . . The rank and file of farmers simply don't understand [the trade agreements program] and it is very difficult to get them to understand." [3]

This information, regularly collected, gave substance to remarks about political realities made by State Department officials to the British, and explains why some concessions were sought and why certain British requests were rejected. The congressional election scheduled for November, 1938, made the administration even more aware of the political framework within which they were operating.

Two of the three leading business organizations in the United Kingdom—the Federation of British Industries, the most influential, and the National Union of Manufacturers, the most "articulate, provocative, and propagandist" [4]—opposed the accord. Only the Association of British Chambers of Commerce favored it, and this body, impressed with the ultimate benefits, admitted that certain businesses would have to make sacrifices. To compound the problem, the center of this opposition was in Birmingham, whose voters had elected to Parliament both Ne-

[3] Memorandum by Alfred D. Stedman, Assistant Administrator of the Agricultural Adjustment Administration, to Wallace, June 29, 1938, *ibid.*; Wallace to Francis P. Miller, Vice-Chairman of National Policy Committee, June 29, 1938, *ibid.*

[4] The characterization of the National Union of Manufacturers was made by James R. Wilkinson, American Consul in Birmingham, in Report to American Embassy, London, Feb. 7, 1938, 611.4131/1311A. In mid-December, 1937, the Federation of British Industries recorded its opposition to the proposed agreement. In a public statement the organization predicted "very serious damage to British internal economy" if imperial preferences were weakened ("World Trade," *Living Age,* CCCLIII [Feb., 1938], 555–556). For general treatments of the negotiations in 1938, consult two works: *The United States in World Affairs: An Account of American Foreign Relations, 1938* (New York, 1939), 190–199, and Arnold J. Toynbee, ed., *Survey of International Affairs, 1938* (London, 1941), I, 17–32.

ville Chamberlain and Anthony Eden. Reportedly the prevailing opinion in Birmingham was that these two Conservatives were not "genuinely enthusiastic" about an agreement.[5]

If enthusiasm was lacking on the Prime Minister's part, the explanation lies elsewhere. It involves his program for the preservation of peace in Europe and the place of the United States in that program. In February, 1938, Chamberlain recorded that since May of 1937 he had "been trying to improve relations with the 2 storm centres, Berlin and Rome." As he saw the situation, the British "were drifting into worse and worse positions with both, with the prospect of having ultimately to face 2 enemies at once." War was abhorrent in itself, and the weakness of France made such a prospect even less attractive. If he could have trusted the United States to support Whitehall, the Prime Minister might not have sought political appeasement, or at least he might have pursued it with less conviction. "The U.S.A. has drawn closer to us," he noted in his diary, "but the isolationists there are so strong and so vocal that she cannot be depended on for help if we should get into trouble."[6] Several weeks earlier he had written in a similar vein to a Bostonian: "I am just now in closer relations with the American Government than has been the case within my recollection. I have made more than one attempt . . . to draw them even closer still and I have had more than one disappointment." He never doubted Washington's "good will." "The trouble is that public opinion in a good part of the states still believes it possible for America to stand outside Europe and watch it disintegrate, without being materially affected herself." Chamberlain's contemporary decision to dismiss an American overture for an international conference makes his next comments interesting. "In spite of my disappointment," the Prime Minister asserted, "I intend to keep on doing everything I

[5] Wilkinson to American Embassy, Feb. 7, 1938, 611.4131/1311A.
[6] Feiling, *Chamberlain,* 322.

can to promote Anglo-American understanding and cooperation. Not because I want or expect America to pull our chestnuts out of the fire for us. . . . But I believe that Americans and British want the same fundamental things in the world." [7]

In January, 1938, Chamberlain was apprised of President Roosevelt's plan to summon a world peace conference, a move Washington hesitated to make without prior approval of the British. The Prime Minister responded unenthusiastically, dampening Roosevelt's hopes and prompting his own Foreign Secretary's resignation from a government with whose foreign policy he had been disenchanted for some time. In Chamberlain's mind American sponsorship of such a conference did not ensure the dependability of American political commitments. Given a choice between cooperating with a well-intentioned President leading a reluctant nation or with two dictators who gave every indication of pursuing their political and economic programs, he took the latter. After the war, Sir Samuel Hoare wrote in defense of his own support of appeasement that he had "sincerely regarded Anglo-American friendship as the very basis of our foreign policy, and it was only with the greatest reluctance and disappointment that I was forced to agree with Chamberlain and admit that in view of the strength of American isolationism, we must for the time being rely chiefly upon ourselves in the immediate crisis that was facing Europe." [8]

Indicative of how these heads of state were uncertain of the courses they were plotting, Chamberlain alleged at this same time that Germany, Italy, Japan, and Russia "pay no heed to reason, but there is one argument to which they will give attention, and that is force. U.S.A. and U.K. in combination represent a force so overwhelming that the mere hint of the possibility

[7] *Ibid.,* 322–323.
[8] Viscount Templewood [Sir Samuel Hoare], *Nine Troubled Years* (London, 1954), 263.

of its use is sufficient to make the most powerful of dictators pause." He concluded, "Co-operation between our two countries is the greatest instrument in the world for the preservation of peace." [9]

What emerges is the frustrating spectacle of two key leaders—Chamberlain in the United Kingdom and Hull in the United States—who never doubted the desirability, if not necessity, of closer relations, but who each assigned different priorities to the proposals of the other. Chamberlain discounted the political significance of the program that obsessed the Secretary of State; Hull frowned on rearmament and wanted no part of any political entanglements that underlay the Prime Minister's hopes. Chamberlain's lack of interest in reciprocity offended Hull, and American refusal to identify with the British in their European struggle aroused Chamberlain's contempt, driving him to make his political peace with Mussolini and Hitler. The Prime Minister killed the January flirtations of Roosevelt by deciding "to enter upon a fresh attempt to reach a reasonable understanding with both Germany and Italy," and he added, "I am by no means unhopeful of getting results." In words reminiscent of Baldwin's, Chamberlain expressed his feeling that "it is always best and safest to count on nothing from the Americans but words." [10]

Hoare noted that in January, 1938, "Chamberlain was convinced that American isolationism made effective American action impossible." The former Foreign Secretary continued, "This conviction more than any other reason . . . made him impatient of American lectures on international conduct, and American reiteration of moral principles . . . [and] more than ever forced his mind in the only direction that then seemed likely to avert

[9] Feiling, *Chamberlain*, 323.   [10] *Ibid.*, 324–325.

war, the negotiation of specific, and probably limited agreements, first with Mussolini, and secondly with Hitler." [11]

While Chamberlain was charting this international course, the Canadian Prime Minister had his own problems. He heard the pleas of the Dominion lumber and fruit-growing people and witnessed a conflict within his Cabinet over the wisdom of granting too many concessions to either Great Britain or the United States. The Conservatives were in the wings waiting for a Liberal blunder that could return them to power. If there were any force that could counteract these considerations, it had to be King's isolationism. In a world terrorized by the fear of war, Canada must draw closer to the United States, even though the price for this comforting prospect was Canadian cooperation in making possible the Anglo-American agreement.

The diplomats had to be certain that they did not agree to something that might retard an economic upswing. Thus, the recession of 1937–1938 in the United States inhibited the negotiations. British officials were reluctant to grant Washington's requests when American purchases of their goods had declined and a more unfavorable trade balance was in sight. Early in March, Chamberlain told Joseph P. Kennedy, the newly arrived American Ambassador in Great Britain, that the British "were being affected a great deal by the business let-up" in the United States, and that he was "very much disturbed at what the inevitable might be if American business did not pick up." [12] Reduced purchasing power in their favorite market also frightened the Canadians. While the economic picture might strengthen the resolve of Washington to effect agreements stimulating the flow of American exports, the other two partners were less willing to

[11] Templewood, *Nine Troubled Years*, 268.
[12] Kennedy to Secretary of State, telegram no. 184, March 4, 1938, 611.41/389.

make the necessary sacrifices in a period of such uncertainty.

The political events of 1938, however, overshadowed the domestic difficulties facing the three governments. Trade agreement negotiations foundered, as London subordinated them to rapprochement with Germany and Italy. An accord with the United States might be desirable to Great Britain for economic reasons, and it might even draw the two governments together politically. In late July, 1938, the Prime Minister himself informed Parliament that relations between his country and the United States "have never been better than they are at the present moment." He continued, "I regard [a trade pact] . . . not merely as an attempt to come to a commercial agreement, which if we could find a fair settlement would be of benefit to both countries, but as an effort to demonstrate the possibility of these two great countries working together on a subject which, if they can come to terms, may prove to be the forerunner of a policy of wider application." [13] In mid-August, William Astor, a key figure in the Cliveden set, told Moffat that Chamberlain was "heart and soul for the conclusion of an agreement in the near future." [14] Reciprocity with the United States was seen to be insufficient, however, when the Austrian and particularly the Czech episodes captured the headlines of the daily press. The appeasers believed—probably correctly—that Washington would not side with the United Kingdom if these European complications resulted in war. This conviction, coupled with lack of confidence in the French, paranoic distrust of the Soviets, and doubts as to support from the Dominions, left the British only one alternative to a European bloodbath—political settlement with the Reich.

Not until after Munich was the Anglo-American agreement concluded, and then it was a secondary maneuver on Whitehall's

[13] Great Britain, 338 *H. C. Deb.* 5 s., 2960.
[14] Moffat Diary, Aug. 15, 1938, Moffat Papers, XLI.

part, a loose end that could conveniently be tied to overall British policy. Disillusionment with the Munich accord and the possibility that a future crisis might not end short of war did not drive the powers together, though this sequence is suggested by such works as the 1938 volume of *The United States in World Affairs* and the biography of Cordell Hull by Julius Pratt. Chamberlain believed—and did so for some time—that the resolution of the Czech problem meant "peace in our time." Munich made possible the Anglo-American trade agreement not because it portended future trouble, thus inviting the comforting feeling of Anglo-American cooperation, but because it promised tranquility in Europe and enabled the British to return to less pressing concerns such as trade with the United States.

Because of these complications, the Canadian and British trade delegations spent many months in Washington wrestling with the challenges given them in November, 1937. Frustration, tension, strain, and hard bargaining characterized these negotiations. The final result—the trade agreements of 1938—was a monumental achievement for advocates of closer relations within the North Atlantic Triangle and a tribute to compromise, patience, statesmanship, and a diplomatic outlook that recognized the mutual interests of the nations.

On January 29, after several weeks of exploratory activity,[15] the State Department formally announced intention to negotiate a trade agreement with Canada and published a list of commodities on which it would consider making concessions. The Committee for Reciprocity Information set March 12 as the deadline for the receipt of written arguments, and April 4 for the opening of oral presentations.[16]

[15] Memorandum of conversation by James C. H. Bonbright, Division of European Affairs, Jan. 12, 1938, *Foreign Relations, 1938*, II, 164–165.
[16] Department of State, *Press Releases*, XVIII (Jan. 29, 1938), no. 435, pp. 156–173.

Shortly before these formalities were completed, a federal by-election in British Columbia had strengthened the Prime Minister's political hand. In a Victoria district, after the "fiercest election contest within memory," the Liberals won a traditionally Conservative seat.[17] The battle gained national notoriety, since both parties had sent eminent spokesmen into the fray. Among the principals in the Liberal party who had campaigned for the trade pacts were Cabinet members Ian Mackenzie and J. G. Gardiner. Richard Bennett had presented the Conservative case in a major speech urging Victorians to sound an emphatic "no" to any attempt by the Dominion government to destroy imperial preferences. "I ask you to use your power," declared the former Prime Minister, "to see to it that this is not done." In an editorial the Vancouver *Daily Province* observed, "Mr. Bennett has put the case of British Columbia's stake in the preservation of Canada's preference in the markets of Great Britain and the Empire with all his characteristic vigor." [18] Too much can be made of one election, but at the very least, as the Toronto *Globe and Mail* put it, "If campaign speeches can be believed, Victoria, B.C., has decided for Canada that the Federal Government is justified in wrecking Mr. Bennett's 1932 Empire pacts to trade with the United States." [19] Though opposition and caution in the Dominion remained and much substantive haggling lay ahead for the diplomats, this by-election was the proper political tonic for Mackenzie King.

On January 24, the State Department had given formal notice of its intention to negotiate an agreement with the United Kingdom, together with the list of possible concession items.[20] In the

[17] Toronto *Globe and Mail,* Dec. 2, 1937.

[18] Vancouver *Daily Province,* Nov. 26, 1937. For the editorial comment, see *ibid.,* Nov. 27, 1937.

[19] Toronto *Globe and Mail,* Dec. 2, 1937.

[20] Department of State, *Press Releases,* XVIII (Jan. 29, 1938), no. 435, pp. 137–156.

latter part of February, after acceding to an American request for delay to allow time for some additional studies, the British trade delegation arrived in Washington.

Two contemporary developments indicated the problems of ever-present concern to Whitehall. On January 17, before a meeting in Birmingham of the National Union of Manufacturers, Sir Patrick Harmon, a local member of Parliament, criticized the proposed Anglo-American agreement. He raised the difficulty of granting concessions to American exporters without injuring domestic producers because of the unfavorable balance of trade with the United States. He continued that the businessman was much better equipped to handle the economic problems of the nation than "the pundits of the Government departments—the permanent civil servants—[who] arrogate to themselves in all these cases the right, because of their assumed economic wisdom and superior intelligence, to decide what is best for the agricultural, industrial, and commercial communities of the land." [21]

At this same time, the National Union of Manufacturers addressed a letter to Oliver Stanley, the President of the Board of Trade, charging that political rather than business considerations had forced Britain's revival of interest in the trade agreement. The letter insisted that because the advantage in the negotiations would thus lie with the United States, they should be dropped. Stanley's subsequent dismissal of the allegation as "complete nonsense" [22] neither allayed the apprehensions of many British manufacturers nor resulted in a diminution of their campaign to discredit the project. Although the President of the Board of Trade had paid little heed to this appeal, similar ones made their point. During the crucial stages of the negotiations Stanley was quite reluctant to accept the essential concessions.

[21] Manchester *Guardian*, Jan. 18, 1938.
[22] *Ibid.*, Jan. 17, 1938; for Stanley's reply, see *ibid.*, Jan. 25, 1938.

In January, while the forces of opposition in Great Britain were directing their fire at the proposed pact, the United States Senate confirmed the nomination of Joseph P. Kennedy as Ambassador to the United Kingdom. Possibly his business background explains in part why he was selected to serve in London. In late 1936, after commiserating about the obstacles impeding a trade pact with Great Britain, James C. Dunn wrote Moffat that many in Washington had finally come to realize that an Ambassador in London who was aggressive in promoting the American standard "would be the most valuable asset the Secretary could have in aiding his program." [23] In any case, Kennedy shouldered some of the trade agreement responsibilities and was willing to shoulder even more. He saw the accord in a slightly different light than did the Secretary of State. Its economic advantages, not its anti-German overtone, appealed to Kennedy. An apologist for the "New Germany" and an advocate of political appeasement for the sake of peace, the American Ambassador favored making a trade arrangement with the Reich as late as November, 1938. With the conclusion of the Anglo-American accord, the United States could seek an economic rapprochement with Hitler and hope for the subsequent return of Germany to political respectability. Like Hull, Kennedy had great faith in the trade agreement program as the road to prosperity and peace. In early March he left his first meeting with the Prime Minister with the impression that Chamberlain was "a very strong individual," reinforcement perhaps for his own conciliatory attitude toward Germany and his belief during the last stages of the trade negotiations that the State Department ought to placate the British. [24]

[23] Dunn to Moffat, Dec. 19, 1936, Moffat Papers, X.

[24] *Documents on German Foreign Policy, 1918–1945* (Washington, 1949), Series D, I, 713–718; IV, 634–636. See William W. Kaufmann's chapter entitled "Two American Ambassadors: Bullitt and Kennedy," in Gordon A. Craig and Felix Gilbert, eds., *The Diplomats, 1919–1939* (Princeton, 1953), 649–681. Kennedy to Secretary of State, telegram no. 184, March 4, 1938, 611.41/389.

A dispute over the exportation of American motion pictures to Great Britain, typical of the problems encountered by the two governments as they moved toward reciprocity, awaited the new Ambassador. In 1927, Parliament had passed the Cinematograph Films Act. Designed to stimulate the flagging domestic industry by controlling the importation of foreign films, the measure required that the subsidiaries of American companies distribute to theaters a certain percentage of domestically produced pictures. The figure varied according to a graduated scale provided by the law. Initially 7 per cent of the total footage distributed, the proportion rose to 20 per cent by March 31, 1938, the expiration date of the act. Percentage requirements for exhibitors were set also, from 5 per cent British films the first year to 20 per cent the last. In order to meet their legal obligations, the American subsidiaries produced cheap, low-quality pictures, usually by contract with small English studios. Interested Britishers, concerned before 1927 with the cultural effects on their country of viewing so many foreign films and so few domestic, now recognized another problem, the influence on their culture of low-grade pictures depicting life in the United Kingdom.

The scheduled expiration of the law in March, 1938, gave groups the opportunity to correct the deficiencies in a revised measure. In the spring of 1936, Walter Runciman, whose department largely administered the law, had appointed a committee, headed by Lord Moyne, to study the act and to make recommendations for future legislation. Following public hearings in May and June, the Moyne Committee submitted its report and recommendations to the Board of Trade, which forwarded them to the House of Commons in November, 1936. To guarantee the distribution of a higher percentage of British films, the committee proposed that quotas be raised to 20 per cent for the first year and to 50 per cent by 1948. To ensure high quality, it recommended a minimum-cost formula, which was applicable to all pictures, and review of films by a films commission.

The movie industry, through Will Hays, president of the Motion Picture Producers and Distributors of America, Inc., informed the State Department of these developments, showed how the proposals, if enacted into law, would ruin its business in Britain, and called for Washington's aid to protect its interests. As early as January, 1937, Hays chose the most effective argument he could employ in dealing with Cordell Hull: more stringent regulations would jeopardize a trade agreement between the United States and the United Kingdom.[25]

The industry got immediate results. On January 15, Hull wired the Embassy in London the instruction to "render all possible and appropriate assistance" to Fayette W. Allport, the representative of the Motion Picture Producers and Distributors of America, Inc. Ray Atherton dutifully sent the Foreign Office an informal note on February 2 requesting a future meeting, along with a memorandum drafted by the American movie industry. In mid-March, just prior to the initial discussion with British officials, the Secretary advised Bingham and Atherton of his great interest in the talks. Action making entry of American films more difficult, particularly when the two governments were attempting to liberalize trade, would be most annoying.[26]

Between March and November, under continued pressure from the movie industry, Washington gradually assumed a more active role in presenting Hollywood's case to Whitehall. It hoped

[25] Atherton to Secretary of State, no. 2079, March 31, 1936, 841.00 P. R./434. See the lengthy memorandum sent to the State Department by the Motion Picture Producers and Distributors of America, Inc., enclosed in Hays to Bingham, Jan. [undated], 1937, 841.4061 Motion Pictures/39.

[26] Secretary of State to American Embassy in London, telegram no. 14, Jan. 15, 1937, 841.4061 Motion Pictures/37; Secretary of State to American Embassy, telegram no. 86, March 16, 1937, 841.4061 Motion Pictures/42; informal note to Foreign Office, Feb. 2, 1937, 841.4061 Motion Pictures/59; Bingham to Secretary of State, telegram no. 156, March 19, 1937, 841.4061 Motion Pictures/43.

at first that the American industry itself could resolve the differences with its British counterpart and the British government. To that end the Embassy arranged meetings between officials of the subsidiaries and the Board of Trade, while private organizations representing the various branches of the industry in Great Britain attempted unsuccessfully to negotiate a settlement. After this frustration, the Americans turned again to the Embassy requesting another communication in their behalf. On June 2, Atherton sent a second informal note, which Allport helped him to draft, spelling out in greater detail for the Foreign Office the American arguments.[27]

Notified of this official interest, the Board of Trade moved to satisfy Washington, while still protecting its own film industry. In June it released a statement of the principal features that ought to be incorporated in the new legislation. Slightly less rigorous than the Moyne Report, it set the maximum quota at 30 per cent, granted double guota-credit for movies which were expensive to produce, left open the possibility of negotiations for some reciprocity arrangement, and differentiated between long and short films, allowing a lower percentage for the latter. At the same time, reflecting a willingness to be fair to all sides, the Board of Trade invited the industry to express its views within ten days. Stanley and his colleagues had obviously not made their final judgments.[28]

At another meeting arranged by the Embassy between film representatives and officials in the Board of Trade, the former inveighed against the proposals that had been made and advanced their own suggestions. They thought a 20 per cent quota

[27] Colonel Frederick Herron to Dunn, April 26, 1937, 841.4061 Motion Pictures/47; Hays to Dunn, May 27, 1937, 841.4061 Motion Pictures/49; informal note to Foreign Office, June 2, 1937, 841.4061 Motion Pictures/59.

[28] Herron to Department of State, June 11, 1937, 841.4061 Motion Pictures/54. He included a cable from Allport listing the eleven points.

—not to mention the higher percentages—to be incompatible with the minimum-cost formula, preferring instead a 10 per cent or at most a 15 per cent figure. The Americans pressed for triple credit when production costs exceeded a certain amount and a reciprocity provision crediting renters in Great Britain for British films distributed in the United States. Finally, they argued against any quotas on short subjects. The spokesmen came away from the discussion considering the Board of Trade to be amenable to the triple-credit and reciprocity propositions but opposed to any changes in the quotas.[29]

Indicative of official involvement, the Ambassador to Great Britain broached the subject with Anthony Eden on June 17 and 24. At the latter meeting Bingham handed the Foreign Secretary a memorandum outlining American attitudes, and Eden promised to distribute the document among members of the Cabinet, which had not yet discussed the problem. Meanwhile a foreign officer of the Motion Picture Producers and Distributors of America, Inc., who was in Washington at the time, brought the State Department up to date. After mentioning the "vigorous" conferences at the Board of Trade, he claimed that "everything possible has now been done to present American position effectively." Thinking that many British functionaries "are apparently not unsympathetic toward it," he wanted more pressure applied to overcome the opposition of "top officials of the Board of Trade who for reasons of political expediency are reluctant to introduce a more favorable measure." He singled out Oliver Stanley as a target for this American pressure. Since direct contact with the Board of Trade was contrary to diplomatic procedures, the State Department carried its latest plea directly

[29] Bingham to Secretary of State, telegram no. 383, June 15, 1937, 841.4061 Motion Pictures/51; memorandum of conversation of Rubin, Allport, Wallace, Brown, and Fennelly (the last three were Board of Trade officials), June 16, 1937, 841.4061 Motion Pictures/59.

to the Foreign Secretary. Stanley got the message, for late in July he replied to the American overtures with a memorandum defending past and current British actions.[30]

On July 30, the Board of Trade presented its bill to the House of Commons. The film industry, though not happy, was optimistic. The proposed measure was an improvement on the June statement, with provisions for a 15 per cent quota the first year and reciprocity in the distribution of British films. The real cause of optimism was the belief that in Commons favorable amendments would be attached to it. In talking with Fayette Allport, a Board of Trade spokesman had said frankly that the triple-credit proposal had merit and that the American companies should try by various means to influence the legislative process. Allport interpreted the remarks to mean the Board of Trade "is in fact washing its hands of the entire matter and giving up in disgust. It is simply passing the buck back to the industry and telling it in effect to get a sensible Bill, if it can, by amending [it] . . . in Parliament." The Motion Picture Producers and Distributors of America, Inc., had several changes in mind. It wanted the maximum quota reduced from 30 per cent, a smaller minimum-cost figure, the addition of triple credit, a stronger reciprocity clause, and the removal of quotas on short subjects. The organization's over-all impression was that the measure as it stood would saddle American subsidiaries with burdens and improve only slightly the quality of films in the United Kingdom.[31]

The State Department's announcement in November of con-

[30] Bingham to Secretary of State, telegram no. 389, June 17, 1937, 033.4111/340; Bingham to Secretary of State, telegram no. 407, June 25, 1937, 852.00/5827; Herron to Dunn, June 18, 1937, 841.4061 Motion Pictures/53; Stanley memorandum in Eden to Bingham, July 30, 1937, 841.4061 Motion Pictures/63.

[31] Allport to Johnson, Aug. 3, 1937, 841.4061 Motion Pictures/63; Allport to Johnson, July 29, 1937, enclosed in Johnson to Secretary of State, no. 3284, Aug. 10, 1937, 841.4061 Motion Pictures/63.

templated trade agreement negotiations with Great Britain gave the movie industry an excellent opportunity to alert Washington again of the pending legislation. Within a few days the British Embassy was told of Hollywood's concern and admonished that it was no time to place additional restrictions on imports. Owen Chalkley, spokesman for the Embassy, replied that his government would treat filmdom fairly and that in any event the Embassy's hands were tied.[32]

A short time later, following a direct appeal from Hays, the Secretary of State instructed Herschel V. Johnson, the Chargé in London, to advise Whitehall formally that the United States wanted the status quo to be maintained during the negotiations. The prospective legislation threatened discussion of motion pictures, a key item on the "non-Ottawa" list of desired concessions.[33]

Hays maintained the pressure, personally reiterating on December 10 his organization's stand to Hull and warning of a movement within the industry to wage a public campaign on the issue. Because of the political implications of such a maneuver and his sympathy with the movie industry, the Secretary, joined by Sayre, immediately sought out the British Ambassador. Sayre and Lindsay differed on a fundamental point. The Ambassador contended that his government was attempting to improve the quality of movies shown in Great Britain, and that the measure was thus unrelated to the trade agreement negotiations. Sympathetic though he was with this purported objective, Sayre argued that anything which affected the entry of an important American product came within the purview of the negotiations. He thought it unwise for the British to pass such legislation. At the

[32] Memorandum by Paul T. Culbertson, Assistant Chief, Division of European Affairs, Nov. 20, 1937, *Foreign Relations, 1937,* II, 88–89.

[33] Secretary of State to Johnson, telegram no. 468, Nov. 29, 1937, *Foreign Relations, 1937,* II, 89–90.

end of a rather cool exchange, the Assistant Secretary emphasized that American overtures to London were not just perfunctory ones to appease the movie industry. Washington was "really anxious" that Whitehall "search for a way of taking such action as they deem necessary by methods which will not increase our difficulties in the coming negotiations." Hull also instructed the Chargé to tell the Foreign Office of the latest developments.[34]

The following day, Johnson reported that the bill, then in committee after its second reading, contained nothing detrimental to American interests. Sir William Brown of the Board of Trade, who knew of the seriousness with which the United States viewed the legislation, had been handed five proposed amendments approved by Allport. He had promised to give them forthwith to Stanley. Johnson believed that Parliament would be reasonable. The measure in its final form would impose no greater restrictions on American imports than its predecessor, and if the proposals were accepted, the industry would be even better off. Since the Board of Trade had been responsive to previous approaches, Johnson suggested that an official statement made to the Foreign Office might "get their backs up" and undermine the gains already made.[35] Hull acceded to the Chargé's request that nothing formal be done for the moment, but repeated that London, unlike the State Department, considered the matter as separate from trade agreement negotiations.[36]

[34] Secretary of State to Johnson, telegram no. 483, Dec. 10, 1937, *Foreign Relations, 1937*, II, 91–92; memorandum by Culbertson, Nov. 22, 1937, 841.4061 Motion Pictures/78; memorandum of conversation with Hays, by Dunn, Dec. 9, 1937, 841.4061 Motion Pictures/84; memorandum by Dunn, Dec. 10, 1937, 841.4061 Motion Pictures/84; memorandum by Sayre, Dec. 11, 1937, 841.4061 Motion Pictures/84.

[35] Johnson to Secretary of State, telegram no. 766, Dec. 11, 1937, *Foreign Relations, 1937*, II, 92–93.

[36] Secretary of State to Johnson, telegram no. 487, Dec. 13, 1937, *Foreign Relations, 1937*, II, 93.

On January 13, 1938, in its initial communication on the subject, the British government notified Washington that it would not withdraw the bill then in Parliament, denying that the bill would inflict undue hardships on the entry of American films if passed.[37] To make a difficult situation even more trying, the two sides became unnecessarily nasty. During his meeting with Sayre on December 10, Lindsay had "mentioned in passing that the British taste was on a higher plane than the American, and there was a strong feeling in England that such American films as were exhibited in Great Britain should be on a higher plane than the general average of quality exhibited in this country." On January 15, the Ambassador wrote Sayre that he hoped the Assistant Secretary was not "still feeling too much agitation about films. I hear that the Board of Trade, who *do* [italics his] know something about this business, are in continuous and friendly consultation with the American interests, and that everything practicable is being done to meet their wishes consistent with the views of Parliament—and with the general objective of maintaining a British film industry." Sayre's initial reaction was to strike back in kind. Upon reflection, he changed his mind, and his letter, dated January 22, was quite conventional. His emotions had not receded completely, though, for he wrote, "I have initialed this redraft most reluctantly. I feel that the British note was meant to be snooty & that there are times when it is wise to show that we have noticed it."[38]

Moffat admitted privately that "one of the stumbling blocks has been the airy way in which Lindsay has kept dismissing the idea as of no importance." The Ambassador, Moffat continued,

[37] Johnson to Secretary of State, telegram no. 28, Jan. 13, 1938, *Foreign Relations, 1938,* II, 5–6.

[38] Memorandum by Dunn, Dec. 10, 1937, 841.4061 Motion Pictures/84; Lindsay to Sayre, Jan. 15, 1938, Sayre to Lindsay, Jan. 22, 1938, 841.4061 Motion Pictures/95.

"frankly admits that he knows nothing about it, and says that he doubts if the State Department knows much more." Because of this, he "has come fairly close to being offensive at times." [39]

By the end of the month, the State Department felt that just two satisfactory courses were open. On February 2, it requested that either legislation be passed consistent with the trade agreement proposals or passage of the measure be delayed. If the British accepted the latter, the trade delegations in Washington or, preferably, Kennedy and appropriate authorities in London could seek a settlement during the interim. Officials in the senior department put much faith in the new Ambassador's experience in the motion picture business to help him iron out the problems. Moffat lamented, "If only Joe Kennedy had been able to reach London a month sooner." [40] He had been detained in the United States, and insufficient time remained before the expiration of the 1927 law for the detailed talks. Kennedy himself was optimistic that once established at Grosvenor Square, he could effect an equitable solution. British cooperation in deferring the death of the films act would give him the necessary two or three months. Lindsay had seemed agreeable to the suggestion, prompting Hull to instruct the Chargé to ascertain the attitude of Whitehall. [41]

Initially, Johnson made little headway. By February 8 he had received no answer to a request for an interview with Oliver Stanley. Supposedly, a reply to an American memorandum left with a Foreign Office representative on February 2 "was on its way," but he had seen nothing. At this stage, Dunn telephoned

[39] Moffat Diary, Jan. 31, 1938, Moffat Papers, XL.

[40] *Ibid.,* Feb. 4, 1938.

[41] Secretary of State to Johnson, telegram no. 42, Jan. 31, 1938, *Foreign Relations, 1938,* II, 10–11; Johnson to Secretary of State, telegram no. 90, Feb. 3, 1938, *ibid.,* 11–12. A further instruction to Johnson to press for delay in conversations with the British was sent February 5 (Secretary of State to Johnson, telegram no. 58, Feb. 5, 1938, *ibid.,* 14).

Johnson, "gave him a pep talk, and told him not to be put off any longer but to demand to see Stanley." [42]

While the Chargé waited patiently in London for word from the British government, Sir Ronald Lindsay informed J. Pierrepont Moffat in Washington that for administrative reasons Parliament could neither postpone passage of the controversial bill nor enact interim legislation. Amendment of the measure was the only alternative. A decidedly chilly exchange followed. Moffat reiterated the American argument that Great Britain was about to injure the motion picture industry and, even worse, to inflict a blow to the trade agreement negotiations. The Ambassador replied that the British had introduced nothing new. "Everybody had known for ten years" of the act's scheduled termination. He noted sarcastically that in the proposed law the quota reserved only "30% of the output in a great cultural product" for the United Kingdom. Moreover, he expected alarmist talk, whether factually true or not, from business spokesmen. Over the years, he added, Hollywood had enjoyed a lucrative market for its movies, and it "should not complain because the [British] public was now insisting on the creation of local film industry." At the conclusion of the exchange, Moffat warned of the obvious effect of the legislation on the American attitude toward certain exports from Great Britain, but Lindsay "shrugged his shoulders and said 'it was too bad.' " [43]

On February 10, Whitehall officially refused to extend the present law but promised to work for a reasonable adjustment. It hoped at the last stages to attach certain mitigating amendments to the final bill. To avoid repercussions in Parliament, the British

[42] Johnson to Secretary of State, telegram no. 112, Feb. 8, 1938, *Foreign Relations, 1938,* II, 14–15; Moffat Diary, Feb. 5 and 6, 1938, Moffat Papers, XL.

[43] Memorandum of conversation by J. Pierrepont Moffat, Chief, Division of European Affairs, Feb. 9, 1938, *Foreign Relations, 1938,* II, 15–16.

emphasized the necessity of secrecy. The State Department remained unhappy, not only because its suggestion had been rejected but also with the proposed amendments which, from its standpoint, left unanswered some important questions. It wanted positive action by London on a fourteen-point program that had been submitted by the movie industry. Washington also informed Whitehall that if it upset the status quo on the eve of negotiations, it could expect increased difficulty in obtaining American markets for British exports.[44]

At this juncture Kennedy assumed his duties at the Court of St. James. In the House of Commons two major amendments intended to appease the United States—triple credit and reciprocity concessions—were withdrawn, though they were to return later in slightly modified form in the House of Lords. The Commons debate had taken place at a most inopportune time. Opposition to the amendments was strong and, as Stanley was retired to the sidelines with gall-bladder problems, the task of defending them was left in the inept hands of a subordinate. The Cabinet crisis prompted by Eden's resignation from the Government was of even more telling effect in bringing about the unforeseen withdrawal. The momentary turmoil within Conservative ranks prevented a resolute push for the unpopular amendments. Faced with defeat, the government withdrew them, although in doing so it reserved the right to reintroduce them in the House of Lords.[45]

[44] Johnson to Secretary of State, telegram no. 118, Feb. 10, 1938, *Foreign Relations, 1938*, II, 16–18, contained the British reply. For the contents of the fourteen-point program, see Secretary of State to Johnson, telegram no. 13, Jan. 12, 1938, *ibid.*, 3–5; Johnson to Secretary of State, telegram no. 40, Jan. 18, 1938, *ibid.*, 6–9; Secretary of State to Johnson, telegram no. 69, Feb. 15, 1938, *ibid.*, 18–19.

[45] Johnson to Secretary of State, telegram no. 158, Feb. 24, 1938, 841.4061 Motion Pictures/109; Johnson to Secretary of State, no. 3968, Feb. 28, 1938, 841.4061 Motion Pictures/111.

Kennedy was of the opinion that the bill, if the two amendments were added, would not seriously injure American interests. He added, moreover, that if Washington accepted the measure, the United States trade delegation would have an advantage to press in the negotiations. In the Ambassador's words, "We have a reasonable bill from any American point of view but not so reasonable that we definitely should not consider that we have made substantial concessions to the British point of view. We therefore have certainly gained for ourselves a credit to be used on the trade agreement." On March 14, in Kennedy's presence, Stanley committed himself to fight for the addition of the two amendments since the bill had now gone to Lords. He questioned, however, whether for bargaining purposes the United States could link the measure to the trade negotiations. He warned of sentiment in Commons that the greater concessions had been made by the British, a feeling that would be accentuated later if, to justify a reduction in some British duty, the American trade delegation pointed to the films act. The Ambassador expected difficult negotiations "to the bitter end," but remained confident that at some later date Whitehall would compensate Washington.[46]

At this moment, the House of Lords staggered the State Department: although the triple-credit and reciprocity features became part of the bill, it appended another provision raising the renters' quota on long films from 15 per cent to 20 per cent for two years. Kennedy was instructed immediately to approach the highest British officials, the Prime Minister if necessary, to get this amendment deleted. Outwardly calm, the Ambassador assured Hull that the Cabinet was cognizant of opinion in the United States and suggested that further protests would accom-

[46] Kennedy to Secretary of State, telegram no. 201, March 11, 1938, *Foreign Relations, 1938*, II, 20–21; Kennedy to Secretary of State, telegram no. 211, March 14, 1938, *ibid.*, 22–24.

plish nothing. He promised to pursue the point with Stanley informally. The President of the Board of Trade, who favored a 15 per cent figure, faced a tough assignment in getting Commons to restore the original formula.[47]

On March 23 the Ambassador reported good news. Stanley had told him of the plans to persuade members of Commons to accept a 15 per cent quota on long films and to retain the provisions desired by the United States. To aid his efforts, Stanley wanted Kennedy to supply him with a memorandum with which to buttress his arguments in Parliament. On March 29 the President of the Board of Trade prevailed with the controversial triple-credit and reciprocity amendments, but the House of Commons accepted a 15 per cent quota only for the first year. The law set the second-year percentage at 20 per cent and provided that the figure could be altered in subsequent years by the Board of Trade. A few days after this enactment, the Chargé dispatched an analysis of how the act compared with the fourteen-point proposal of the United States. Although seven points were not met and four more were met only in part, he wrote, "It is the consensus that American interests can look forward to carrying on their business in Great Britain without fear of substantial loss of revenue. . . . [Some observers believe] that their position is better than it was under the 1927 Act." [48]

By April 25 a draft agreement was ready for submission to the British delegation in Washington. Because of the complicated

[47] Secretary of State to Kennedy, telegram no. 113, March 15, 1938, *Foreign Relations, 1938*, II, 24; Kennedy to Secretary of State, telegram no. 221, March 16, 1938, *ibid.,* 24–25.

[48] Kennedy to Secretary of State, telegram no. 242, March 23, 1938, 841.4061 Motion Pictures/126; Kennedy to Secretary of State, telegram no. 258, March 29, 1938, 841.4061 Motion Pictures/129; Johnson to Secretary of State, no. 140, April 4, 1938, 841.4061 Motion Pictures/134. A much too brief, and thus distorted, account of this problem appears in Pratt, *Hull,* I, 128.

situation, the Americans decided to postpone their requests on motion pictures, a maneuver with which Kennedy agreed. In fact, he suggested negotiation of a separate accord confined solely to that item. The Ambassador doubted that the British would alter existing legislation, and he believed the Board of Trade would probably administer the law fairly. Possibly his government might persuade the department to keep quotas from rising above 20 per cent, but he reaffirmed that the United States could not realistically expect more. Any compensation would have to come during trade agreement bargaining.[49]

Within the week, the persistent Hull wanted Kennedy to discuss proposed film negotiations with the British government. If London agreed, they would be conducted concurrently with the general negotiations, and the terms might hopefully be incorporated in the general trade agreement. Deferring to Kennedy's experience, the Secretary of State gave the Ambassador a free hand, mentioning only the desirability of a permanent quota of 15 per cent.[50] Kennedy informed Hull at once that for political reasons particularly, a comprehensive arrangement was unlikely. Under no circumstances would Whitehall freeze the renters' quota at 15 per cent. On June 2 he brought this diversionary issue to an end. His talks with Board of Trade people had convinced him that nothing could be done, and he recommended that the whole project be dropped.[51]

That the trade delegations and the ambassadors of the two countries engaged in this kind of activity explains in part why a

[49] Sumner Welles, Acting Secretary of State, to Kennedy, telegram no. 172, April 25, 1938, *Foreign Relations, 1938*, II, 26; Kennedy to Secretary of State, telegram no. 340, April 26, 1938, *ibid.*, 27.

[50] Secretary of State to Kennedy, telegram no. 190, May 3, 1938, *Foreign Relations, 1938*, II, 28–29.

[51] Kennedy to Secretary of State, telegram no. 373, May 5, 1938, *Foreign Relations, 1938*, II, 29; Kennedy to Secretary of State, telegram no. 477, June 2, 1938, *ibid.*, 33–34.

year elapsed between the announcement of contemplated negotiations and the signing of the final instrument. The film discussions had lasted from February, 1937, to June, 1938, and the two
sides were able to show little for the expenditure of their time
and effort. Hollywood could boast that it had friends in Washington, but Hays was not completely satisfied with the outcome.

Technically, the Canadian- and Anglo-American negotiations
were carried on separately, but in actual practice they were
trilateral. In order to grant certain concessions to Washington,
the British had to obtain the approval of the Dominions. Although it favored an Anglo-American agreement, Canada
wanted, and politically needed, compensation in the United
States market for its losses.

Divisions within the Dominion Cabinet continued to plague
Mackenzie King. Indications are that late in March the question
of whether to consent to British requests was the principal topic
of a Government caucus, where the forces of protection scored a
notable victory. The individual carrying their banner was the
redoubtable Charles Dunning, who in the past year apparently
had relaxed little in his efforts to protect Dominion interests. A
newspaper article of March 4 by Chester Bloom of the Sifton
chain prompted the battle within the caucus. According to the
correspondent, protectionists, led by the Minister of Finance,
had risen to party prominence at the expense of those who had
traditionally favored low tariffs. The leading antagonists in
Bloom's political drama were Dunning and J. G. Gardiner of
Saskatchewan, the Minister of Agriculture. The ambitious Gardiner, having failed to obtain the Finance portfolio in 1937,
became a major force in the Cabinet, broadening the scope of his
department's activities. Unfortunately, his attempts to enlarge its
marketing functions aroused the ire of William D. Euler, the
Minister of Trade and Commerce, with the result that "the two
most extreme right wing members of the Cabinet" were allied

against him. In turn, political realities deprived Gardiner of the support of two like-minded colleagues, J. L. Ilsley, the Minister of National Revenue, and Norman Rogers, the Minister of Labor. The forceful and aggressive Dunning, aided by the political support of Euler and Conservatives disillusioned with their own fragmented organization, and by Mackenzie King's reluctance to dominate Cabinet ministers, prevailed in this rivalry with Gardiner. In the opinion of Bloom, the defeat of advocates of low tariffs had been followed by "a profound change in the orientation" of the Liberal party which jeopardized conclusion of a meaningful trade agreement between the United States and Canada.[52]

Whereas the American Chargé in Ottawa discounted Bloom's analysis, Norman MacLeod, a reliable journalist, concurred shortly thereafter with certain portions of it. According to Mac-Leod, the westerners in the Cabinet, irked by the Bloom article, tried to reverse the trend in the caucus later that month only to witness a complete Dunning victory, "the greatest which the Finance Minister has enjoyed since he re-entered public life." MacLeod balked at Bloom's pessimistic conclusion that Dunning's influence precluded a comprehensive trade accord.[53]

In any case, these glimpses into Ottawa's inner sanctum reveal that Dunning played a decisive role in the 1938 negotiations. Although the record is meager, several letters provide corroborative testimony. On August 30, Dunning, citing ill health, expressed to King a desire to retire from public life. In the first of two replies, the Prime Minister explained why in the future he wanted this colleague "at my side, indisposed or not." He men-

---

[52] Bloom's article originally appeared in the Saskatoon *Star-Phoenix,* March 4, 1938; it was reprinted in the Ottawa *Citizen,* March 16, 1938.

[53] John Farr Simmons' observations were in Simmons to Secretary of State, no. 2085, April 7, 1938, 611.4231/2345. Norman MacLeod's article, entitled "Victory behind Doors," appeared in Toronto *Saturday Night,* March 26, 1938.

tioned the trade negotiations with the United States as one of the "important decisions" that had to be made, and added, "I want to feel free to quote your views to [other Cabinet members] . . . as from time to time they and I would wish to know them." King continued that Roosevelt hoped to have the agreement signed in late September or early October and wanted the Prime Minister to visit Hyde Park at that time. Though he doubted that the signing could take place that quickly, King wrote, "[If it happens] I would like to communicate with you concerning what may be best to do in some of the difficult situations that will arise." His second letter is even more suggestive. Fearing that he had granted approval to Dunning's request too precipitately, the Prime Minister declared that Dunning's retirement would be a loss to nation, party, and to him personally. "The truth is, as you must know," he went on, "that, for years past, I have lent more upon you and Lapointe than upon any other members of the Government." [54]

On April 26, following several weeks of discussions, the Department of State submitted a draft agreement to the British trade delegation. [55] Whitehall found it unacceptable, largely because of the meagerness of the American concessions proposed on such items as cotton and woolen textiles, commodities which were as essential to Great Britain as expanded markets for agricultural products were to the United States. It was thought that acceptance of the proposals would result in "only a trifling increase in trade," hardly an attractive prospect to the British public when the United States maintained a decidedly favorable balance in its commercial exchanges with the United Kingdom. British export trade needed further stimulation to warrant the

[54] Dunning to King, Aug. 30, 1938, King to Dunning, Sept. 3, 1938, and King to Dunning, Sept. 10, 1938, Dunning Papers.

[55] Department of State to the British Trade Delegation, April 26, 1938, *Foreign Relations, 1938*, II, 27–28.

concessions which the proposal would grant American exporters and to overcome local political opposition.[56]

The most troublesome item for the negotiators was lumber. American companies, penalized by the imperial preferences that had encouraged the competitive Canadian industry, wanted the State Department to reconcile the irreconcilable—to open wider the door of the British market to American products, while leaving the domestic door closed to further imports from Canada. Dominion firms preferred that no relaxation be made in the preference or, if that was impossible, that entry into the United States be made easier as compensation for the sacrifice. The Canadian government was acutely sensitive about its lumber industry. In March, 1938, it had protested as inimical to the export of this important commodity a provision in the proposed Revenue Bill requiring marking of lumber imports to show national origin.[57] By the middle of April this continuing concern had strengthened Canadian resistance to concessions in the British tariff.

While the State Department skirmished with Ottawa, lumber associations in the United States exerted counterpressure. On May 2 leading representatives of the industry met with Francis B. Sayre and Alger Hiss. Their principal spokesman, Wilson Compton of the Lumber Manufacturers Association, concentrated on the retention of the marking amendment. As this proviso jeopardized concessions by Canada in the trade negotiations, Sayre had pressed for its deletion before the congressional conference committee. While supposedly more interested in ob-

[56] British Trade Delegation to Department of State, May 6, 1938, *Foreign Relations, 1938,* II, 30–33.

[57] Memorandum of conversation by Constant Southworth, Division of Trade Agreements, March 5, 1938, *Foreign Relations, 1938,* II, 165–167; Herbert Marler, Canadian Minister to the United States, to Hull, March 17, 1938, *ibid.,* 167–168; memorandum of conversation by Southworth, April 19, 1938, *ibid.,* 169–171.

taining "equality of treatment" for their exports in Great Britain than in retaining the clause, Compton and his colleagues raised every conceivable argument against its elimination. One representative of the West Coast Lumber Association warned that the industry would endanger a trade pact with Canada rather than surrender in the fight. When they learned that the Canadian and American negotiators had not yet discussed lumber officially, the lumbermen urged the State Department to use the marking issue as a weapon to extract more concessions from the Dominion. They refused to make further "sacrifices" in the interest of the larger accord, asserting that lumber companies had not benefited from the 1935 agreement.[58] The Assistant Secretary, appalled at some of what he heard, debated ably, but in the end his antagonists prevailed. The Revenue Act of 1938 stipulated that imports had to be duly marked.

In June the State Department tried a new tack to expedite the negotiations. Although inconsistent with a literal interpretation of the most-favored-nation principle, Washington wanted the British to classify for tariff purposes lumber products imported from the United States and those from other countries. London rejected the request: Lindsay argued that this form of discrimination against Baltic lumber could not be justified. He did not say so, but if the original American request of a 5 per cent duty were accepted, imports from the Baltic states would more freely enter the United Kingdom—a possibility which excited even more apprehensions among Canadian exporters. The Secretary of State claimed that cheaper lumber would encourage construction, which would be good for the economies of both countries. That special interests might keep a lumber concession out of the agreement especially annoyed him. Hull wanted a comprehen-

---

[58] Memorandum of conversation by Alger Hiss, May 2, 1938, 611.4131/1521. See also an earlier memorandum by Hiss, 611.426 Lumber/516.

sive effort to be made by the trade experts to resolve a question which was, in his opinion, "five percent . . . economic . . . [and] ninety-five percent . . . more or less political or psychological." To do otherwise would allow "a few lumber barons" to determine the course of the two governments.[59]

Lumber was only one of the products hampering the negotiations. On July 1 the British trade delegation transmitted additional offers on American industrial commodities that fell considerably short of what the State Department considered essential.[60] Officials closest to the scene had not anticipated the delays, hoping to conclude the arrangements well before the congressional elections of November. Late in 1937, Sayre himself had set May as the probable date for signature. On July 12 the British Ambassador confessed to a State Department representative that he had expected the negotiations to be completed by that time. Earlier he had informed his government of the American wish to have an agreement by the middle of June, nearly six months before the administration had to face the electorate. June had passed, and now he saw neither an early termination of the bargaining sessions nor an inclination by Washington to expedite them. The latter surprised Lindsay, who had understood that the forthcoming political event troubled the administration. The State Department spokesman denied this, alleging that greater public acceptance of the reciprocity program had diminished the program's vulnerability.[61]

Lindsay's pessimistic forecast proved accurate. Curiously, how-

[59] Department of State to the British Trade Delegation, June 14, 1938, *Foreign Relations, 1938*, II, 34–35; British Embassy to Department of State, July 5, 1938, *ibid.*, 35–37; memorandum by Hull, July 7, 1938, *ibid.*, 37.

[60] Hawkins and Hickerson to Kennedy, telegram no. 320, July 2, 1938, 611.4131/1625A.

[61] Sayre to Phillips, Dec. 2, 1937, Sayre Papers, Box 5; memorandum by James C. Dunn, July 12, 1938, 611.4131/1683.

ever, Oliver Stanley startled Kennedy two days later by revealing his understanding that except for five or six items, the agreement was nearly settled. Because of the imminence of Parliamentary adjournment, scheduled for July 29, and the consequent exodus of personnel from London, the American Ambassador wired Hull immediately for instructions.[62] On July 21 Kennedy suggested a meeting with Chamberlain to discuss the latest British offers and American attitudes.[63]

The prevailing opinion among the American negotiators at this time was that the British were "stalling interminably; that they won't budge an inch from their present position until they hear from Chamberlain." These men could not predict future British policy, but they speculated, "As matters stand now [the British have] gone very little of the way, and there doesn't seem to be any immediate prospect of consummation." If Chamberlain "agreed on a rather small group of important conditions, which they [the British] have given no indication of conceding at the moment, and appear to be in no hurry" to concede, an agreement could follow quickly.[64]

On July 22, Hull instructed Kennedy to speak "clearly and frankly" to the Prime Minister at once, even though other pressing developments might have prevented him from being fully informed of the details of the negotiations. He was to impress on Chamberlain that the United States considered a satisfactory agreement to be one in which the British accepted substantially the American requests which had been transmitted to the British trade delegation. The State Department would not yield on these requests just to make possible the conclusion of an arrange-

[62] Kennedy to Secretary of State, telegram no. 636, July 14, 1938, *Foreign Relations, 1938*, II, 38.

[63] Kennedy to Secretary of State, telegram no. 664, July 21, 1938, 611.4131/1681.

[64] Memorandum, July 14, 1938, Morgenthau Diary, Book 134, pp. 203–204.

ment within the next few days. Nor would it agree to any suspension of the negotiations unless Chamberlain accepted the responsibility. To dissuade Whitehall on this score, Hull wanted any interruption to be made public and the Prime Minister to know of the criticism, particularly sharp in the United States, that had already been leveled at the protracted nature of the negotiations. The business community's uncertainty about the trade pact, a by-product of the delay, was retarding financial recovery. Suspension of six weeks for ministerial holidays would intensify both the criticism and the business uncertainty.[65]

On July 24, via transatlantic telephone, the Secretary of State told the Ambassador to first see Stanley to inform him of American disenchantment and of plans to carry the problems directly to the Prime Minister. To keep the head of the Board of Trade happy, Kennedy was to report to him also the contents of his conversation with Chamberlain. The Secretary then outlined the format for the Ambassador's exchange with Chamberlain. Initially, the Ambassador was to emphasize that only the keen disappointment in Washington with the sessions had prompted the visit. Had the many time-consuming European matters not diverted the Prime Minister's attention, the Americans felt, an agreement would have been a reality already. Then the Ambassador could proceed to the fundamentals. First, the British negotiators had not bargained in good faith, refusing in the course of negotiations to expand their concessions as they had promised and as the United States delegation had done. Second, and more important, the political health of the world depended upon the conclusion of a comprehensive agreement. In the Secretary's words, "No single act would contribute so much to quieting and stabilizing the threats to peace and political stability, not only in Europe but in other parts of the world, than the announcement

[65] Secretary of State to Kennedy, telegram no. 379, July 22, 1938, *Foreign Relations, 1938,* II, 38–39.

that these two great countries had come together with a broad, basic trade arrangement." That was America's "big objective," and Hull warned that if Chamberlain failed to see the accord in its larger context, "it might well be charged in Germany, Italy, Japan, and other countries that our two countries are utterly incapable of sitting down" and concluding a mutually profitable trade pact. "I have not the slightest doubt," he asserted, "that these negotiations are being watched by those countries to see whether we are capable" of effecting a worth-while agreement. "I think that it would greatly harm not only our two countries but also the whole outlook for peace and economic improvement" if Great Britain and the United States, after the many months of effort, could produce only "a little, narrow, picayunish trade agreement." Hull wanted to make certain that Chamberlain would believe this point, if he believed nothing else. He thought the two nations could build a foundation upon which to erect "a restored structure of world order," but that British refusal to act would encourage German and Japanese aggression. At the same time, it would strengthen the "forces of isolation" in the United States, thus undermining the cause of closer Anglo-American cooperation. The Secretary felt that Chamberlain must be brought to realize that "now is the one and only time . . . during this generation" when the United States and Great Britain "are publicly on trial with respect to the whole movement for economic rehabilitation and a restored fabric of world order." [66]

The next day the Ambassador talked with Stanley. The President of the Board of Trade, "surprised and grieved" at Hull's feeling that the British had not made enough concessions, said that they had moved considerably in Washington's direction.

[66] Telephone conversation between Kennedy and Hull, July 24, 1938, 611.4131/1706; Secretary of State to Kennedy, telegram no. 387, July 25, 1938, *Foreign Relations, 1938*, II, 38–42.

They were "pained" that he thought differently. The Secretary of State promised to show Kennedy the specific items in question, since London remained convinced that it was innocent of the American indictments. Hull deduced that Whitehall was not convinced of the "broad purposes" of an agreement, but Kennedy, who believed the British were sincere, disagreed. The Ambassador doubted the wisdom of telling Chamberlain that Hull was dissatisfied and of instructing the British what to do. He much preferred the "soft" approach, exploring the Prime Minister's opinions and determining precisely how interested Whitehall was in an agreement. He hoped that the trade delegations could resolve most of the issues shortly, enabling himself and Chamberlain to accommodate differences on the few remaining commodities. At any rate, the Ambassador expected that Chamberlain, if he knew of Hull's anger, would say "to Hell with the whole business," and, Kennedy cautioned, "We don't want the whole thing to blow up." In reply to the Secretary's query whether the British recognized the "peace" aspects of an accord, he suggested that this consideration was secondary to that of Hull's prestige among Britishers: London wanted the arrangement primarily because the much-respected Secretary of State wanted it. Although upset at British disregard of the international implications of an agreement, Hull told Kennedy to emphasize the argument anyway during his conversation with Chamberlain.[67]

Later in the day the Secretary directed the Ambassador to contrast for the Prime Minister the attitudes and actions of the two parties: the United States had made major concessions, while Great Britain had not met the main American requests. On none of the important agricultural items had there been any improvement during the past few months, despite British acceptance of the State Department's condition in November that

[67] Telephone conversation between Kennedy and Hull, July 25, 1938, 611.4131/1723.

without certain liberalizations in the United Kingdom schedules there could be no agreement. Whitehall had since discussed them, but apparently only moderate changes would be forthcoming, not enough certainly to compensate the United States for its grants. Chamberlain had to understand that a one-sided accord would destroy the American program. Hull pointed out again that Washington sought the trade pact primarily for its long-range political and economic effects. If Chamberlain and his fellow ministers, not discerning this, failed to act, the Axis powers would conclude that the democracies paled before their challenges, unable even to negotiate a trade agreement successfully. Future decisions predicated on that assumption could be disastrous for the entire world. When confronted with alternatives of peace on the one hand and further animosities and possible war on the other, the two governments must not allow vested economic interests to shape their destinies.[68]

On July 26, the day Kennedy met with Chamberlain, A. E. Overton, the head of the British trade delegation, warned Harry Hawkins of the State Department not to expect major concessions on the outstanding items. His government had given what was politically and economically feasible, and pressure from Washington could only force the British into concessions detrimental to domestic businesses. Hawkins doubted that his country's proposals were excessive when compared with its offers, and contended that anything less than substantial improvement by Great Britain would produce an agreement unfair and prejudicial to enterprise in the United States. The two governments diverged fundamentally on what constituted a fair accord. After shadowboxing over the question which had the greater political problem to surmount, the officials returned to their basic difference. Overton denied that to make an equitable pact the British must accept every important American request. Hawkins count-

[68] Secretary of State to Kennedy, telegram no. 387, July 25, 1938, *Foreign Relations, 1938,* II, 39–42.

ered that though generally refusals in one area could be balanced elsewhere, there were no adequate compensations for the failure to obtain lower duties on some commodities. The conversation had come full circle with no solution in sight. J. Pierrepont Moffat, who late in July returned to his desk following vacation, expressed thinking in which Hawkins would probably have concurred when he wrote that the negotiations were still continuing, "Great Britain not yet having receded from her position that the United States should play Santa Claus." [69]

Kennedy's meeting with Chamberlain had not produced any immediate results, but the Ambassador left his host believing that Hull's arguments had impressed the Prime Minister. The British planned to grant more concessions, though Kennedy held out little hope for lumber or tobacco and the question remained whether the concessions would satisfy Washington. At least Chamberlain had decided to support the agreement; the Ambassador thought that already the Prime Minister had urged Stanley to work for the pact.[70] The next step was for the Cabinet to review the entire problem.

Before it could assemble, Hull handed the British Ambassador a memorandum requesting reconsideration of the proposal to classify lumber products to facilitate the entry of American varieties. The Secretary renewed his appeal for a mutually profitable settlement, provoking the Ambassador to inveigh "against the [lumber request] . . . in language that became somewhat disagreeable." [71] The American formula would retain the reductions

[69] Memorandum of conversation by Hawkins, Chief, Division of Trade Agreements, July 26, 1938, *Foreign Relations, 1938,* II, 42–44; Moffat Diary, July 28, 1938, Moffat Papers, XLI.

[70] Kennedy to Secretary of State, telegram no. 678, July 26, 1938, *Foreign Relations, 1938,* II, 44–45.

[71] Department of State to British Embassy, July 27, 1938, *Foreign Relations, 1938,* II, 45–47; memorandum of conversation by Hull, July 27, 1938, 611.4131/1710.

incorporated in the Canadian-American agreement of 1935, reduce from 10 per cent to 5 per cent the British duty on Douglas
fir and other American softwood exports, and grant free entry to
these goods if Washington removed the remaining excise tax on
imports of Canadian lumber. Moreover, the United Kingdom
would lower the rate on Baltic softwoods to 7½ per cent.[72]

Whitehall remained adamant. On July 27, the Cabinet acceded to other requests but rejected the lumber proposal. That
the United States had made a similar accommodation for British
textiles made little impression.[73] London considered the other
concessions to be important, however, and a few days later Lindsay pointed out Britain's recent grants to Hull. He hoped that
this action would make possible an early termination of the
negotiations. Certainly as eager as Lindsay for a prompt resolution of the issues, the Secretary noted that the State Department
was no longer pressing the British on large numbers of items, but
concentrating just on those which it felt to be "absolutely and
unconditionally" necessary. Washington would persist with
these few requests until it was satisfied.[74] The most important
was lumber. With the passage of time the United States
strengthened its determination to accept no compromise.[75]

Even the crisis prompted by Hitler's Sudetan demands failed
to break the stalemate. On August 19, during a talk with Hull, a

[72] Department of State to British Embassy, June 27, 1938, *Foreign
Relations, 1938*, II, 45–47; Secretary of State to Kennedy, telegram no.
395, July 27, 1938, *ibid.*, 47–48.
[73] Memorandum of conversation by Welles, July 29, 1938, *Foreign
Relations, 1938*, II, 48–49.
[74] Memorandum of conversation by Hull, Aug. 1, 1938, *Foreign Relations, 1938*, II, 49–50.
[75] Secretary of State to Kennedy, telegram no. 444, Aug. 12, 1938,
Foreign Relations, 1938, II, 50. Kennedy was to learn whether the
British refusal of July were final and whether other lumber-exporting
countries knew of the American proposal. He was answered in Johnson to
Secretary of State, telegram no. 764, Aug. 15, 1938, *ibid.*, 50–51.

worried Lindsay related the trade pact to the current situation. Unable to resist the temptation, the Secretary reminded his guest of the American efforts of the past three and a half years to persuade Whitehall to think of the accord as a contribution to the political climate of the world. Nevertheless, he noted that present proposals did not provide for a balanced agreement. Something more had to be granted on four items—lumber, rice or lard, tobacco, and hams. Potential political opposition in the Middle and Far West left no alternative. As this conversation progressed, Hull criticized not only the reluctance of the British to accede to the requests, but also their public silence on his project of promoting peace through commercial reciprocity. He linked the two, suggesting that London's "paltry" concessions reflected its indifference to the "wholesome peace-making program of trade restoration." In conclusion, he urged the Ambassador to press the British for acceptance of the proposals.[76]

A short time later Hull reverted to the British government's "lack of interest" in his program, telling Lindsay, "If one—if only one—great British statesman would come out of the woods and proceed to make himself a crusader in the name of his government for the economic and peace program for which we are crusading in this country . . . there could be no more important step in the direction of stabilizing dangerous conditions on the continent of Europe." [77] The Secretary had apparently not lost faith in his prescription for the international maladies of

[76] Memorandum of conversation by Hull, Aug. 19, 1938, *Foreign Relations, 1938*, II, 51–53. Four days later, Lindsay talked with J. Pierrepont Moffat. The Ambassador "went back to the urgency for haste, and said that any day trouble might break out in Europe and all our labors would be compromised, if not destroyed. Furthermore, the mere fact of concluding an agreement would have a stabilizing effect" (memorandum, Moffat to Hull, Aug. 23, 1938, 611.4131/1756½).

[77] Memorandum of conversation by Hull, Sept. 3, 1938, 760 F. 62/1037.

frustration and expansion, but he was almost alone. Norman Davis, for example, now believed that trade agreements were "not enough" to "ease the pressure of world conditions today." [78] Roosevelt, never so confident as Hull in the political effects of reciprocity, reportedly told Secretary of the Treasury Morgenthau, "Henry, these trade treaties are just too goddamned slow. The world is marching too fast. They're just too slow." [79]

It was quite clear that "early signature [depended] primarily on a satisfactory answer to . . . [American] proposals on a short list of agricultural products and lumber." [80] On September 9, Francis Sayre expressed to Lindsay his concern and discouragement over the lack of progress in the negotiations, which he felt was a tragedy in view of the German challenge in Europe. The Assistant Secretary thought the two countries "were descending too much into a horse-trade . . . when the whole future of the world [was] at stake"; unless something lifted them above that level quickly, the whole plan would collapse. He even suggested a direct appeal by telephone to Chamberlain, occasioning Lindsay's reply, "Oh, don't do that. The Foreign Office never does business that way. I do not think it would do any good." Sayre also underlined the political reasons for the American failure to better present terms. Opposition in New England to the tariff relaxations on British textiles could be offset by support for the agreement and the administration from the Far West and agricultural regions. Thus, the concession on lumber was essential, improvement in duties on rice and lard important. The Ambassa-

[78] Moffat Diary, Sept. 15, 1937, Moffat Papers, XXXIX.

[79] Entry, Oct. 11, 1938, Morgenthau Diary, Book 145, p. 287. Following the quote in the text, Morgenthau continued, "Now, he's told me that." Harry Dexter White repeated, "Too slow and too ineffective," to which Morgenthau replied, "Right." See also Blum, *Years of Crisis*, 524.

[80] Secretary of State to Kennedy, telegram no. 490, Aug. 31, 1938, *Foreign Relations, 1938,* II, 53.

dor thought his government might accommodate the lumber request, but not the additional proposals as well.[81]

One week later, Sayre and Hawkins told Lindsay that there was nothing new in the negotiations, noting that they were awaiting the British answer to a modified lumber proposal. After London had balked at the earlier formula, the State Department most reluctantly had adjusted it slightly. Much depended on the British response. Sayre also warned that Secretary of Agriculture Henry A. Wallace, who would have a voice in the final American decision, felt that Whitehall must grant the requests on farm goods.[82]

In this continued effort Washington had a valuable ally in Canada—so valuable, in fact, that American officials closed their eyes to a diplomatic indiscretion committed by Sir Herbert Marler, the Canadian Minister in the United States. Early in September, unknown to the State Department, Marler had gone directly to the Treasury Department to discuss marking of lumber imports. When Morgenthau learned of this "back door stuff," he immediately notified Hull who, in turn, referred the Secretary of the Treasury to Sayre. Sayre was extraordinarily frank. Although he admitted the impropriety of Marler's bypassing normal diplomatic channels, he was not about to make an issue of it. The Assistant Secretary of State informed Morgenthau that "our real troubles [in the negotiations] are with U.K. on lumber. . . . The Canadians have been playing the game very fairly. . . . [In] our pending Canadian trade agreement, the Canadians have given us all kinds of things. The Canadian trade agreement is bully. The trouble we're having is with U.K." Reaching the crux of the matter, Sayre said, "We're getting the Canadians to gang up with us against U.K. on this lumber

---

[81] Memorandum of conversation by Sayre, Sept. 9, 1938, *Foreign Relations, 1938*, II, 53–55.

[82] Memorandum of conversation by Sayre, Sept. 16, 1938, *Foreign Relations, 1938*, II, 55–56.

situation." Neither Sayre nor Hull wanted anything "to cross wires" and get the Canadians "peeved" at such a crucial time. A telephone call to Marler from Morgenthau settled the episode on a cordial and friendly note.[83]

During the latter half of September, with its principal attention directed to the parleys at Godesberg and Munich, the Foreign Office wondered if the United States, because of its pending congressional elections, would "become more and more exigent in its demands" and take advantage of British involvements in Europe to "force an unfair agreement down . . . [their] throats." Sayre assured the British Ambassador that Washington would never resort to such diplomatic blackmail, a token of the good will that, though sometimes well concealed, underlay the negotiations. The Assistant Secretary reminded Lindsay, however, that the State Department considered the latest American proposals to be fair to both parties.[84]

The European flirtation with war temporarily passed, though at Czechoslovakia's expense, and in the aftermath the trade agreement was finally concluded. Even then the negotiators could not escape last-minute difficulties and frustrations. Moffat wrote at the time, "The British seem to feel that we are raising the ante on them whereas we feel they are deliberately refusing to meet us on agricultural items which from the very beginning was explained as the essential of a trade agreement." He concluded forcefully, "Thank God, however, that the trade negotiations center up elsewhere and that we only have to observe them from afar!"[85]

[83] A very favorable construction of events permitted Marler to discuss the matter in the future with subordinate Treasury officials (telephone conversations of Morgenthau with Hull, Sayre, and Marler, Sept. 15, 1938, Morgenthau Diary, Book 141, pp. 1–5, 10–13).

[84] Memorandum of conversation by Sayre, Sept. 19, 1938, 611.4131/1792.

[85] Moffat to Robert T. Pell, American Embassy in London, Oct. 4, 1938, Moffat Papers, XIV.

On October 5, Hull wrote to Lindsay that he could not sign an accord so shallow as the present one. Included was a memorandum spelling out the items still causing problems.[86] The following day Sayre passed along to the Ambassador both documents together with another draft agreement. The final British statement on lumber, a compromise solution to the thorny question, demanded additional concessions by the United Kingdom mostly on agricultural exports. The new duty on softwood lumber of certain specifications, rather than all varieties, would be approximately 4½ per cent. If the United States removed its excise tax on Canadian imports, American exporters could ship the specified products freely into Great Britain.[87] Whereas Washington had retracted also on rice and tobacco, it raised the value attached to free entry of lard.[88] The State Department was making it easier to conclude an agreement by forfeiting earlier stands, but to justify these shifts, there had to be some "give" by London.

Getting these last concessions was not a simple matter. The American Ambassador made the task no easier for Washington when he consistently urged acceptance of the British proposals. According to Kennedy's analysis, Chamberlain led a Cabinet either opposed to or dubious about the present arrangement. Oliver Stanley, a particular target for the Ambassador's critical

[86] Hull to Lindsay, Oct. 5, 1938, *Foreign Relations, 1938*, II, 57–58; Department of State to British Ambassador, Oct. 6, 1938, 611.4131/1807B.

[87] For the details of the complicated lumber formula, see Department of State, *Press Releases*, XIX (Nov. 19, 1938), no. 477, Supplement A, "The Trade Agreement with the United Kingdom."

[88] Hull to Lindsay, Oct. 5, 1938, *Foreign Relations, 1938*, II, 57–58; memorandum of conversation by Sayre, Oct. 6, 1938, *ibid.*, 58–59; Sumner Welles, Acting Secretary of State, to Kennedy, telegram no. 612, Oct. 8, 1938, *ibid.*, 60–61; memorandum, Department of State to British Ambassador, Oct. 6, 1938, 611.4131/1807B.

comments, was "definitely against" the pact, construing the American proposals of October 6 as "the last drop in the bucket." In Stanley's opinion, acceptance of them, besides causing charges of "complete sell out" in Parliament, would aggravate an already unfavorable balance of trade. Nor was the load lessened when the prestigious economist John Maynard Keynes published a letter in the *Times* (London) citing passive trade balances and advising that Britain buy where it sells, all of which appeared to corroborate Stanley's principal fear.[89] If the Prime Minister wanted the Anglo-American accord, he would have to dominate his fellow Cabinet member.

On October 8, Lindsay asked Sayre and Hawkins whether the requests of October 6 were an ultimatum that the United Kingdom had to accept completely or whether there was still room for maneuver and modification. Sayre rejected Lindsay's choice of words, but dispelled any doubt that acceptance of these proposals by the British was indispensable to political acceptance of the document by the American public. The Ambassador suspected that Washington would deem Whitehall's reply unsatisfactory.[90] His thinking had not changed when, several days later, he said that his official statement would be ready about October 22. It

[89] Kennedy to Secretary of State, telegram no. 1141, Oct. 7, 1938, *Foreign Relations, 1938,* II, 59–60. Kennedy wired Hull a few days later the contents of a conversation with Lord Halifax, the Foreign Secretary, which is indicative of the sentiments within the Cabinet. Halifax introduced the trade agreement into the discussions "and spoke very discouragingly about it. He had been talking to Stanley and rather indicated that the whole pact was being weighed with the political advantages on one side and the trade disadvantages as they saw them on the other. My impression is that they think rather badly about the whole situation, not so much blaming us but I think blaming themselves for having got into a situation that is so difficult to get out of" (Kennedy to Secretary of State, telegram no. 1168, Oct. 12, 1938, 611.4131/1812).

[90] Memorandum of conversation by Hawkins, Oct. 8, 1938, *Foreign Relations, 1938,* II, 61–62.

would reflect London's inability to accede to some of the American formulas.[91]

From Grosvenor Square, Kennedy, still ready to appease the British, urged his superiors in the Department to be reasonable in their attitudes and requests. In his opinion, the tone of the memorandum of October 6 had been that of an ultimatum, which was just the thing to avoid. He reminded them of the reactions of some people when, as in cards, "they are called." Clearly reflecting his pique that he had not been delegated greater authority and the belief that he would have successfully concluded the accord had he been so authorized, he forecast accurately that the British would not grant everything. His final recommendation, never acted on by Hull, called for additional pressure on Stanley. Kennedy, who remained unimpressed with Stanley's ability, felt that this Cabinet official's "standing" with Chamberlain was "a little shaky, due to his opposition to the Munich agreement." Under the circumstances, the Ambassador thought that Stanley "would hesitate a long time before being responsible for breaking off negotiations." [92]

On October 25, when he transmitted Whitehall's official answer, Lindsay intimated that it was "virtually the last word." London's only partial acceptance of the State Department's proposals disappointed Hull, who nevertheless promised to study

[91] Memorandum of conversation by Hawkins, Oct. 11, 1938, *Foreign Relations, 1938*, II, 62–64. For later discussions of the tobacco formula, which was causing considerable trouble, see memorandum of conversation by Hickerson, Oct. 18, 1938, *ibid.*, 64–65. Annexed to this memorandum was the Tentative Tobacco Formula, Oct. 17, 1938, *ibid.*, 65.

[92] Kennedy to Secretary of State, telegram no. 1206, Oct. 18, 1938, *Foreign Relations, 1938*, II, 65–66; telephone conversation between Kennedy and Hull, Oct. 14, 1938, 611.4131/1832; Kennedy to Secretary of State, telegram no. 1212, Oct. 19, 1938, 611.4131/1837; Kennedy to Secretary of State, telegram no. 1221, Oct. 21, 1938, 611.4131/1839; Secretary of State to Kennedy, telegram no. 649, Oct. 22, 1938, 611.4131/1839.

the British position. To Lindsay and Overton he voiced his inability to understand Britain's rationale and his fear that it did not really want a comprehensive trade agreement. The only pleasant remark to emerge from this exchange was Hull's compliment to Lindsay: had Lindsay been both the ambassador and the president of the Board of Trade, the pact would be behind them.[93]

Moffat immediately supported acceptance of the British proposals. He recognized that they did not meet American requests completely, but said, "I favor going ahead and signing as I fear a situation exists where . . . the golden moment might be past." [94] The Secretary of State agreed and, in spite of his frustration, decided to sign the trade accord. He felt that its present terms represented everything Washington could obtain without reopening the question of proposed American concessions to the United Kingdom. Opposition to the agreement in the British Cabinet might grow if negotiations continued. In the United States dissatisfaction with the delays and uncertainty about the future among business elements retarded economic expansion, or so Hull believed. Finally, the political significance of such a pact had not diminished. Given these factors, the Secretary thought it better to accept an agreement not wholly to his liking rather than to prolong the discussions and risk the economic and political consequences of their collapse.[95] A consistent theme throughout the negotiations, in both their informal and formal stages, was concession and retreat by the State Department in the interest of economic recovery at home and abroad and, hopefully, of international peace.

[93] Memorandum of conversation by Hull, Oct. 25, 1938, *Foreign Relations, 1938,* II, 67–68; Lindsay to Hull, Oct. 25, 1938, *ibid.,* 68–69.
[94] Moffat Diary, Oct. 25, 1938, Moffat Papers, XLI.
[95] Secretary of State to Kennedy, telegram no. 675, Nov. 3, 1938, *Foreign Relations, 1938,* II, 69–70; Secretary of State to Kennedy, telegram no. 679, Nov. 3, 1938, *ibid.,* 70–71.

By early November the difficult Anglo-American bargaining thus came to an end. Concurrently, American negotiators had been working with the Canadians on their pact. During these protracted discussions the tariff rates on lumber proved to be the principal problem, but the complicated formula finally adopted removed this obstacle. On October 5, Mackenzie King was quoted in the Canadian press as saying that, although there was no final word from Washington, the negotiations might be completed any day. He added that the Canadian-American agreement had been practically concluded.[96]

The last troublesome item was anthracite coal. In order to grant the United States easier entry, Ottawa had to be released from its commitment to Britain. Pressed by the State Department on August 12 to comply, Overton several weeks later pointed out the difficulties. South Wales, which would feel the effects of the concession, was the most "depressed area" in the United Kingdom, already the recipient of much public expenditure for social and economic uplift. The criticism certain to follow a further blow to its health was more than the government could handle; and Overton justified British reluctance on commercial grounds as well.[97] For the next three weeks, the State Department tried diligently, but abortively, to persuade Whitehall to reconsider.[98] As expected, the absence of any liberaliza-

[96] Simmons to Secretary of State, telegram no. 105, Oct. 5, 1938, 611.4231/2507.

[97] This issue had come up as early as July 26, when Overton and Hawkins devoted part of their discussion to the American request (memorandum of conversation by Hawkins, July 26, 1938, *Foreign Relations, 1938*, II, 43–44). For the later and more detailed negotiations, see Overton to Hawkins, Sept. 2, 1938, 611.4131/1822.

[98] The modified proposal called for free entry during the months of December to April with no reduction in the duty during the other months (Hull to Lindsay, Oct. 6, 1938, *Foreign Relations, 1938*, II, 174–175). The British refusal was enclosed in Lindsay to Hull, Oct. 25, 1938, *ibid.*, 176–177.

tion in the Canadian tariff evinced strictures from the executive director of the Anthracite Institute.[99]

Of the two agreements that were now ready for signature, Roosevelt was supposedly partial to the one with Canada. At least Morgenthau quoted the President to that effect, although it is possible that he used the argument to guide the accords past the dubious and hesitant Morgenthau. Throughout the negotiations, the Treasury Department had played a small role. The Secretary freely admitted that reciprocity was "the apple of . . . [Hull's] eye" and that he did not want to interfere. When the value of sterling fell late in the year, Morgenthau became concerned and alerted the State Department. Discussions with the British followed. On November 15, Roosevelt told Morgenthau that he hoped the Anglo-American agreement would be concluded. "Very much between us," the President said, "I'd like to sign it. I can't get a trade treaty with Canada unless I get one with England, and I very much want one with Canada. If you'll tell me that the Canadian dollar is all right, let's let this thing go."[100] As Roosevelt probably knew, the Canadian dollar was stable. A provision in the United Kingdom agreement momentarily resolved the exchange-rate problem, and only the formalities remained.

On November 17, in the East Room of the White House, Hull, Lindsay, and King signed the agreements. "Today was the big day in Mr. Hull's career," wrote Moffat. "There was quite a ceremony at the White House. The old Lincoln table was brought down and at it sat the President, the British Ambassador, the Canadian Prime Minister, the Secretary of State, and

[99] The New York *Times*, Nov. 19, 1938, quoted Louis C. Madeira, the executive director of the Anthracite Institute, as having said that the agreement "does not touch the duty of 50 cents a ton, which is the big obstacle to a greater movement of anthracite coal into Canada."

[100] Memorandum, Sept. 8, 1938, Morgenthau Diary, Book 139, p. 13; memorandum, Nov. 15, 1938, *ibid.*, Book 151, pp. 1–2.

Overton. . . . Chairs were arranged in a big semi-circle around the table and everyone who had anything to do with the Treaty from the Assistant Secretary of State down to the copyists was invited. The press turned out in full force." [101]

Of the essential items besides lumber, Great Britain abolished duties on wheat and lard; reduced them on rice, apples, some machinery, tractors, and tools; increased the quota on hams; and bound on the free list pork products, corn, and cotton. Canada lowered schedules on fruit and vegetables, fish, paper, certain chemicals, wood, and iron and steel products; froze levels on automobiles; and, very important, abolished the 3 per cent excise tax that had plagued American exporters since 1932. In return, the United States guaranteed free entry for all Canadian goods presently on the list; reduced duties on key Dominion farm exports—cattle, hogs, cheese, eggs, potatoes, and pork—and certain metals; and removed the quotas on western hemlock and Douglas fir, while increasing them on other products. The British gained lower American tariffs on textiles, metals, and metal manufactures.[102]

Nevertheless, the Anglo-American agreement was not so broad as the State Department had originally envisioned. The lumber formula opened the British door only slightly, and congressional refusal in July, 1939, to repeal the excise tax on Canadian lumber imports punctuated its limited nature. Nothing was done for tobacco beyond a promise by the United Kingdom to act in 1942 when its formal pledge to the Empire tobacco exporter had expired. Anthracite producers had only the removal

[101] Moffat Diary, Nov. 17, 1938, Moffat Papers, XLI.

[102] Department of State, *Press Releases*, XIX (Nov. 19, 1938), no. 477, Supplement A, "The Trade Agreement with the United Kingdom"; *ibid.*, Supplement B, "The New Trade Agreement with Canada." The terms are discussed also in Soward *et al.*, *Canada in World Affairs: The Pre-War Years*, 212–224, and Kreider, *The Anglo-American Trade Agreement, passim.*

of the excise tax to show for their and Washington's efforts, whereas the American motion picture industry had even less. Other tariff relaxations fell short of levels sought by the United States during most of the negotiations. In sum, American officials preferred to think of its political rather than its economic significance. To them it was a belated strengthening of the bonds among the three English-speaking peoples and a counterweight to the expanding totalitarianism of the day.

Newspapers in both the Dominion and Great Britain adhered to the same theme even though Whitehall had given little encouragement to the notion that the pact heralded a new political era. The Canadian-American agreement was warmly received in Canada, obtaining the endorsement of even the Montreal *Gazette* which, a month before the signing, had denounced any relaxation of imperial preferences. "On the whole," the *Gazette* admitted, "it is still possible to hope that there will be no loss to this country." This Conservative organ felt that British and American opinion would welcome the Anglo-American accord, not only for its economic effects, but also because of its importance as a "signal of a new unity of policy between the two leading democracies." [103] Equally remarkable was the reception in industrial Ontario. The Toronto *Evening Telegram*, also a Conservative paper, bypassed the ostensible purpose of the agreement—improving trade—to concentrate upon its presenting to the world a new axis between London and Washington that was regarded as an answer to the ideologies of the totalitarian states.[104] Privately, the Tories expressed similar thoughts. In reply to Robert Manion's query about his opinion of the agreements, H. H. Stevens, Minister of Trade and Commerce during the Ben-

[103] The Montreal *Gazette*, Nov. 18, 1938, printed two editorials of interest, "Reciprocity Broadened" and "The Anglo-American Agreement."

[104] Toronto *Evening Telegram*, Nov. 18, 1938.

nett regime, advised the party leader, "The main thing to keep in mind is that by this Treaty the Canadian Government has made a contribution to closer commercial relations between Great Britain and the United States. It is my firm opinion that this achievement is of peculiar significance at this time of world distress." Furthermore, he added, "It may well be the initial step which will ultimately result in a growing and more intimate association of the United States with the British Empire." For these reasons, Stevens cautioned against any attempt by his party to take the agreement into the political arena.[105]

Liberal newspapers, wih the exception of the Ottawa *Citizen,* were even more enthusiastic. They anticipated increased trade and substantial economic advantages for Dominion interests, but also saw in the agreement a tangible expression of unity of purpose within the North Atlantic Triangle.[106] Unquestionably the world political situation, highlighted by the recent Munich crisis, helped to shape attitudes in Canada. Where there had been opposition, there was now support; where suspicion, now trust; where futility, now hope.

[105] Stevens to Manion, Nov. 23, 1938, H. H. Stevens Papers, CLIII, Correspondence 1938 K-M.

[106] For example, the Winnipeg *Free Press,* Nov. 18, 1938, asserted that the "rejoicing will be increased by the fact that on its political side these treaties will have a beneficial effect upon the general world situations. . . . May it presage the beginning of a return to sanity and more stable conditions." On November 19 the Ottawa *Citizen* argued that "something more than ballyhoo is needed on Parliament Hill to save the economic situation in this country." In Simmons to Secretary of State, no. 2752, Dec. 7, 1938, 611.4231/2626, the Chargé wrote, "During the interval which has elapsed . . . nothing has occurred which would indicate any perceptible lessening in the general enthusiasm initially accorded the pacts. . . . In the press and elsewhere . . . the preponderance of opinion in Canada continues to be favorably inclined towards the revised agreement." The principal dissenting voice came from the Vancouver *Daily Province,* which questioned the Canadian-American agreement's merits.

In Great Britain the political implications of the arrangements were given as much or more prominence than the economic. The Manchester *Daily Dispatch* thought that the Anglo-American agreement's political significance matched its economic value, asserting, "The closer the United States stands with Great Britain—in commerce and in politics—the more powerful will be the democratic influence for stability and peace in a world sadly in need of both." [107] The Manchester *Guardian* called it a good agreement, which would be welcomed by most people not so much for the accelerated trade that might result, but for its political symbolism.[108] The London *Daily Telegraph* declared that first and foremost the accord was an "outward and visible expression of solidarity" between Great Britain and the United States and, like other London newspapers, thought that it lowered tariff barriers significantly to the benefit of the entire world.[109] Lord Beaverbrook's London *Express* raised a dissent, but this editorial took issue with the most-favored-nation clause, not with the over-all agreement itself.[110] Partisanship in the United Kingdom was blessedly absent; Liberal and Labor politicians and organs had consistently supported the negotiations, in some cases more enthusiastically than officials of the party in power.

The same cannot be said of the political scene in the United States. Important Republican papers continued their opposition to all New Deal actions, whereas those with Democratic affiliations praised the result. The majority of newspapers, however, gave their editorial support to the agreement. Altogether only 16 per cent of the American press viewed it as definitely "unfavorable," with the highest percentages in New England and the Far

[107] Manchester *Daily Dispatch,* Nov. 18, 1938.
[108] Manchester *Guardian,* Nov. 18, 1938.
[109] *Daily Telegraph* (London), Nov. 18, 1938.
[110] *Daily Express* (London), Nov. 18, 1938.

West. There 37 per cent and 50 per cent respectively were hostile. Obviously editors in these regions were unhappy with the concessions on textiles to the United Kingdom and on lumber to Canada, and with the failure of the American negotiators to lower the British tariff further. Not unexpectedly, these editorials paralleled closely the attitudes and arguments of the special interests in the sections they represented. The greatest support came from papers in the South and Southwest, the Middle Atlantic, and the Midwestern states, where spokesmen anticipated expanded trade for natural products.[111] Certainly the politi-

[111] Restrained or cautious acceptance marked the response of the journals representing the Middle Western farmer. The *Wallace's Farmer and Iowa Homestead* (Dec. 3, 1938), saw some benefits for the corn-belt farmer, but "not a great deal." The Anglo-American trade agreement's "main value . . . is that it shows two great nations are willing to cut down tariff barriers and to move toward greater freedom in international trade." Reciprocity with Britain certainly was not the complete answer for the farmer's ills. The *Prairie Farmer,* the most important of the publications, refused to commit itself on the economic gains or losses. "Time will tell," wrote its correspondent, Julian Bentley, on December 3, 1938. "The important thing," he continued, was the "effort on the part of three great nations to promote the flow of business, to change conditions so that the results are better for all concerned." The Ohio *Farmer* (Dec. 3 and 17, 1938) also felt that the future would render judgment on the agreements, but held that "anything that will tie the democracies of the world more closely together in times like these and break down barriers between nations is a good thing."

Obviously, those newspapers reflecting the opinions of farmers faced with greater competition from Canada expressed themselves differently. The influential *Hoard's Diaryman* remained neutral on the Anglo-American accord, but attacked the Canadian pact. "Objections to the concessions by the dairy industry received the same consideration by the state department as has occurred previously," it complained on December 25, 1938, finding little logic "in making it easier to import dairy products at a time when we are burdened with a surplus that it is difficult to dispose of, even at low prices." The conservative editor of the *American Agriculturist,* a New York publication, was uncomplimentary, endorsing on December 17, 1938, the National Grange's recent call for Senate approval of trade treaties.

cal speculations expressed during the negotiations had been vindicated. Support in the other regions had more than offset the opposition in the Northeast and West.[112] George Gallup provided another index: a nationwide survey made by the American Institute of Public Opinion in November, 1938, found that of those Americans interviewed, 86 per cent approved Hull's efforts to obtain an Anglo-American trade agreement.[113]

Thus the year of formal negotiations, characterized by delays, diversions, haggling, and political apprehensions, and conducted in a time of international crises and uncertainties, the business recession, and the fall in the value of sterling,[114] ended on a happy note. The three nations, having successfully removed economic irritants from their relations, were about to enter the period of their closest collaboration in history.

[112] For a statistical analysis of press opinion in the United States, see Kreider, *The Anglo-American Trade Agreement*, 42.

[113] "American Institute of Public Opinion—Surveys, 1938–39," *Public Opinion Quarterly*, III (Oct., 1939), 593.

[114] This problem, which, as noted, caused some concern late in the negotiations, is explored in Feis to Morgenthau, Sept. 12, 1938, 611.4131/1776A. Sayre broached the topic with Lindsay at that time. See also Morgenthau to Hull, Nov. 16, 1938, Morgenthau Diary, Book 151, pp. 109–110.

Conclusion

While significant, the Anglo-American agreement left unful-
filled the hopes of Hull and some of his colleagues. It only
slightly weakened the imperial preference system and did not
completely reverse the protectionist trade policy of Great Britain.
If State Department officials expected the British to refrain
henceforth from bilateral arrangements antagonistic to American
business, they were to be disappointed. In March, 1939, industrialists from the United Kingdom and Germany, representing the
Federation of British Industries and Reichsgruppe Industrie,
concluded an agreement at Dusseldorf, with the blessing of
Chamberlain, designed to improve German foreign-exchange
holdings. At the same time, London sought accords with the
Balkan states.[1]

Most important of all, the trade pacts of 1938 had little effect
on political developments in Europe, a disappointment to those
who thought that economic rapprochement and the symbolic

[1] Kreider, *The Anglo-American Trade Agreement, passim* (see particularly the discussion of the Dusseldorf Agreement of March, 1939, pp.
74–78); Feiling, *Chamberlain*, 396; Margaret George, *The Warped
Vision: British Foreign Policy, 1933–1939* (Pittsburgh, 1965), 195–196;
Martin Gilbert and Richard Gott, *The Appeasers* (Boston, 1963),
207–208.

Conclusion 273

expression of North Atlantic solidarity could deter war. The Chamberlain government, not yet disenchanted with the security that greater Anglo-German collaboration seemed to offer, hoped that the Dusseldorf conference would lead to a trade agreement with the Reich. Although the Nazi coup in Czechoslovakia in March, 1939, prevented the planned Anglo-German negotiations, the Prime Minister continued to believe for some time that economic appeasement was a necessary concomitant of the political detente.[2] These answers to European problems— Hull's Anglo-American reciprocity and Whitehall's accommodation with Germany—fared poorly. In September, 1939, German armies rolled into Poland, beginning a six-year struggle that profoundly changed the map and the balance of power both in Europe and Asia.

Beliefs, particularly if they border on obsessions, die hard. After the war, the Secretary of State wrote that international economic collaboration could have prevented much of the revolution that followed. The Anglo-American agreement, had it come earlier in the decade, might have arrested the disastrous political trends, which, by November, 1938, were already too long in the making. It is lamentable that history cannot disclose what the ultimate repercussions of an Anglo-American accord of the mid-thirties might have been. The result of such speculations would depend on whether one accepted, as did Hull, the notion that the seeds of international discord germinated in economic soil. Preceding pages have indicated that key individuals in the British Foreign Office had doubts about the agreement's political efficacy, much preferring to see the United States adopt policies more attuned to the British interpretation of the problems. Repeal of the American neutrality legislation, allowing the United States to use its economic power against any

[2] George, *The Warped Vision*, 196–202; Gilbert and Gott, *The Appeasers*, 189–208.

threat to European stability, had greater attraction than a trade pact. There is no evidence that an agreement signed earlier would have had any effect on Whitehall's attempt at appeasement of Germany. Everything points in the other direction; the pressing problems were felt to require political solutions.

While reciprocity failed to avert war, it brought the three governments closer together at a crucial moment. Some of the differences within the triangle had been resolved and the German thrust in 1939 encountered adversaries more politically and economically united than before. Yet this was more a fortuitous than a preconceived by-product. As shown repeatedly, the leading British policy makers viewed the negotiations primarily in an economic, rather than a political, context. They never lost sight of the possibility that American isolationism would preclude any move by the Roosevelt Administration toward greater collaboration with the United Kingdom. No trade pact could subvert this aversion to entanglements and to the probability of involvement in a major war.

The arrangements with Canada and the United Kingdom were no panacea for the exporting interests within the bloc. Quotas, currency exchange problems, and passive trade balances remained. One cannot predict definitively what the long-range consequences might have been if war had not intervened. Probably these accords would have improved considerably trading opportunities for American businessmen and farmers. Some annoyances, and thus political opposition, would have lingered. A second arrangement with the United Kingdom would quite likely have come more easily, but not necessarily automatically.

What instructive lessons does this study offer in retrospect? First, it seems clear that concern about political tensions in Europe underlay Hull's devotion to the Anglo-American agreement. Had it not been for this disintegration and the importance of a cooperative response, he might have relaxed the pressure to conclude the agreement, and favored interests in Great Britain and the Dominions would have defeated the project. Even with the world situation then prevailing, members of the British Cabinet moved only deliberately. Their primary objective was to prevent a world conflagration by political settlements with their adversaries, not by the conclusion of a trade pact with a partner that might not prove reliable.

The two great tragedies of the period were the breakdown of Anglo-American unity and the inability of the leaders to repair the breach until war had been forced upon them. Harold Macmillan, sympathetic with Winston Churchill's critique of appeasement, expressed this thought well when he wrote, "I firmly believed that the peace and prosperity of the world depended upon close co-operation between Britain and the United States." [3] The depression and subsequent divergent policies of Washington and London shattered this ideal. What followed were wasted years as officials in the two capitals questioned, insulted, and generally distrusted the actions of each other. Trade agreement negotiations, rather than having the desired cathartic effect, blended into the background of suspicion, doubt, and contempt. As late as May, 1938, Moffat recorded that at a lengthy meeting in Hull's office, the Secretary had been "upset at the way the British are up to their old tricks." After citing some of the more irreconcilable problems, for example Chamberlain's and Halifax's response to Roosevelt's qualified approval of the recently signed Anglo-Italian treaty, Moffat concluded, "You can see that the picture is not 'all beer and skittles.' " [4]

Eventually international tensions had a centripetal effect. German officials in the United States discerned this fact, if somewhat prematurely. In late September, 1937, reporting a recent conversation with Sumner Welles, Hans Dieckhoff, the Ger-

[3] Harold Macmillan, *Winds of Change, 1914–1939,* 28.
[4] Moffat Diary, May 12, 1938, Moffat Papers, XL.

man Ambassador in Washington, noted the progress made in Anglo-American trade agreement discussions. The United Kingdom "finally recognized," he wrote, "that conclusion of the trade agreement was a necessary condition for Anglo-American cooperation on a wider scale." During the crisis over the Sudetenland, the German Chargé in Washington went even further: "The history of Anglo-American relations since 1914," he perceptively observed, "teaches us that in normal times they occasionally become strained, but that in a crisis the principle of solidarity is forthwith adopted." Citing "the parallelism" in recent policies of the two countries, he continued, "The imminent conclusion of a trade agreement has a significance which goes far beyond economic matters." He predicted that in the event of war the United States would do everything to prevent British defeat.[5]

Second, Canada served as a useful channel of communication to the United Kingdom for the United States, but forces shaping Canadian policy limited its effectiveness. At the Imperial Conference of 1937 the senior Dominion could not accomplish what Hull had hoped it would. King could interpret American thinking to London and he could even attempt to meet Washington's requests for reduced preferences, but Canada is an independent nation with indigenous economic and political considerations that its statesmen must weigh. A more forceful man than Mackenzie King might have expedited the trade agreements by wielding greater influence within the Cabinet. It is doubtful, however, that any political leader would flout economic interests and traditions without first making a proper study and surveying national opinion. Unquestionably King was tardy in bringing his govern-

[5] *Documents on German Foreign Policy*, Series D, I, 631, 726–732. Hitler paid scant attention to such reports; an Anglo-American agreement in 1936 or 1937 probably would have altered his plans for Europe very little, if at all. See the chapter by Gordon A. Craig in Craig and Gilbert, eds., *The Diplomats*, 406–436.

ment to the bargaining table, but there were real problems confronting him in the Dominion, and Great Britain provided him with little practical aid in surmounting them. In sum, while it has at times played a valuable role in Anglo-American relations, Canada cannot automatically reconcile every difference between London and Washington. Ottawa has to operate within a framework shaped by internal forces. As a result, historians should discard the term "linchpin" when describing Canada's ties to the United States and the Empire. The relationship is much more complex.

Third, though exaggeration of its long-range meaning must be avoided, King and Roosevelt, two men with very conflicting personalities, had strengthened their personal bond of friendship and trust. Unfortunately, Chamberlain's aloofness kept this understanding from becoming trilateral. The Prime Minister should have pursued the President's feelers in 1937 and 1938. He forfeited the opportunity to build the bridge, later credited to Churchill, between London and Washington. The absence of Anglo-American summitry, however, must not discount Chamberlain's limited contribution to bilateral solidarity. After Eden's resignation in February, 1938, the Prime Minister saw more than any other individual in the British government the advantages of the trade pact, and pressed for its completion. He had less faith in the arrangement than the American Secretary of State, and throughout the negotiations he sought accords with Germany and Italy. The rumor of his "anti-Americanism" has to be modified as the story of his Cabinet battles over reciprocity unfolds. The initiative and the pressure for the agreement came from Hull,[6] but Chamberlain, whatever his shortcomings, deserves some credit for his readiness to brave political opposition

---

[6] An informative article dealing with this topic is H. B. Elliston, "Mr. Hull Calling London," *Atlantic Monthly*, CLXI (Jan., 1938), 72–76.

at home and within the Empire to respond, if not always enthusiastically, to the Secretary's call.

Fourth, Canadian-American relations became increasingly cordial after 1935, as the two governments corrected the errors of the early thirties. This was not always easy. Amicable ties have been the result of hard work by diplomats, of recognition of the respective economic needs, political pressures, and emotional makeup of the two peoples, and, sometimes, of political risks taken by their leaders. Undeniably there were risks in King's course, and Roosevelt probably would have had less misgivings had he deferred his final decision on the first Canadian-American agreement until after November, 1936.

Fifth, the political influence that private interests wield was evident throughout these developments. Problems in American diplomacy, like those in domestic affairs, are fair game for organized pressure groups. When they see a threat to their privileged positions, they campaign to shape opinion or alter the course of legislation. People in the Departments of State and Agriculture, as well as the President himself, spent no little time collecting and evaluating material measuring public attitudes of the trade agreement program in general and the Anglo-American pact in particular. With this information they advanced politically judicious requests, fought politically unwise concessions, and undertook a campaign of their own to educate the American voter. Similar organized efforts to preserve or alter the status quo affected the democratic process in Canada and the United Kingdom. In short, the role of political partisanship is fundamental and must be assigned high priority when assessing the foreign policy decisions of the United States.

Finally, because the negotiation of trade agreements was the responsibility of the State Department, not the President, the focus has been on Cordell Hull. The Secretary was free largely to formulate policy. How well did he perform this task? The

Secretary's differences in 1940 and 1941 with Stimson and Morgenthau over the proper diplomatic course with respect to Japan, especially his aversion to economic sanctions, are well known. Yet, when dealing with a program that was so close to his heart, the adoption of which would supposedly turn nations from war to peace, he reflected the same cautious attitudes and actions. When he proclaimed to the world the benefits of rehabilitated international commerce or preached moral sermons regarding international political behavior, he perhaps had no equal. When the questions became less academic and more practical, he revealed his indecision. Hull was not a strong, persevering individual who, convinced that he had an answer to the world's ills, fought unswervingly for its acceptance. He persevered in homilies, thinking that verbal endorsements had moral force, but he faltered when he had to make decisions. Reciprocity was Hull's substitute for more responsible involvement in contemporary turmoils with their risk of war. Fearful that such was the case, Britain attributed much less importance to the plan than did Hull. Perhaps his performance prompted and justified Roosevelt's turning to other advisers and assuming certain functions himself when the great prewar and wartime decisions had to be made.

Bibliography

This study is based largely on primary sources. The central files of the Department of State, indispensable to historians of nineteen-thirties diplomacy, form the bulk of the documentation. Although only a small number of these items are published in the *Foreign Relations* series, the volumes include nearly all of the significant documents relating to the Anglo-American trade agreement of 1938. Similarly, they present reasonably well the story of the negotiation of the Canadian-American pacts. The originals in the files have been checked, but the citations in the footnotes are to the published source. The greatest benefit of the files is the access they provide to a broad spectrum of foreign newspapers. With some exceptions—the Toronto *Mail and Empire,* Toronto *Globe,* Toronto *Globe and Mail,* Ottawa *Journal,* and *Times* (London)—the editorials and articles cited in the text were taken from the original clippings sent to Washington by the Department's foreign service officers.

The Franklin D. Roosevelt Papers in Hyde Park, New York, some of which were made available on microfilm, contain useful documents. Since Roosevelt kept neither a record of his conversations nor a diary, the full import of his chats with Mackenzie

King must await the opening of this portion of the King Papers. That collection, in the Public Archives of Canada, is open through 1932, but it will be a few years before historians can see materials germane to this study.

Also in the Roosevelt Library are the Morgenthau Diaries, open through Roosevelt's second term. A careful examination of the approximately 150 volumes that cover developments through 1938 revealed little of substance not presented in Blum's published volume. In the footnotes I have cited both the original diary entry and the published account when the two sources paralleled.

The J. Pierrepont Moffat Papers at the Houghton Library, Harvard University, containing the often quoted Diary and perceptive correspondence with friends and colleagues in Washington and abroad, are another indispensable source. The published volume by Nancy Harvison Hooker, while useful on occasion, hardly scratches the surface. One of the most rewarding adventures in research was reading these vital documents. It is unfortunate that more foreign service officers did not keep similar records of this eventful period.

The Cordell Hull Papers in the Library of Congress were generally disappointing, with the exception of certain letters from Norman Davis and a 1937 epistolary exchange with King. Most of the items are copies of dispatches and memoranda housed in the State Department's central files.

The Francis B. Sayre Papers, also in the Library of Congress and only recently opened, contained very few documents dealing with the trade agreements program.

The Norman H. Davis Papers, another Library of Congress collection, were an important source on the tariff truce negotiations prior to the World Monetary and Economic Conference and on developments in London in 1937.

The William Phillips Diary, the 1933–1936 portion of which was read on microfilm, added depth to the account of the Canadian-American trade negotiations in those years.

The public papers of both the Canadian Department of External Affairs and the British Foreign Office are closed, but some private manuscripts are available. Perhaps the most disappointing collection is the Richard B. Bennett Papers. Though voluminous, they have obviously been expurgated by someone to shield the Prime Minister from anything damaging to his career. Bennett, a bachelor, apparently had few friends in whom he could confide his inmost thoughts, and the infrequent notations in his diary are useless. The most valuable materials in the Bennett Papers are the letters to Bennett from his brother-in-law, William Herridge, the Canadian Minister to the United States from 1931 to 1935. These letters leave little doubt that Herridge was the architect of Bennett's "New Deal" of 1935, and that he was the most important force in Canadian official circles behind the 1934–1935 negotiations with Washington.

The John W. Dafoe Papers, available on microfilm in the Public Archives of Canada, are very helpful, particularly for gaining insight into the Ottawa Conference of 1932 and the trade negotiations with the United States in 1934 and 1935. Dafoe, editor and long-time Liberal, not only offered perceptive analyses of current issues in his letters but also employed astute journalists to observe developments for the Sifton newspapers.

The Charles A. Dunning Papers, which belong to Queen's University at Kingston, Ontario, are another disappointment. Except for some correspondence with King, they contributed nothing.

The Robert Manion Papers, H. H. Stevens Papers, C. H. Cahan Papers, and Ernest Lapointe Papers, all at the Public Archives of Canada, contained little of value. Manion was a prominent Conservative and Bennett's successor as party leader.

In certain letters to his son James, a Canadian diplomat serving in Japan, he made some interesting commentaries on Bennett, particularly on his physical and mental problems in 1935. The Stevens collection—he was Minister of Trade and Commerce during Conservative control—is silent on the trade negotiations with the United States. Unfortunately, there is nothing in the Lapointe Papers about the Imperial Conference of 1937.

The following list of sources used in the preparation of this study is selective. It cites just those items which directly pertain to the topics developed in the text.

MANUSCRIPT SOURCES

Bennett, Richard B. Papers. Harriet Irving Library, University of New Brunswick.

Cahan, C. H. Papers. Public Archives of Canada, Ottawa, Ontario.

Dafoe, John W. Papers. Public Archives of Canada (available on microfilm), Ottawa, Ontario.

Davis, Norman H. Papers. Division of Manuscripts, Library of Congress.

Dunning, Charles A. Papers. Queen's University Library, Queen's University.

Hull, Cordell. Papers. Division of Manuscripts, Library of Congress.

Lapointe, Ernest. Papers. Public Archives of Canada, Ottawa, Ontario.

Manion, Robert. Papers. Public Archives of Canada, Ottawa, Ontario.

Moffat, J. Pierrepont. Papers. Houghton Library, Harvard University.

Morgenthau, Henry, Jr. Diary. Franklin D. Roosevelt Library, Hyde Park, New York.

Morrison, Alfred Eugene. "R. B. Bennett and the Imperial Preferential Trade Agreements, 1932." M.A. thesis, University of New Brunswick, 1966.

Phillips, William. Diary. Houghton Library, Harvard University.

Roosevelt, Franklin D. Papers. Franklin D. Roosevelt Library, Hyde Park, New York.

Sayre, Francis B. Papers. Division of Manuscripts, Library of Congress.

Stevens, H. H. Papers. Public Archives of Canada, Ottawa, Ontario.

United States Department of Agriculture. Archives. Washington, D.C.

United States Department of Commerce. Archives. Washington, D.C.

United States Department of State. Archives. Washington, D.C.

PUBLISHED SOURCES

Allen, H. C. *Great Britain and the United States: A History of Anglo-American Relations* (1783–1952). New York: St. Martin's Press, 1955.

"American Institute of Public Opinion—Surveys, 1938–39," *Public Opinion Quarterly*, III (Oct., 1939), 581–607.

Amery, L. S. *My Political Life*. 3 vols. London: Hutchinson, 1955.

Beaverbrook, Lord. *Friends: Sixty Years of Intimate Personal Relations with Richard Bedford Bennett*. London: Heinemann, 1959.

Beckett, Grace. *The Reciprocal Trade Agreements Program*. New York: Columbia University Press, 1941.

Bidwell, Percy W. *Our Trade with Britain: Bases for a Reciprocal Tariff Agreement*. New York: Council on Foreign Relations, 1938.

——. "Prospects of a Trade Agreement with England," *Foreign Affairs*, XVI (Oct., 1937), 103–114.

Blum, John Morton. *From the Morgenthau Diaries: Years of Crisis, 1928–1938*. Boston: Houghton Mifflin, 1959.

Brebner, John Bartlet. *North Atlantic Triangle*. New Haven: Yale University Press, 1945.

Butler, J. R. M. *Lord Lothian (Philip Kerr), 1882–1940*. London: Macmillan, 1960.

Canada. *Debates, House of Commons*. For the year 1931, Vol. III; 1932–1933, Vols. II, IV, V; 1934, Vol. I; 1935, Vols. I–IV; 1936, Vols. I, II; 1937, Vols. I, II, III; 1938, Vol. I.

Churchill, Winston S. *The Gathering Storm.* Boston: Houghton Mifflin, 1948.

Council on Foreign Relations. *The United States in World Affairs.* New York: Harper (annual survey published in each succeeding year). Volumes for the years 1932–1938.

Craig, Gordon A., and Felix Gilbert, eds. *The Diplomats, 1919–1939.* Princeton: Princeton University Press, 1953.

DeConde, Alexander, ed. *Isolation and Security.* Durham: Duke University Press, 1957.

Documents on German Foreign Policy, 1918–1945, from the Archives of the German Foreign Ministry, Series D. Washington, D.C.: United States Government Printing Office, 1949–1956.

Drummond, Donald F. *The Passing of American Neutrality, 1937–1941.* Ann Arbor: University of Michigan Press, 1955.

Eayrs, James. *In Defense of Canada: Appeasement and Rearmament.* Toronto: University of Toronto Press, 1965.

Eden, Anthony. *The Eden Memoirs: Facing the Dictators.* London: Cassell, 1962.

Edminster, Lynn R. "Agriculture's Stake in the British Agreement and the Trade Agreements Program," *International Conciliation,* CCCXLVII (Feb., 1939), 79–94.

Elliston, H. B. "Mr. Hull Calling London," *Atlantic Monthly,* CLXI (Jan., 1938), 72–76.

Esthus, Raymond A. *From Enmity to Alliance: U.S.-Australian Relations, 1931–1941.* Seattle: University of Washington Press, 1964.

Feiling, Keith. *The Life of Neville Chamberlain.* London: Macmillan, 1946.

Feis, Herbert. "A Year of the Canadian Trade Agreement," *Foreign Affairs,* XV (July, 1937), 619–635.

———. *1933: Characters in Crisis.* Boston: Little, Brown, 1966.

Ferrell, Robert H. *American Diplomacy in the Great Depression.* New Haven: Yale University Press, 1957.

Gallup, George, and Claude Robinson. "American Institute of Public Opinion—Surveys, 1935–38," *Public Opinion Quarterly,* II (July, 1938), 373–398.

Gardner, Lloyd C. *Economic Aspects of New Deal Diplomacy.* Madison: University of Wisconsin Press, 1964.

George, Margaret. *The Warped Vision: British Foreign Policy, 1933–1939.* Pittsburgh: University of Pittsburgh Press, 1965.

Gilbert, Martin, and Richard Gott. *The Appeasers.* Boston: Houghton Mifflin, 1963.

Great Britain. *Parliamentary Debates, House of Commons.* Vols. 245, 261, 278, 281, 314, 317, 318, 321, 324–331, 333–336, 338–341.

Halifax, Lord. *Fullness of Days.* New York: Dodd, Mead, 1957.

Hancock, W. K. *Survey of British Commonwealth Affairs.* 2 vols. New York: Oxford University Press, 1940.

Hirst, Francis W. "Cordell Hull and Cobden," *Contemporary Review,* CLV (Jan., 1939), 10–17.

Hooker, Nancy Harvison, ed. *The Moffat Papers.* Cambridge: Harvard University Press, 1956.

Hull, Cordell. *The Memoirs of Cordell Hull.* 2 vols. New York: Macmillan, 1948.

Hutchison, Bruce. *The Incredible Canadian.* New York: Longmans, Green, 1953.

Ickes, Harold L. *The Secret Diary of Harold L. Ickes.* 3 vols. New York: Simon and Schuster, 1953–1959.

Imperial Economic Conference, 1932. *Report of the Conference.* Ottawa: King's Printer, 1932.

Jones, Joseph M. *Tariff Retaliation: Repercussions of the Hawley-Smoot Bill.* Philadelphia: University of Pennsylvania Press, 1934.

Jones, Thomas. *A Diary with Letters, 1931–1950.* London: Oxford University Press, 1954.

Keenleyside, Hugh L., and Gerald S. Brown. *Canada and the United States.* rev. ed. New York: Knopf, 1952.

Kottman, Richard N. "The Canadian-American Trade Agreement of 1935," *Journal of American History,* LII (Sept., 1965), 275–296.

Kreider, Carl. *The Anglo-American Trade Agreement: A Study of British and American Commercial Policies, 1934–1939.* Princeton: Princeton University Press, 1943.

——. "Democratic Processes in the Trade Agreements Program," *American Political Science Review*, XXXIV (April, 1940), 317–332.

Langer, William L., and S. Everett Gleason. *The Challenge to Isolation, 1937–1940*. New York: Harper & Bros., 1952.

League of Nations, Monetary and Economic Conference. *Draft Annotated Agenda*. Geneva, 1933.

——. *Journal of the Monetary and Economic Conference*. London, 1933.

——. *Reports Approved by the Conference on July 27, 1933, and Resolutions Adopted by the Bureau and the Executive Committee*. Geneva, 1933.

Lindley, Ernest K. *The Roosevelt Revolution: First Phase*. New York: Viking, 1933.

MacLeod, Iain. *Neville Chamberlain*. New York: Atheneum, 1962.

Macmillan, Harold. *Winds of Change, 1914–1939*. New York: Harper and Row, 1966.

Mansergh, Nicholas. *Survey of British Commonwealth Affairs: Problems of External Policy, 1931–1939*. New York: Oxford University Press, 1952.

Massey, Vincent. *What's Past Is Prologue: The Memoirs of the Right Honourable Vincent Massey*. Toronto: Macmillan, 1963.

Moley, Raymond. *After Seven Years*. New York: Harper & Bros., 1939.

Nicholas, Herbert. *Britain and the U.S.A.* Baltimore: Johns Hopkins University Press, 1963.

Nichols, Jeannette P. "Roosevelt's Monetary Diplomacy in 1933," *American Historical Review*, LVI (Jan., 1951), 295–317.

Ollivier, Maurice, ed. and compiler. *The Colonial and Imperial Conferences from 1887 to 1937*. 3 vols. Ottawa: Queen's Printer, 1954.

Parkinson, J. F. "Memorandum on the Bases of Canadian Commercial Policy, 1926–38." Toronto: Canadian Institute of International Affairs, 1939. Mimeo.

Phillips, William. *Ventures in Diplomacy*. Boston: Beacon, 1952.

Pratt, Julius W. *Cordell Hull.* 2 vols. New York: Cooper Square, 1964.

Rauch, Basil. *The History of the New Deal, 1933–1938.* New York: Creative Age Press, 1944.

Riddell, Walter, ed. *Documents on Canadian Foreign Policy, 1917–1939.* Toronto: Oxford University Press, 1962.

Roosevelt, Elliott, ed. *F. D. R.: His Personal Letters, 1928–1945.* 2 vols. New York: Duell, Sloan and Pearce, 1950.

Royal Institute of International Affairs. *Survey of International Affairs.* London: Oxford University Press (annual survey published in each succeeding year). For the year 1933, Vol. I (1934); 1937, Vol. I (1938); Vol. I (1941).

Russett, Bruce M. *Community and Contention: Britain and America in the Twentieth Century.* Cambridge: M.I.T. Press, 1963.

Safarian, A. E. *The Canadian Economy in the Great Depression.* Toronto: University of Toronto Press, 1959.

———. "Foreign Trade and the Level of Economic Activity in Canada in the 1930's," *Canadian Journal of Economics and Political Science,* XVIII (Aug., 1952), 336–344.

Sayre, Francis Bowes. *The Way Forward: The American Trade Agreements Program.* New York: Macmillan, 1939.

Schlesinger, Arthur M., Jr. *The Coming of the New Deal.* Boston: Houghton Mifflin, 1959.

"So that Nations May Trade," *Business Week,* no. 325 (Nov. 23, 1935), 44.

Soward, F. H., Parkinson, J. F., MacKenzie, N. A. M., and T. W. L. MacDermot. *Canada in World Affairs: The Pre-War Years.* Toronto: Oxford University Press, 1941.

Stone, Shepard. "Anglo-American Economic Issues," *Current History,* XXXVIII (July, 1933), 399–405.

Tasca, Henry J. *The Reciprocal Trade Policy of the United States.* Philadelphia: University of Pennsylvania Press, 1938.

———. *World Trading Systems: A Study of American and British Commercial Policies.* Paris: International Institute of Intellectual Co-operation, 1939.

Templewood, Viscount. *Nine Troubled Years*. London: Collins, 1954.

Towle, Lawrence W. *International Trade and Commercial Policy*. New York: Harper & Bros., 1947.

"Trade Pact Controversy Bubbles," *Literary Digest*, CXX (Nov. 30, 1935), 35–36.

"Treaties of Alliance," *Business Week* (Jan. 29, 1938), 15.

United States Congress. *Congressional Record*. Washington, D.C.: United States Government Printing Office. For the year 1936, Vol. 80; 1938, Vol. 83.

United States Department of State. *Foreign Relations of the United States: Diplomatic Papers, 1932–1938*. 34 vols. Washington, D.C.: United States Government Printing Office, 1948–1955. For the year 1933, Vols. I and II (1949–1950); 1934, Vol. I (1951); 1935, Vol. II (1952); 1936, Vol. I (1953); 1937, Vols. I and II (1954); 1938, Vols. I and II (1955).

———. *Press Releases*.

Wallace, Henry A. "How the Canadian Trade Agreement Will Affect Farmers," *Vital Speeches*, II (Dec. 2, 1935), 151–152.

Watkins, Ernest. *R. B. Bennett: A Biography*. Toronto: Kingswood House, 1963.

Wilbur, J. R. H. "H. H. Stevens and the Reconstruction Party," *Canadian Historical Review*, XLV (March, 1964), 1–28.

Willoughby, William R. *The St. Lawrence Waterway: A Study in Politics and Diplomacy*. Madison: University of Wisconsin Press, 1961.

"World Trade," *Living Age*, CCCLIII (Feb., 1938), 555–556.

Index

Acheson, Dean, 69
Agricultural Adjustment Act (1933), 53-56, 65, 66, 70
Allport, Fayette W., 230, 231, 233, 235
American Institute of Public Opinion, 212, 213, 217-218, 271
Amery, Leopold S., 20, 24, 29, 213
Anglo-American trade agreement (1938), 5, 7-9; initial efforts, 117, 120-148; controversy over divergent trade policies, 126-138, 141-144, 149-150, 157, 159-160; preliminary exchanges, 139-143, 146-147, 165-166, 172, 186-189, 194-195, 202-205; Canada as an intermediary, 151-156, 161-165, 167-172, 179-182; negotiations accepted by the United States, 208-209; negotiation of, 227-243, 245-264; terms of, 266; reaction to, 267-271
Anglo-Canadian agreement (1932), 32-33, 38, 108, 109, 121, 122, 154, 159
Anglo-Canadian agreement (1937), 151-152, 154-158, 169, 171, 180, 197
Anti-Comintern Pact, 205, 207
Armour, Norman, 100-103, 105-107, 152-155, 157, 159, 164-165, 169-170, 182, 185, 189-190, 192-193, 197, 199-201, 208

Association of British Chambers of Commerce, 219
Atherton, Ray, 50, 128-130, 135, 184, 185, 230, 231
Attlee, Clement, 209
Australia, 18, 173, 179, 181, 195, 204, 216-217

Baldwin, Stanley, 3, 6, 19, 20, 22, 23, 25, 30-34, 36, 141, 153, 171, 176, 184
Baruch, Bernard, 69
Beaverbrook, Lord, 15, 20, 269
Bennett, Richard B., 14; and Imperial Conference of 1930, 17; and Imperial Economic Conference of 1932, 17-19, 21-32, 34-35, 38; and World Monetary and Economic Conference, 68-69, 77; and commercial reciprocity with the United States, 83-85, 87, 90-95, 97-105, 109, 113-114; and Canadian-American trade agreement negotiations of 1937–1938, 211, 226
Bingham, Robert W., 76, 132-137, 143-145, 167, 171-174, 203-204, 230, 232
Bloom, Chester, 87 n, 90 n, 243-244
Boal, Pierre de L., 35, 37
British Empire Committee, 121-122
Brown, Sir William, 179-180, 203-204, 235

290